THE
ANALYSIS
OF
FANTASY

THE
ANALYSIS
OF
FANTASY

The Thematic Apperception

WILLIAM E. HENRY, Ph.D.

The Committee on Human Development
and
The Department of Psychology
The University of Chicago

Technique in the Study of Personality

ROBERT E. KRIEGER PUBLISHING COMPANY
MALABAR, FLORIDA

ORIGINAL EDITION 1956
REPRINT 1973, 1987

Printed and Published by
ROBERT E. KRIEGER PUBLISHING CO., INC.
KRIEGER DRIVE
MALABAR, FLORIDA 32950

© COPYRIGHT 1956 BY
JOHN WILEY & SONS, INC.
Reprinted by arrangement
L.C. #56-7157

SBN #0-88275-114-X

PRINTED IN THE UNITED STATES OF AMERICA

10 9 8 7 6

Dedication

To

Jean Walker Macfarlane

and

W. Lloyd Warner

In dedicating this volume to Professor Jean Walker Macfarlane of the University of California and to Professor W. Lloyd Warner of the University of Chicago, I wish to express my gratitude for their attempts to impart to me some segment of their knowledge. Professor Macfarlane has introduced me to the complexities of the individual personality and Professor Warner to the compelling continuities of group life. I trust that they will find it appropriate that I have attempted to utilize both of these facets of behavior in the study of fantasy, although neither can be held responsible for the way in which I have done so.

Preface

Stories told to pictures represent a symptomatic by-product of the interaction of individual personality and the stimulation represented by the pictures. Any effort to interpret responses must thus have a firm base in the psychodynamic principles of personality. It must similarly be closely attuned to the realities of the stimulating circumstances. In this volume I have attempted an approximation to three significant areas relevant to this interpretive task. The first of these areas lies in the general principles of interpretive psychodynamics. These I have stated in a form which, while clearly incomplete, is, I hope, appropriate to the analysis of data of this sort. The second area deals with the understanding of the ways in which variation is present within the basic data themselves, the stories proper. Here I have presented a number of variables of the content and the form of Thematic Apperception Technique (TAT) stories and suggested some tentative principles for relating these to attributes of persons. The third area lies in the characteristics of the stimuli, the pictures proper. Here I have attempted an analysis of some variables of the pictures which present to the subject differential external circumstances and suggested some ways in which differential selection and differential response to these stimuli may bear significance for the interpretive task.

Throughout this volume, two special interests will be noted. First, I have at all times attempted to keep interpretation close to data, feeling that progress in research in this field will benefit most by the close association of evidence and inference. To this end, I have deliberately restrained myself in the face of the temptation to make secondary interpretations based upon first-order interpretations. Rather, I have constantly attempted to criticize all interpretations on the basis of story data. Where more meaningful interpretations appear to be those derived from prior interpretation, I have indicated the nature of the inference and noted its unstable base in evidence. Unfortunately, it cannot be concluded from this intention that the interpretations thereby derived are more nearly true of the person whose fantasy is analyzed. My intent to keep interpretations close to data should not be taken as an assumption of validity. Second, the central concern of the volume is with nonclinical formulations of personality. This reflects my own strong interest in research in normal personality and my feeling that we are sadly in need of theoretical formulations based solidly upon the normal. This is not to suggest that the systematic study of the nonnormal personality is not a vital research area, but rather to highlight our need for concepts and techniques which will permit us to understand and predict the communalities and the idiosyncrasies of everyday life. To this end, I have also focussed somewhat more than is usual upon the relevance of the communalities of group life and upon the necessity for understanding social events in their relation to personality. To no small extent, the features of personality which find support in external circumstances constitute major segments of ego strength and normal personality functioning.

It is the impelling hope of workers who utilize the projective instruments in the study of personality to be able to formulate their practices and principles in ways sufficiently clear to permit both systematic investigation and a transmittal of these principles to their colleagues and students. It is that hope which motivates this volume. I do not envision it as a manual, in the sense of a precise guide to the novice to the principles and facts of fantasy interpretation. Rather I see it as an effort of one worker to formulate with increasing precision his own practices and principles. If this effort seems to stimulate other workers to the same task and permits them to criticize, experiment with, and reformulate these principles or others, I shall feel it has been worth while. Above all, I hope that this effort, though it lacks a systematic treatment of issues of validity, will assist in providing a conceptual basis upon which studies of the validity of interpretations may be founded.

WILLIAM E. HENRY

Chicago, Illinois
April, 1956

Acknowledgments

I wish to express my great indebtedness to Mrs. Alice Chandler for her very considerable assistance in the preparation of this book; to Dr. Robert McFarland for the assistance he gave in preparing the material from which Chapter 12 has been written; to Gerald Handel for his helpful comments during the preparation of the book; to Ruth Doman Handel for her careful reading of the proofs; and to Dr. Adrian Vandervere who, while at the University of Chicago, provided greatly appreciated criticism and encouragement during my first efforts at interpreting fantasy material. In addition, I wish to express my gratitude to the many students who, through their constant questions and criticisms, have aided immeasurably in formulating this interpretive procedure.

WILLIAM E. HENRY

Contents

Part 1

THE PROCESS
OF INTERPRETATION

CHAPTER 1

The task of interpretation: its social and psychological nature

The analysis of fantasy is a problem in the interpretation of symbolic statements. When in story form, these statements are organized by the intellect but take their meaning from the emotions. The interpretive significance of themas perceived and stories told to pictures is thus to be derived from the understanding of the ways in which emotional preoccupations are symbolized in words and plots, from the ways in which emotions bow to propriety in overt expression, and from the ways in which each individual lessens his own burden by expressing his feelings, though disguising them for himself and for others.

The technique of thematic apperception takes much of its particular relevance to the study of personality from this dual aspect of fantasy expression. On the one hand, fantasy in storytelling derives from the less conscious and less structured aspects of the individual's personality. To these areas of personality the rules of logic and propriety do not apply. On the other hand, the task set for the storyteller is one that requires him to organize his fantasy into a recognizable story form and to verbalize this story for the inspection of others. To this latter requirement the rules of logic and propriety do apply, at least those particular rules of logic and propriety that the subject has found applicable to his own life. Thus interpretation of thematic apperception must take place within these overlapping frameworks: the more nearly private and less conscious motives and generalizations derived from past life experiences, and the public, socially determined, more nearly rational frameworks of convention.

This seeming distinction between the personal and the social is of course artificial. It is made here primarily to emphasize the fact that the basic data of the TAT, i.e., the stories, are a derivative. They are a derivative of the personal phrased in terms of the social. While this fact does in a sense obscure personal motive, it is only through an analysis of the manner in which the person manipulates the symbols of conventional communication that one derives insight into these personal motives. This suggests that the social forms, the rules of logic and propriety which are used to structure the individual's fantasy, are in themselves deeply rooted in personal motive. Only if this is true can they serve as a guide to the very motives they are partially designed to obscure. The developmental training of the individual provides ample evidence that this is indeed the case. Child training in the ways of the adult society may be seen conceptually in terms of the long-range goals favored by the society. Yet in terms of the individuals who live in it, the demands of the society are in no sense abstract; they consist of the very personal *day-to-day interaction with people.* Through these daily interactions, the individual learns what his society expects of him and, of course, what he will expect of himself. These training situations have two special characteristics relevant to TAT interpretation. They teach skills and they teach feelings. They teach the forms of behavior proper to the social group, and they teach the feelings and attitudes that the adult thinks appropriate to the situation. The mother warning her child not to slip and fall while running down a grassy slope is not only suggesting care in a physically dangerous situation but is also inhibiting a spontaneous impulse. When her child dashes up to a friendly dog and pats it, the mother's warning that dogs may bite is a suggestion of controlling affect and impulsivity as well as a lesson in realistic caution. Thus each experience, whether private in the sense of being unique to that person, or public in the sense of being a common, expected event, is an experience with both rational and emotional connotations. Whether an event is unique in occurrence or public, it is still a personal event, invested with emotional meaning specific to the individual who experiences it. It is, of course, relevant that the experience is one encountered by many others, but this communality does not alter the essentially personal nature of the experience, nor does it make the affect associated with it less vital. Thus each person, regardless of the nature of his life experience or of his personal adjustment to it, invests meaning and affect in the ordinary symbols of communication in his society and in the relationships presumed to exist between those symbols.

During the processes of adapting to the demands of one's society, one learns both skills and feelings. And, in a sense, one learns them in that order, skills first and feelings second. Or, perhaps more exactly phrased, one learns skills directly and feelings indirectly. The training agents—parents, school teachers, other adults and children—generally teach the skills consciously and intentionally: how to eat and when, where to eliminate, how to dress, how to greet a relative or a stranger, when to play with the neighbor's children, how to behave on a date, etc. These things are taught directly and are learned directly, consciously. But along with each of these experiences, and in a sense as a generalization drawn from many such experiences, feelings are also learned. These feelings which attach to the many varied life experiences are seldom taught directly. More usually they are only implications or conclusions derived by the individual himself. As such, they remain only partially conscious and most frequently are not stated explicitly. Certain of these feelings are deeply threatening and tend to be repressed or grossly transformed, thus becoming less clear and making their recognition by the individual himself less likely. Many are not in themselves threatening to the individual, even though remaining implicit. But regardless of whether these underlying feelings are routine and rather close to awareness, they act as guiding principles and give direction to the individual in situations of choice. Some operate well within the critical gaze of rationality. Some are more disturbing and offer severe challenge to rational control and the dictates of reality observation. Yet in either case, their expression takes place in terms of the situations in which they were initially experienced. Much as it is possible to think rationally only in terms of the concepts and symbols provided by your society, similarly it is possible to express feeling only in terms of the ideas, personal relationships, symbols, and symbolic interactions in connection with which feelings have been connected in the past. As feelings are learned implicitly through skills and techniques taught overtly, so these same implicit feelings can be expressed overtly only through the manipulation of the skills and techniques with which they are associated.

From the point of view of the individual learning or behaving in terms of the patterns set by his society, the basic directives which give consistency to his behavior are essentially emotional in nature. These directives may be subsumed under two generalizations: what the individual feels and believes the world of people and things outside him to be like, and what he feels and believes himself to be like. Thus, each of the societal continuities that is relevant to the life of any given individual has its substructure in the emotional life of that individual. Presumably, then, each patterning of societal expectancies receives a major portion of its substance and coercive power from the emotional involvement, partly conscious and partly unconscious, which individuals have in it. Thus it is that societal expectancies, which for the individual are essentially personal and emotional in nature, are an integral part of the personality of the individual. The basic story plots of that society and the assumptions of feeling and action attached to them are utilized by the individual to symbolize and express meaning and intent. In many instances, the utilization of themes and ideas found to have cultural communality should not be seen as an evasion on the part of the subject. All individuals express their desires and needs in the symbols provided by their society, some being less imaginative or complex and hence forced to use concepts and symbols which are of more general currency. Yet individual significance will still be carried in these common plots and concepts.

In the interactive system individual-society, the individual is viewed as attempting to satisfy his desires within the society of which he is a part. To this end he utilizes those social groups, occupations, and social institutions whose activities and interests most nearly provide the satisfaction he seeks. In the most extreme case the individual attempts to complete his wishes with whatever means his society provides and at any cost to the society. It is for this reason that the individual develops strong interest in certain selectively perceived plots, activities, or idea-systems prevalent in his society, involving himself with those that, at the time at least, seem to intrigue him. Similarly he ignores or develops contempt for those that seem to him unrelated or opposed to his aims.

On the other hand, the society makes demands and has needs that must be fulfilled. It * demands at least outer conformity to its values

---

* This temporary reification of the concept of culture is recognized and will perhaps be permitted in the interests of grammatical simplicity.

and modes of living, and it punishes, by ostracism or social disgrace or personal distortion, those individuals who fail to attain a sufficient degree of that conformity. The task of the society, in a sense, is to perpetuate that society by a continuance of those values and modes of living that have been found satisfactory in the past.

Yet it should not be assumed that the interests of the individual and society are necessarily in opposition, as tempting an idea as this is to the modern American mind. The individual requires a social framework and a series of reasonably certain rules and codes by which to guide his behavior. And the society requires the active belief and participation of individuals within it and the spark of individually creative minds.

Yet the process by which society gains an individual's conformity and the individual gains the satisfaction of his personal needs is a process of coercion, sometimes of distortion, of partial conformities and partial uniqueness. During this process the society attempts to mold the individual to the pattern of its values, and the individual attempts to achieve a satisfying uniqueness within the bounds of social comfort. In the individual this process is one of continual learning and adjustment out of which the individual gradually develops and organizes his own personality.

The personality which emerges through the process of adapting to experience may be seen as the psychological counterpart and residue of the individual's life history of experiences. The personality, composed of an interrelated series of generalizations, convictions, fears, hopes, loves and hates, may be seen as taking on a certain consistency, developing along with this consistency boundaries between it and the stimulation of outer reality. There are two special features of the personality tendency toward consistency which are of crucial significance for TAT interpretation. These features are: first, *a resistance to repeated change,* and second, *a tendency to reproduce itself.* This first tendency is a direct reflection of the development of consistency within the personality and the gradual reduction over time of the ability of the personality to change. As consistency develops, flexibility decreases. With this reduced flexibility, an additional feature appears, the tendency to reaffirm the present consistency. This tendency is the mechanism of *projection* and may be defined as the inclination to see in all outside reality the values and convictions that are already a part of the personality. Thus the individual interprets reality to conform with the reality he expects, he sees in the outer world (and in himself) only what he wants and is able to see. Further, he responds to that personally defined reality in terms of his own feelings, values, and convictions.

The personality thus operates to screen, select, and interpret stimulation from outside. But another process would also seem to be in operation, a process equally vital to the interpretation of fantasy. Not only does the personality select what stimulation will be recognized; there is also a demand for a more direct and overt expression of the feelings and values which constitute the personality. A screen for stimuli is not enough; it is necessary that those feelings and convictions be acted out in the public world. This *projection outward* of the individual's personality is readily seen in behavior. Behavior, including that behavior which is the response to a TAT picture, is thus to be seen as symptomatic of the underlying characteristics of the personality. Yet that behavior is at the same time a reaction to the immediate social situation, since the individual lives at all times under the effect of social stimulation. It is not only the unique aspects of the personality which are projected into behavior—in slips of the hand and tongue, in unique choice and arrangements of objects, in body movement and stance, in imagination and fantasy. Also projected are those aspects of the individual which, because of much common training and background, are similar to the personalities of other individuals.

A special feature of the projection into behavior consists of the retesting and reaffirming of the convictions and feelings of the personality and the experimentation with variations on these feelings and convictions. No one is so sure of himself and his goals that he does not, to a greater or lesser degree, challenge and test his ambitions and assumptions. Both areas of acute conflict and areas of positive, unconflictful values are subject to this testing and reaffirming process. The stress of the interplay of personal and social demands raises many problems in the mind of the individual, presents many questions, and in some instances gives rise to much conflict and anxiety. Making up his mind about these problems, and often merely living in peace with the solution derived, requires a certain amount of acting out, an opportunity to gain confidence by testing alternatives or of exorcising the devil through confrontation. The testing of these areas takes place on at least two levels: first, that of introspection, and second, that of the manipulation of the people, objects, and institutions composing the social world around the individual. Both consciously and unconsciously the individual reflects upon his adjustment to his own life. And both consciously and unconsciously he reacts to and manipulates the social world to the same end: that of contemplating his adjustment to life and, by a continuous expression of its dominant characteristics, reaffirming for himself the wisdom of this adjustment.

The projection and reaffirmation of the individual's personality is accomplished in symbolic form. That is to say, the manifestation of the individual's feelings, values, and conflicts is expressed indirectly through the manipulation of people and events, and through the evaluation he puts upon the stimulation from outside. The behavior of the individual is thus symbolic of his underlying personality adjustment; the observed behaviors are to be thought of as symbols that stand for personal motivations, symbols whose meanings are defined by the personality. These symbols have the same two aspects previously described for the personality itself: some of these symbols are public, and others are private. Thus certain behaviors and social participations of the individual are similarly interpreted and similarly experienced by all individuals of the same social group. This is true because of the similarity of training of individuals within the same social group. Because of their communality of training, all individuals within a group will interpret certain behaviors in the same way and, further, will express certain commonly felt conflicts in the same way. These common behaviors constitute the recognizable characteristics of the group—features that make all members of that group identifiable as such and serve to differentiate them from members of other groups. In addition to these common public modes of behavior, and the common interpretations of symbols, each individual also develops his own private meanings and symbols. These private symbols are expressive of personality trends which are unique to him. This uniqueness derives from the idiosyncratic aspects of his bodily constitution and his life experiences. Not only will each individual develop for himself purely private symbols but he will also utilize the common public symbolic modes of behavior in individually unique ways. This latter fact serves partially to obscure the individuality of behavior, to make behavior seem less unique. But it also enables the individual to obtain for himself greater individuality within the framework of convention.

The Thematic Apperception Technique is a device for the analysis of these underlying psychological needs and feelings and the ways in which they are handled by the individual. Whether pathological or within the limits of normality, these underlying trends are manifested in terms of the ideas and symbols with which the individual communicates with others in ordinary nontest situations. While somewhat unusual, the telling of stories to pictures is not basically different from the tasks required of a person in regular social interaction. And, similarly, the formulation of interrelated ideas in story form reflects the pattern of ideas habitually utilized by the individual—full or constricted, rich or impoverished, distorted or overly cautious, reality-oriented or bizarre. The enthusiasms, the hesitancies, the experiential gaps in awareness which give direction to the subject's ordinary action and conversation will similarly influence and direct his storytelling.

In this sense, the TAT stories may perhaps be best viewed as reality stimuli, portraying in cryptic outline certain basic life events. The organized response of the individual thus portrays his usual definition of and usual manner of responding to such reality events. The range of situations portrayed in the TAT pictures extends somewhat the limits of ordinary reality demands, both in kind of situation normally calling for response and in time, in that situations dealt with in the historical past are now brought again into awareness and demand reaction. Yet the manner of response remains much the same, whether usual or unusual demands are made by the pictures. Regardless of whether a picture is viewed by the subject in a form prototypical of a present life reality or as a reflection of a past, almost forgotten situation, the manner of response now in the test situation is in terms of the present working vocabulary and pattern of associations. To the extent that these present views of reality and the ways of dealing with it are distorted, so may we expect the TAT stories to be similarly distorted. And to the extent that the present ways of defining and responding to reality demands are not distorted, so may we expect to find in the TAT a reflection of the normal and ordinary.

This does not mean that the normal and ordinary should be discarded and only the distorted and anxiety-ridden data sought. To do so is to neglect the resources of control and future change. In either a normal or pathological subject, the common, normal responses are of great importance in showing the setting within which deviancy occurs and in analyzing the techniques of adjustment and ego strength.

The framework of convention is the basic one in terms of which the TAT story is formulated. The irregularities, the distortions of emphasis, the imputing of motive, the introduction of figures not present in the pictures, all these represent the subject's effort to speak in terms of conventional symbols and ideas, while still conveying his personal feeling and motive. This is not a reflection of an intellectual caution on the part of the subject. While persons vary greatly in the manner in which their personal motive is diffused with conventional symbol, except in the case of the most distorted subject, they have no choice.

There is no other way for the individual to convey his personal feelings except in the ways in which he has been taught to communicate with others: in the public symbols whose core of meanings is generally understandable. This means, of course, that each story told by a subject portrays his personal affect through a screen of public affect. In each instance in which the subject portrays his reaction to a particular figure or event in the TAT picture, the response is a blend of his private feelings and of the public feelings traditionally (in his culture) associated with this figure or event. To the extent that the subject can manipulate public symbols readily, to that extent can he use them to convey more of his personal meaning. Similarly, to the extent that his lack of common social training or his unique view of common moral issues obscures his understanding of the general core of affect and meaning attached to these figures and events, to that extent can he similarly convey his personal meanings through distortions of these common meanings. It is vital to bear clearly in mind that the point of departure in each instance is the body of symbols and their general core of meaning traditional in the subject's general culture. Variations, blendings, and arrangements of these common meanings will reveal the subject's integration with his social group and the nature of his various deviations from it. His individuality thus consists of both his unique ideas and feelings and his particular version of the common cultural meanings and assumptions.

In this connection it will perhaps be well to comment briefly on the general nature of the stimuli provided by the TAT, leaving a more detailed analysis of the pictures to later chapters. As Dr. Henry Murray remarks in his Thematic Apperception Test Manual,* the TAT pictures were designed to present the subject with "certain classical human situations." The subject, in responding to the pictorial representation of these basic dramas, reveals his own formulation of them and the private meanings which he attaches to them. Yet in so doing he does not start *de novo*. He starts on the basis of the pattern of meaning and affect which his past cultural training has taught him should characterize such human situations. This is not to say that each person repeats verbatim the standard cultural versions of the basic dramas, though certain highly stereotyped subjects would indeed seem to approach this degree of cultural identity. Rather it means that each picture must be seen as presenting two stimuli, one, the visual stimulus, and two, the stimulus of the emotional assumptions and dramatic plot development which, because of past cultural training, tend to adhere to the particular human situation portrayed. In

* Murray, Henry A. *Thematic Apperception Test.* Pictures and manual (20 pp.). Cambridge: Harvard University Press, 1943.

responding to each picture stimulus, the subject thus utilizes his rational and imaginative skills to bring his private feelings into line with both the pictorial form demands of the picture—the picture's manifest content—and to fit his personal convictions into the emotional complex presented—the picture's latent content.

The interpretation of the subject's responses thus is to be seen in terms of an interactional system composed of four basic parts: the subject's underlying psychologic structure, his techniques of adapting to his own feelings and emotions and to external demands, the manifest content of the picture stimulus, and the latent content of the picture stimulus. The final response is the resultant of these four parts, each obviously varying in its contribution to the final story created by the subject.

It is apparent that almost infinite variation can occur in the manner of interaction of these basic response determinants. The manifest stimulus (cf. Chapter 12) of the picture may be such as to dictate the core of the story told. Thus, picture 1, a boy with a violin, obviously suggests a story dealing with a boy-violin situation. Similarly, picture 4, a scene of a woman restraining a man, while permitting a wide range of response, nonetheless does demand a story including an explanation of this somewhat dramatic heterosexual scene. Picture 3BM, less clearly structured than many, permits the subject greater leeway, in that the figure may be seen as a boy or a girl, or possibly an older person, in a situation permitting wide variation in interpretation. Yet the picture does demand reference to the figure in some sort of situation that accounts for the huddled form and the bowed head. Similarly the object on the floor, often referred to as a gun, though lending itself to many other interpretations, tends to demand some explanation. Thus each picture makes demands of a contentual sort, suggesting the basic setting of the story and to some extent the characters to be involved in it. The manifest stimulus of the picture also involves demands of a form character. That is, certain pictures present a simple form pattern. Others are more complex in form, requiring more of the subject who tells a story about it. Thus, 8GF, a young woman looking off into space, presents only one major form aspect to be accounted for, a seated woman. On the other hand, picture 2, a country scene, has in it three central figures, in addition to many fairly apparent large details, such as a horse, barns, and trees, and a number of quite small details not often observed by the ordinary subject, which are a second man and horse, a lake and reflection in the background, and details of the furrows of the plowed field. Pictures such as 19, with its weird cloud formations, or 16, a blank card, present a quite different form, allowing greater freedom for the subject to imagine, yet giving less specific form to guide him. Thus, each picture makes its own demand in terms of form, much as it sets the general scene in terms of content.

The pictures exert an influence upon the final story in yet another way: their latent stimulus. It seems important to observe that each picture tends to set an emotional as well as a form or content demand upon the subject. This emotional demand we call the latent stimulus of the picture. The manifest stimulus of a picture refers to the objects and forms presented visually to the subject. The latent stimulus refers to the emotional issue presented by each picture. This latent stimulus cannot usually be defined by inspection of the picture, though a person with a thorough knowledge of the psychological assumptions of the subculture of the subject to be tested can often make a good guess. The latent stimulus can be defined only in terms of the analysis of stories told by individuals. The latent stimulus is defined by the answer to the question: What is the basic emotional problem being discussed when subjects tell stories to this picture? In picture 1, the boy and the violin, the manifest content is a boy seated in front of a violin. The manifest stimulus demand is satisfied by reference to the boy, to the violin, and to some connection or relationship between them (contemplating, admiring, hating, planning to break, seeing as a symbol of a great musician, etc.). Yet this seems an insufficient description of the stimulus presented to the subject. Also an integral part of that stimulus is the set of assumptions usually made about the emotional problem at issue. Thus in picture 1, the latent stimulus * is one dealing with the relation of instinctual or self-

---

* It is difficult at this point in our work with TAT to say "for whom" this definition of latent content holds. Most likely this is a useful definition for the broad American middle classes. It is apparent from some lower class records taken in the Chicago area that such a dilemma is not taken as the core of the stimulus. In addition to the social class dimension, there is undoubtedly also an age dimension along which variation in latent meaning occurs, though this does not hold for all pictures. In picture 4, for example, the postpubescent subject defines this as an adult heterosexual scene in which disharmony is a central feature. In the prepubescent, however, the adult heterosexuality is replaced as an emotional focus by the parental conflict focus. It is also possible, to illustrate from this same picture, that for the lower class person, the drama which the middle-class person sees would be less intense and viewed more as an ordinary adult scene. In 17F, to illustrate further, the background female figure is quite generally seen as a negative force, a witch, the symbolic restraining superego, etc. Only recently,

expressive drives to the demands of some external societal force. One
is presented in picture 1 with not only the necessity of telling a story
about a boy and a violin but also a story in which a solution must be
made to this instinctual outer demand issue.

The remaining two major determinants of the story response, the
subject's underlying psychological structure and his techniques of
adapting to these emotions and to outer reality, are to be approached
through whatever theoretical position the interpreter finds useful. In
general, it should be said that any theory justly described as psychodynamic will provide the flexibility necessary to interpret fantasy
material. The manner of interpretation will of course vary with the
constructs and assumptions of the theory applied.

however, we have begun to see responses of women over 70 who see her as
quite benign and helpful.

CHAPTER 2

Principles of
the interpretive process

It is the hope of workers in the field of the projective instruments
that they will some day be able to state explicitly and in testable
form the system of dynamics which forms the basis of their interpretive
schema.   It is probably true that artistic judgment and intuition will
always remain a part of the process of interpretation of behavior.
Nonetheless, it is apparent that the tenets of dynamic psychologies
are being subjected increasingly to both clinical and experimental
analysis.   As experience widens and as critical studies progress, the
delineation of interpretive principles can become specific and pointed.
This gain will be derived, clearly enough, not only from studies in the
interpretation of the projective instruments but from all increase in
the knowledge of personality dynamics, especially as they are related
to observable and describable behavior.   In the present chapter an
effort will be made to set forth a series of interrelated principles and
assumptions which it is believed form a workable base for the analysis
of fantasy.   No particular claim to originality is made for these principles.   It will be apparent that many of them are either explicitly
stated principles of psychodynamics or at least would find recognition
and acceptance among workers in the field.   They are, of course, proposed for their direct relevance to the interpretation of fantasy, though

they serve only as a scaffolding for such analysis. If any uniqueness lies in them, it is in the fact that they include many concepts normally thought of as "sociological" rather than "psychodynamic."

Such concepts can obviously be as "dynamic" as are those more traditionally associated with dynamic psychology. They form an adjunct to the concepts of personality depth necessary for the relating of dynamic concepts to behavior and for the understanding of behavior in its social context.

The interpretation of behavior, whether the sample we call fantasy or in another form, is itself a dynamic process characterized by an interaction between three major variables: the behavior sample selected, the knowledge of the interpreter, and the empathic qualities of the interpreter. The attempt is made here to deal with a limited aspect of the first variable. The third, often referred to as intuition, will not be considered. This is not to imply that guided, critical intuition is not a vital part of the interpretive process. It is, and is well worth quite separate, intense study. The second variable, the psychodynamic knowledge of the interpreter, is a similarly integral and vital part of the interpretive process. The task of summing the knowledge relevant to interpretation is not only beyond the skill of the author but out of place in this volume. An approach will be made to this goal only in so far as the principles of interpretation discussed in this chapter involve the facts and assumptions in current psychodynamic theory.

There is one further way in which the knowledge and assumptions of the interpreter are relevant to the process of interpretation. This is in the way in which he views human personality and in the way in which he conceptualizes the relation of the individual to the persons, objects, and events around him. In this conceptualization there are of course many formulations. Undoubtedly, a considerable variety is possible within the formulations, all of which will permit the interpreter to give significance in personality terms to a subject's fantasy. It seems probable, however, that the more explicitly these formulations are stated the easier it may be to understand the process of interpretation and the sooner we will derive statements of fantasy analysis which are specific and testable. To this end, we will here present a formulation of the dynamic organization of the individual and attempt to show how this view leads to procedures and a logic of the interpretive process.

The Basic Assumptions Regarding the Relation of the Individual and His Environment

The distinction traditionally made between the individual and his environment is recognized as less clear than these concepts would imply. The environment is an integral part of the individual whose ideas, feelings, and values can most often be clearly seen only as they are referred to events, people, or objects technically "outside" the person himself. There is therefore no advantage to be gained by making too sharp a distinction between "inside" and "outside" the person, though this dichotomy may be useful for indicating emphasis on sources of motivating action. The manner in which the individual and the environment are related may best be formulated by seeing them as foci within a field, all parts of which are interactive and all parts of which potentially influence other parts. It is perhaps for this reason that the individual is often best described in terms of the interaction which he holds with other persons, events, or objects. Thus a vital part of the personality of the person is found in the feelings and ways of acting with which he is related to significant figures in his past and present life. This is not to deny that the person may and does develop a patterning of feelings and action tendencies which may be described independently of the external circumstances with which they may have been associated historically. In fact, it is characteristic that the complex of person-centered or environment-centered forces tends to develop consistencies. These consistencies represent the facts or conclusions derived from repeated experience. In spite of the interactive nature of the individual and his setting, he tends toward a patterning which represents his effort to simplify the complexity of this setting and to concentrate upon remembered repetitive aspects of that environment. Thus with time the perspective narrows and the motivating forces shift from external to internal.

The tendency toward internal consistency, discussed in more detail in the section on "The Patterning of Self," represents a continual motivating force in the individual's relationship to his environment. In the analysis of fantasy, it is well to assume that an effort in this direction is being made by the subject, whether conscious or not. The concept of equilibrium is also of relevance here. To some extent the establishment of a pattern of reasonable consistency is made through a process of balancing forces, of contrasting good with evil, of overstressing and understressing.

Characteristics of fantasy should be carefully analyzed in terms of their place in this balancing process and their role in the description of the person's tendencies toward consistency evaluated. As the individual reacts to his experiences and attempts to establish a direction for himself that seems proper, his deviations from the central core of his consistency reduce. The hazard to be avoided in fantasy interpretation is that of confusing the swings made in the interest of balance with the central direction of the personality. This is particularly apt to occur with subjects at times of sharp developmental change or idiosyncratic trauma.

The use of the concepts of equilibrium and consistency should not lead us to assume any *a priori* nucleus of consistency or point of balance. In the description of the personality, some value is certainly placed on sufficient internal consistency to prevent distressing contradictions and the waste of energy resulting from this. However, it is probable that great lack of consistency can be tolerated by many persons. The ability to satisfactorily encompass great complexity is a personality attribute of importance. This ability should not be confused with disorder and distress. Further, it should not be assumed that the concept of equilibrium implies that the swings resulting in balance are necessarily short, minor swings. It is often true, of course, that the internal consistency of the individual is so great that very few behavioral or feeling contradictions appear. However, a quite functional and satisfactory equilibrium can occur in personalities where the consistency is a very complex one and the seeming deviation can be significantly related without crippling conflict or energy waste. It is in this connection that attention should be drawn to a possible inclination to consider normal adjustment as identical with a state of calm acceptance and defined by an absence of pathological symptoms. The illusion of the rural pastoral seems possibly to have led us to overlook much that is distorting in the ordinary uncomplex states and similarly to prejudge certain personality complexities as pathologic.

In sum, it is assumed that the individual represents a complex blend of internally and externally motivating forces to which patterning is given by the tendency toward equilibrium and toward the establishment of an internal consistency.

Basic Assumption of Constant Emotional Movement

Constant emotional movement characterizes the general state of the individual. The specific character of the emotional state of the individual will vary from person to person and, within the individual, from time to time. This constant emotional movement has several sources and characteristics. For our purposes three general bases for this emotional movement will be described. First, there is the notion of *psychic energy,* a basic part of most psychodynamic theories. Second, there is the notion of *expectancy sets,* foci of emotional energy best described as centered in patterns of organized role-systems external to the individual. And third, there is the notion of *anxiety and movement-limitations,* a contributing mobile emotional state related to difficulties and failures in role-pattern integration.

It is of course entirely possible to conceive of the latter two categories as essentially part of category one, psychic energy. If the objective here were to reduce variables to their simplest form, it would perhaps then be best to assume only category one. We should then posit all energy which is related to external objects and events to be a reflection or cathexis of basic psychic energy. In the same manner, anxiety, whether conflictful or constructively adaptive, may be similarly collapsed into the notion of psychic energy. However, the author believes it is very helpful to utilize these three breakdowns, largely on the grounds that they are distinguishable both theoretically and practically and they provide useful leads to the dynamics of interpretation.

Psychic energy

The assumption of a constant emotional energy which remains unidentified as to source seems somewhat less than satisfactory scientifically. Nonetheless, it appears to be a necessary assumption if we are to explain the interrelationships of behavior and motive and the continuity and consistency of personality through time. The practical implications of this assumption of psychic energy are, for our purposes, two in number. First, that behavior (including the telling of stories to pictures) is motivated and bears a meaningful relationship to that motivation. Second, that the individual maintains a constant effort to deal emotionally with issues presented to him by either internal or external stimulation. The importance of the first implication, that of psychic determinism, is obvious. It is the logic which permits us to examine bits of observed behavior, and to draw from them generalizations representing the directions and goals of individual motivation. The second implication stresses the probability that the individual, in his selective perception of himself and the world about him, will perceive events in terms of their relevance to him at the time of their occurrence. This means that some events will be perceived as relevant and others as not relevant. However, all events perceived as relevant will be invested with emotion. As time passes, the residue of the emotional investment tends to remain more impelling than the cognitive recollection of the events themselves.

It is for this reason that in the analysis of fantasy the interpreter should seek more the emotional conclusions derived by the subject than he should the factual bases or events which may have given rise to these emotional residuals. It is in this sense that the interpreter seeks the subject's *image* of male and female, the *feeling* of power or impotence, the *assumption* of inevitable disaster or fateful intervention. These will represent, in the present fantasy of the subject, the conclusions and emotional issues which, for that subject, are of importance.

Expectancy set

A second focus of constant emotional movement may be seen in the institutions which are external to the subject. Each institutionalized role or set of events in the world external to self consists of an organized pattern of interrelated behaviors. As the individual grows, or as at any time in his life cycle he becomes initially aware of an organized role-pattern external to him, he may recognize the presence of a meaningful patterning. To the extent that the perceived role-pattern is of relevance for him, to that extent does it serve as a motivating goal. By processes of imitation and role-assumption, the individual attempts to internalize the meaningful attributes of the organized external role-pattern, and to bring this pattern and his present emotional assumptions into line. Depending upon the individual, this is a process leading to change and growth, or one leading to rejections and the crystallization of present affect.

The importance for fantasy interpretation lies in the reminder that clues to the personal emotional significance of fantasy may be found as often in an awareness of the institutionalized organization of outside events as in the purely "internal" dynamics of the individual. This will be particularly true at age periods of change, when the balance of internal consistency to apprehension over new events is disturbed. It will also be true in areas in which relationship to outside events is of importance. The analysis of relations to other persons, especially peer relations, for instance, requires emphasis upon the pull of an as yet noninternalized external pattern. The final analysis will depend as much on this as upon an understanding of the push of already formulated internal assumptions. It will be especially true whenever prediction of behavior is involved, since observed behavior is most frequently the result of the interaction of self and the perceived external events.

A further notion should be specified here to give meaning to the foregoing observation regarding the external institutionalized events. This is the possibility that these external events establish a sort of "expectancy set." By this is meant an assumption that each individual will know how to play the game in all its intricacies. Our culture would appear to assume that whenever a person is operating within the sphere of a particular institution he will operate according to the (usually implicit) rules at the core of that institution. Few institutionalized patterns are set up to account for persons who are on the fringe of that same institution. This "expectancy set," i.e., the expectation upon the individual to behave in the manner most generally expected by the sphere of activity in question, is a powerful draw and keeps the individual constantly on his emotional toes. Whether or not he successfully imitates the expected roles, he is constantly aware of the presence of a pattern of expected behavior.

Possibly the clearest example of this expectancy set is to be found in adult-child relations, in which the child is frequently told that certain behaviors are not "grown-up." The strong implication of this is that there are a set of "grown-up" behaviors, from which vantage point it is presumed the parent is talking. Motivating power is given to the image by frequent admonitions, or promises as the case may be, of "wait until you're grown up." Thus the parent presents an implication of a consistent organized pattern of desirable behavior into which status the child can presumably some day be admitted. Other examples of the same idea may be seen in the area of sex training, in which the image of "little boys" as different from "little girls" sets a similar expectancy. There is presumed to be a "little boyness" that is potentially learnable and different, not only from "little girlness" but from the present state of the individual in question. The motivating set, of course, lies in the image of attaining this "little boyness" state.

In adult spheres, similar sets are made by many of the organizations to which one can belong. The rules of behavior vary in their degree of explicitness, but there are almost always such rules and they set a standard of behavior. Thus a "good Kiwanian" is a fairly clear-cut thing which sets a pattern for the person who aspires to this status. Similarly a "good Catholic" can be discerned from a "good Unitarian," even though their stated values and goals may not be greatly dissimilar. Less apparent but possibly more generally important are the expectancies set by the images of properness in the social class or occupations scene. Thus the lower-middle-class housewife is set an image of respectability potentially obtainable and not defined by her ability to cook and keep house. Similarly, a doctor is set a pattern of good middle-classness which is not identical with his medical skills or the quality of his diploma.

The important point is not that differential role-patterns exist, though it is clear they do, *but that each of them implies a pattern of organized behavior which can be learned by the individual for whom that particular pattern has relevance.*

It should further be pointed out that, for children and adults alike, there is a strong expectancy on the part of the society for the individual to properly aspire to learn the role-patterns in question. *This expectancy is conveyed to the individual in a variety of ways and serves to develop in the individual a kind of leaning-into-the-wind, an expectant anticipation that contributes to the constant emotional state and increases his readiness to respond in ways characteristic of his personality organization at the time.*

Anxiety and limitations upon free movement

A third factor involved in the continuous emotional movement of the individual is the energy derived from anxiety. Anxiety is aroused by the inability to cope with the need for continual adjustment to unclear standards, and the lack of clear-cut evidence of adequate role-assumption. The energy so developed contributes to the maintenance of the emotional tone of the individual. In some instances this energy is constructive and adaptive and, in others, conflictful and productive of further anxiety. It seems wise to distinguish this type of motivational energy. Its usefulness lies in the emphasis it places on energy derived neither from the striving from inner needs nor from the expectancy orientation suggestive of attempts to integrate into externally perceived role-patterns. Rather this anxiety is seen as a reactive energy derived from efforts to integrate basic needs with external realities or from inconsistencies in, or failures to learn, desired external role-patterns. Its dependence upon the notions of psychic energy and expectancy set is clearly recognized. Its utility in fantasy analysis lies in its presence as a facilitating or limiting force: facilitating one individual in his adaptation to external demands, limiting the freedom of movement of another. It should not be confused with the basic assertiveness of psychic energy, nor with the constant need for role-definition seen in the concept of expectancy set. Rather this anxiety may be seen as a kind of omnipresent sensitization to stimuli selectively perceived as relevant to the particular inner needs and life goals of the individual.

The emphasis upon the concept of expectancy set and a reactive anxiety will serve to stress that one major lifelong goal is the need to define roles and to organize behavior. The breakdown of the energy involved in this continual role-defining serves to bring into focus the distinction between an externally oriented striving and the secondary energy derived from the particular experiences the individual has had in this direction.

The Patterning of Self

The sense of self-identity, the development of the self as an object possible of goal direction and attainment, emerges through experience and maturation. The process of this emergence is one of the drawing of generalizations from repeated affect-laden experiences. While it may be difficult to say at what point in time changes or reorientations of the self no longer occur, it is probable that the childhood and adolescent years are the ones during which the greatest developmental changes take place. It also seems likely that the formulation of the self as a work-oriented and financially self-supporting object, occurring normally in the early adult years, brings to a near close the major self concepts which may be expected to guide the individual in his adult years. It should be recalled, however, that possible major questionings of the self may occur in at least two subsequent periods: the time at which children leave the home and the change in the notion of self as responsible for the support and development of the young, and the climacteric in which may occur reorientation of the concept of self as a sexual object and possible threats to the feeling of function and worthwhileness. With these possible exceptions, and of course the possibility of change through psychotherapy or traumatic experience, the major structural characteristics of the self may be seen as generally well formed by the late adolescent or early adult years. It is with the presence of an organized self and with some of its major structural characteristics that we will deal here. The data and theories regarding the phases of self-development and the experiences relevant to them are of course vital to estimating the nature of the self. They are, however, in the realm of all other knowledge of persons and their interactions. Such knowledge is vital. It serves as a general framework within which to place the individual personality description rather than as specific principles of interpretation.

For a lucid analysis of the structure and developmental characteristics of this notion of self, and for one particularly suited to the
psychosocial viewpoint of the Thematic Apperception Technique, the
reader is referred to the writings of Erik H. Erikson.°

It has been observed that the self emerges with experience and
evaluation. This emergence may be seen as one resulting from the
interaction of the persons and ideas representative of the culture,
the physical organism and its rhythm and developmental changes, and,
at a certain point, the accumulating generalizations drawn by the
individual which represent his rudimentary self. This process is one
in which, 1. distinctions and delimitations are observed between the
individual and other persons and things; 2. content generalizations
are drawn as to the specific nature of the individual self; and 3.
generalizations are drawn as to the nature of outside events and
persons. In the description of the individual personality, it is important
to attend to all three of these structural characteristics and, from the
fantasy, to estimate the generalizations drawn by the individual with
respect to each. The interdependence of all three is apparent, yet
differential evaluations are necessary, particularly when prediction of
behavior or past relationships is required. The advantage of these
distinctions arises from the differing influences which these self-oriented
generalizations make in individual behavior. Thus wide variations
appear in the degree to which individuals perceive of themselves as
distinct from others and, conversely, in the extent to which the individual does not separate himself from other persons or influences in
his environment. The behavior reaction which an individual may
be expected to have to environmental changes will vary materially
with the extent to which he perceives himself as identical with or
highly distinct from that environment. Similarly, the specific content
characteristics of the self will contribute to this reaction, regardless
of the total amount of self-directed influence which the individual
may feel to be his. The generalizations drawn about the nature of
the significant others in his environment will again be relevant in
determining the course of the person's behavior. The image of the
goodness of other persons, of the receptivity which he feels they have
to stimuli from him, the reaction which he expects them to have, all
these, whether true or not, will markedly influence the course of his
behavior.

It is apparent that wide variations exist in the view which persons

° Erik H. Erikson, *Childhood and Society* (New York: Norton and Co., 1950).

have of the external world. Whether primarily factual, in the sense of concurring with the :udgments of others, or fanciful, in the sense of deriving primarily from distortions determined by the residuals of earlier events, the world and its events are differentially perceived. In ego identity there are also similarly wide variations. These occur not only in the self-referent content of identity, but also in the extent to which the individual has defined the boundaries of self and other.

It should specifically be noted that the definition of self and the individual's perception of his own sense of identity need not be thought to reside entirely "within" the person. The permeability of the boundaries of self and nonself is such that with great frequency an important part of the events or systematic ideologies that lend stability and definition to self are found external to the person. This is perhaps clearest in the ease of attachment to an ideology, yet it can be equally true in instances of major cathexis to, for example, one's children and their development, one's ideas and creative products and their fate, involvement with the physical world of objects, and attachment to and occupation with organized groups and societal institutions. Certainly most persons maintain some aspects of their self-image through such "ritual" events. The resistive power of the self-boundaries, however, varies greatly from person to person and, further, these boundaries vary both in the direction of obtaining identity from cathexes to such external events as those just described, as well as in the direction of permitting "internally" defined self-convictions to define and interpret external events. In the latter instance, the individual does not so much gain identity from the systematic characteristics of the external as he does consolidate his own internal image by a selective perception of the external.

Within individuals of comparable firmness of self, further variation will occur in the areas of self in which identity is clear and those in which it is not. In some areas, let us say those of the directive influences which one has over one's actions and those of others, the individual may feel distinct and directive. He thus is able to move with energy and vigor in his relationships to others, causing movement within these relations and maintaining for himself a feeling of personal power. Yet for the same person the sense of distinction in areas of goals and values may be so vague that his strivings are either inchoate and ill-defined or, more frequently, become identical with the average or dominant values of the social group in which he finds himself. While he sees himself as different from others in power and influence, he tends to perceive the goals for which he strives as "natural," as indistinct from the goals maintained by what he would see as "all good people."

The converse might be the person whose sense of identity is such that he feels he blends with all others, desiring the same things and seeing no distinction in his power to guide and influence others. Yet this person, in the area of goals and values, may hold a quite unique philosophy, perceived by himself and others as distinct and different. Thus, though he feels identical with others in his relations with people, he senses a malaise, derived possibly from the fact that others, while accepting his definition of identity in matters of influence, sense his distinctive system of values and continue to react guardedly.

This selective principle, which helps to determine how the individual will perceive and define external stimulation, is not to be seen as identical with body limits, but as potentially extending beyond them and defining external objects as part of self. Thus, one's creative products, work, home, children vary in the extent to which they are seen as distinct or the extent to which they are seen as part of self. The implication of this extension of self to external objects is to be found in the assumption that events which relate to them are seen as also relating to the self. Criticism of one's creative product and the failure or success of social causes to which one is attached are seen as directly self-referent and as influencing personal esteem. Especially where one's children are seen as extensions of self, the assumption seems to be made that the desires and motives which influence the self are also the values which motivate the other person.

It is apparent, of course, that not all persons assume this degree of identity with selected external objects. In these persons, success or failure of such external objects is perceived with greater objectivity and as less related to the sense of identity and personal esteem. It is probable that these are persons who attach greater importance to events motivated by other persons and see behavior, even as it relates to objects or events of personal importance, as determined as much by outside events as by personal desire and motive.

The involvement of the self in fantasies told to pictures undoubtedly varies from person to person. Yet it is suggested that the involvement in the storytelling task is generally characteristic of the ego-involving processes of the individual. The individual who views himself clearly and marks himself off distinctly from persons and events of his environment is one who can describe distinct events, persons, and sequences in his fantasies. Conversely, the person whose sense of self-identity is vague and undefined describes events in the stories without clarity, persons do not stand out, action and motivation are obscured.

In the developmental phases of personality, sometimes lasting well into early adulthood in some groups, the contradictory and still unformulated aspects of self may well be reflected in fantasy in exaggerated or depreciated form. Thus emotions or themes strongly highlighted in the stories of such persons may reflect more the uncertainty of the self-image than any final state. It is perhaps for this reason that it is often deceptive to assume that the prevalence of a great deal of references to any particular emotion indicates a similar preponderance of such emotion in the personality of the subject; or that the characteristics of a clearly perceived hero-figure are the characteristics of the storyteller; or that the dominant themas represent the action sequences which feature the real life-space of the subject. It should be assumed that the subject will permit himself in his fantasy an amount of imaginative leeway comparable to the complexity level of this total personality and proportionate to the extent to which he wishes to keep unconscious certain features of his self-image or personal motivation. For at least these reasons, the relationship between self and actions portrayed in stories should not be assumed to be direct. In personalities whose image of self is uncomplex and bears a very direct relation to events in the outer world, the parallel may be close. In more complex personalities, however, experimentation with tempting or only half-believed ideas may well represent the self-critical ego in stages of trial. Personalities in temporary stress often experiment wildly with certain emotions, notably aggression, in manners quite uncharacteristic of their past or future states.

The relevance of the patterning of self for the interpretation of fantasy is, of course, that it suggests the necessity of deducing from the data of the stories a central guideline, a level of communality always less specific than the level of the data themselves. As the storyteller illustrates in symbolic communicable form his self-convictions, so the interpreter must re-evaluate the outward symbols and reconstruct the guideline.

For purposes of suggesting some ways in which the concept of self may have relevance for the interpretation of fantasy, it may be well to show some parallels between processes of ego development and characteristic features of fantasy. For this purpose, the following concepts will be considered: *identification, projection, impulse denial and rejection,* and *role-assumption.* Each of these processes has relevance for the organizing of self during its developmental phases.

Identification

Identification with significant figures in the child's environment, notably parents, provides the child with an initial sense of direction and gives him the assurance of a temporary fully made identity. From the vantage point of this assumed identity, the child may experiment and as his capabilities and range of experiences grow, develop for himself an identity in part different from the models presented by his parents. In spite of the distinctness of self which may develop in the individual subsequently, it seems probable that he will retain to some degree certain features of affect and conviction which were characteristic of the models with whom he so closely identified in his early years. These external figures of identification will be selected by the person to some extent according to the preoccupations current for that individual. That is to say, the individual does not identify with all the figures available for identification, nor in fact need he identify with all aspects of any single person toward whom he feels some emulatory drive. Depending to some extent upon his developmental preoccupations, the individual will selectively choose those persons or aspects of persons which will provide him with the most relevant externalized image of an at least partially satisfying resolution of these preoccupations. It is possible that in this lie some of the reasons why fantasied-persons, mythical figures created in the folklore of the present or the past, are of interest at certain stages. To some extent this will further vary with the characterization of the actual persons available for identification. It should be observed that this same tendency may be partly responsible for the overelaborated identification with public figures (real and present—war heroes, flyers, movie stars, business tycoons—or mythical and historical—Horatio Alger, Cinderella, Bunyan, the Devil). With these, as distinct from the persons present in the immediate environment of the individual, the imagination may elaborate the desirable or undesirable features of the identification-object without the often disillusioning corrective of presently observed behavior. It should not be assumed that the individual's choice of identification-objects is always a conscious choice, nor, in fact, always a felicitous choice. The individual will initially develop cathexis towards such external objects as may bear a protective relationship to him.

In many instances, these persons will encourage such identification. In others, they will not. Yet some degree of identification will take place nonetheless. It seems probable that in most societal groups the individual can no more afford to be without some identification-objects than he can without the clothes thought appropriate in that group. While they may turn out to be scanty or unbecoming, the individual can only select those clothes which his circumstances permit. And, in any case, while his range of realistic choice may be limited, choose he must. The richness of choice of identification-objects will undoubtedly influence the complexity level of his adult personality. But, *faute de mieux*, the individual will identify, at least in part, with whatever is available. It perhaps therefore follows that the individual will at first be unable to select only those persons, or those attributes of persons, that will subsequently be thought desirable by him. Most identification patterns are thus "tie-in" deals in which for a rate he can afford he is able to emulate one attribute of a person yet must also accept another attribute less desired. The "tie-in" analogy is apt in expressing the necessity of often taking a second-rate product in order to receive a first-rate one. It breaks down, however, in that it implies a conscious awareness of the second-rate quality of the tied-in product. Unfortunately, in identification this is seldom the case.

The implication of these observations is that we should not always assume a pattern of emulative identification with a single or limited range of real persons. The child who can identify in a clear-cut and positive fashion with his mother and subsequently his father is possibly fortunate. He is probably also rather rare. In fantasy, the reflection of these identification patterns can be expected to be similarly dispersed, not, in the majority of cases, being embodied in each story in a clear-cut hero-figure whose attributed features represent those of the storyteller. It seems important to re-emphasize the observations made in Murray's manual,[129] to the effect that the attributes of a well-defined hero-figure are of particular relevance to the storyteller. However, it should not be assumed that every set of stories will be characterized by such well-defined heroes. The telling of stories with well-defined hero-figures is in itself a personality characteristic and not a necessary feature of the storytelling task. Also, it should be recalled that the feelings and actions attributed to the hero need not be the direct counterpart of the feelings and actions of the subject. These are not infrequently the reverse of the action tendencies of the subject and, in many cases, they are at best a simple distortion of affect areas in which the subject experiences concern. In any case, the statement of feeling and action attributed to the hero will be in symbolic form, in some persons at a high order of abstractness and in others at a fairly direct reflection of real feelings with only minor changes of locale and *dramatis personae.*

It has already been observed that persons may identify with only parts of people, selected attributes that are outstanding or that are of psychic interest for the individual. This may appear, of course, to be an identification with the total person in that affect is directed toward him, concern is felt about his actions and feelings, and some imitative behavior is present. In so far as identification is with an essential totality of identification-objects, to that extent may we expect clear-cut images of heroes to emerge in fantasy. The individual himself, of course, may be confused about the extent of his identification, assuming that the emulated object is interesting *in toto,* rather than that, as is perhaps more frequently the case, he is interesting in a number of specific attributes and that affect then generalizes to encompass the whole. The reversals of affect noted frequently in adolescence may be reflective of this confusion. The adolescent, in his efforts to establish a functional identity, experiments with his affect by emulating persons who represent for him the particular affect or action area with which he is concerned. Being often unable to distinguish those aspects that are of significance for him from those that are not, he reacts to the person as though it were the totality that was of interest. He thus invests the other person with generalized positive (or negative) affect and reacts to him on that basis. A shift in the roles with which the adolescent is experimenting, however, can result in complete reversal of this affect, former positive interest turning to rejection or to indifference. The fluctuating ambivalence often noted in adolescents again suggests that the identification is a mixed one, that the identification-object represents two characteristics about which the person holds contradictory feelings and about which he is unable to make up his mind. The complexity of feeling perhaps results from his inability to realize that two affect areas are represented. The burden of the confusion thus falls on the adolescent himself, who has the choice of projecting his ambivalence upon the other person and thus concluding that he is inconsistent and unreliable, or of rejecting the person entirely, searching for a model in another person who does not present him with these conflicting images.

The likelihood of mixed and part identification suggests that, in the analysis of fantasy, we could more profitably look for these partial identification-patterns than for identifications totally embodied in a hero-figure. A productive approach is to focus upon patterns of cathexes to interpersonal relations and of attributes systematically attributed to specific categories of persons and events. This is not to deny the presence of clear-cut hero-figures in some stories of some persons. Their appearance, however, is in itself a personality characteristic suggestive of storytellers who, more than other persons, identify readily with persons and tend to permit their own cathexes to be symbolized by single individuals. In persons and groups given to fairly intense interpersonal relations, of whatever quality, such whole-person identifications occur. They are less characteristic of persons inclined to be more objective in their approach to personal relations or in those whose earlier experiences with significant figures in their environment have been traumatic. In sum, the writer wishes to emphasize that one should analyze whatever pattern of identification characterizes the stories of a particular person and view such a pattern as descriptive of the personality. In so doing, one should anticipate wide variations from the image of total identification with single persons and expect to find patterns of mixed or partial identification. One should further expect to find these patterns evidenced in all descriptions of persons, actions, feelings, and objects, and not merely in the attributes noted of a central herolike figure.

Projection

The word projection in the field of projective techniques has taken on a meaning somewhat less specific than its original psychoanalytic focus. This original meaning assumed that projection referred to attributing to other objects feelings and actions characteristic of but rejected by the self. A more generally used meaning in the projective field would broaden this significance to imply what may be called *habituated response tendencies.* These habituated tendencies are then seen as characteristic modes of response descriptive of the individual's emotion and behavior in situations broader than the test but parallel to the particular stimulus situations provided by the pictures from which such habituated responses are deduced. It is certainly true that some subjects will at some time *project,* in the original sense of the term. Such technical *projecting,* however, should be viewed as only one possible mode of response and not as a necessary or characteristic approach to the picture. In the response to pictures ambiguous as to content or action, the individual may be seen as *projecting* in the sense in which this term may be used in geometry: to externalize or perceive as spatially and sensibly objective. Such a use of the concept of projecting retains at least two features of the psychoanalytic term: 1. the stress upon the fact that the subject need not be consciously aware of the systems of content or form by which he orders outside events, and 2. the subject, in ordering such outside events, "externalizes" in the sense that the order which he attributes to the outer event is already to some extent "within" and characteristic of the subject. It loses, of course, one special feature of the analytic notion: the need for the projected material to be denied by the subject.

The emphasis upon externalization and objectification is the principal use of the concept projection here. It is assumed that the characteristic modes of response of the subject are made *external* by the storyteller, in that they are attributed by him to persons and events in the picture. These modes of response are seen by the subject as *objective,* in the sense that they are perceived as *"really true"* of the outside person and events to which the subject attributes them. The attributed characteristics are "really true" of the outside events primarily in that they are not seen by the subject as representing the self. They become "objective" and "outside" because the subject specifically states that they apply to figures in pictures, descriptions produced "voluntarily" by the exercise of the subject's rational imagination. Occasionally, of course, there is some realization that that which the subject attributes to outside events is in some ways true of himself.

In the interpretation of fantasy, it is most productive to view the stories as a set of personal and social interactions with a reality defined by the picture. As the subject selectively redefines the stimuli and reacts to them by the attribution of action and feeling, he defines for us, the interpreter, his habitual modes of reaction to situations parallel to the pictures. To the extent that the pictures cover the range of major personal interactions important to the subject, to that extent will an interpretation of his externalized habitual responses, the stories, provide for us an image of his personality.

The individual may externalize (in the sense of the broader definition of projection) many aspects of his personality to include habituated intellectual response tendencies, assumptions of affect and action expected from various categories of people, cathexes of persons and nonpersons, his preoccupation with specific events or action sequences, and his perspective on past, present, and future. These varied aspects of personality will be objectified in a wide variety of ways. These will be discussed in some detail in later chapters. Here it should suffice to say that all describable aspects of the story are important to the diagnosis of projected affect, whether content characteristics or form.

Rejection and impulse denial

The patterns of identification and the reflection of projected person-ality attributes constitute, in a sense, some direct evidence of the personality underlying fantasies. In the areas of rejection and impulse denial lie some of the indirect evidences. It seems sound to assume that some areas of importance in the analysis of a personality may be perceived by the subject as undesirable, terrifying, or be so paralyzing to him as to bring forth only responses of rejection and denial. In fantasy, rejections may vary from the neglect of a positive, or more frequently a negative, aspect of a picture to a complete denial that a given situation or picture has any describable meaning at all. Such denial will include the "protest too much" reactions of the subject who insists upon positive affect in a "negative" * picture, as well as the subject who describes constructively a picture yet, in so doing, refuses to utilize segments of the picture frequently described by subjects: the "gun" in 3BM, the "other woman" in 4, "close affect" in 11. It is, of course, frequently difficult to determine with confidence the interpretive significance of such rejections. They have the quality of "no data" rather than of observable attributions of specific feeling or action. At the least, however, they should be noted as gaps in the personality picture or as areas of unusual response requiring further study. At the most, they can provide significant clues to be explored in other aspects of the stories. It should be assumed that rejections do not occur randomly, but rather that they occur with pattern. The determination of this pattern is the interpretive problem. Not infre-quently, such rejections will occur in locations from which some sug-gestive clues may be drawn. Some general suggestions for determin-ing what meaning rejection may have will be given later, especially in the discussion of negative content.

Closely related to rejections of pictures or specific parts of them are the more generalized but psychologically related denials of impulse. Both of these categories are suggestive of areas of repression and blocked affect. It seems profitable to separate these two categories, primarily to stress the fact that generalized impulse denial may be characteristic of the entire approach of a subject to the storytelling task and be evidenced in less clear-cut fashion than are specific rejections.

---

* The designation of a picture as positive or negative refers to the tendency of subjects to give positively or negatively toned stories to it. This point is referred to further in Chapter 12 under the discussion of "Latent Stimulus Demand."

These may include a general tendency to omit all reference to impulse categories in storytelling, a tendency to systematically obstruct all action which is based on impulse expression, or, particularly in subjects given to projection (in the analytic sense) and reaction formation, the specific verbalized denial that a figure in a story feels specific emotions. The general importance of the areas of denial lies in its relevance for determining sources of data in fantasy. As is suggested, it is not sufficient to analyze only those attributions of specific meaning which occur in the description of a picture and the relating of a story. It is further necessary to observe specifically the responses or notable failures to respond which suggest blocked and/or unexpressed affect. In the analysis of such responses one must rely more heavily upon normative data and past experience with characteristic topics or areas of blocking in specific pictures.

Role-assumption

As the individual matures, or as at any time in his career new life tasks are presented to him, he attempts to integrate these new experiences. All of the generalized processes described in the foregoing, and of course many others related to these, are helpful. One further process, which in a sense is a principle guiding the interaction of other processes, may be described as *role-assumption*. This refers to the likelihood that the individual is at all times attempting to carry into action some general set of hypotheses as to how he should act. These hypotheses are organized, with greater or lesser success, into some pattern of roles which the individual conceives as appropriate to him. These roles need not at all times be explicit; they may be only dimly perceived. They are not always directly social, in the sense of being a recognizable social category: mother, father, the prankster, the brilliant young man, the moral being. They are often merely guides to self-definition, often temporary and having the quality of an experimental tryout session. As the individual establishes an identity for himself, these experiments in role-assumption reduce and an over-all characteristic identity is apparent. It is important to view processes of identification, projection, and impulse denial in the light of this process of role-assumption. As the individual experiments with these images of his future self, his pattern of identifications and rejections will change. The pattern running through specific response tendencies is often best seen in terms of those hypotheses by which the individual attempts to give himself direction and consistency. One of the major tasks of fantasy interpretation is to see the central pathways of the individual's behavior, to deduce the general directives which give meaning to specific details of fantasy. One should continually ask of the specific data of the stories: What assumptions about himself does this person seem to be making? What roles are serving as his guides? What kind of consistency is he striving for?

External Press as Guides to Roles

The data of the TAT stories are not exclusively personal; they are social as well. They reflect both inner feelings and external social interactions. For at least this one reason, the broader the knowledge of the interpreter about processes of social groupings and interaction, the more precise and comprehensive can be his analysis of the TAT. This does not necessarily mean that the interpreter must know specifically the social group from which the subject comes and the nature of his position within it. Such information is indeed useful, but of more general importance is the interpreter's knowledge of social processes as such, whether or not specific to the social experiences of the subject in question. We should assume the presence of an environment of press and see the stories as a resultant of interaction between self and external press. Interpreters of the TAT, and other similar data-gathering devices, differ in the extent to which they utilize this interactive principle, although the author doubts if any reject this general notion of the interaction of self and external press. *The writer proposes specifically that the stories are not exclusively a projection of inner states. They are rather a resultant of these inner states, in response to a personal definition of generalized social situations, as represented by the pictures.*

The specific interpretive value of this notion is to be derived from envisioning the subject as moving through a personal life-space which is at all times inhabited—inhabited by the subject's images of real persons and events. It is important to recall that these real persons do not exist merely to provide projection-objects for the subject, but that they hold their own on-going goals and objectives. The effective image of these persons for the subject in all likelihood includes this image of these persons as moving, so to speak, as having goals and objectives toward which they are continually striving. It is also clear that the subject quite frequently misperceives these persons, attributing to them characteristics they do not hold, or that they hold in either lesser or greater intensity than the subject imagines. To attempt to describe the personality of a subject on the basis of the assumption that the stories represent exclusively inner states is analogous to trying to describe the functioning of the lower half of the human body without reference to the top half. In this sense the TAT stories stand intermediate, descriptive of both the inner states and of the perceived outer world.*

The perceived outer world reflected in TAT stories is generally a world of residual images of past experience and only occasionally are real-life events (in the sense of independently discovered actual occurrences) utilized as plot or characters. While there is personal variation in the closeness with which residual images parallel actual events, we may assume generally that fantasies represent a series of generalizations drawn from experience, rather than experiences themselves. It is at least in part for this reason that the prediction of specific behavior should be made with great caution. In many instances, varying intercase and intracase, predictions of specific externally observable behavior depend upon the interpreter's knowledge of characteristic psychodynamic underpinnings of overt behavior. To a large extent, also, correct behavior predictions depend upon knowledge of the counter- or facilitating forces present in the environment in which the individual is acting. A further modifier is to be found in the extent to which the personality of the storyteller is a highly malleable one or, conversely, highly rigid or self-determined. To describe the personality of a subject is an easier task than describing the projection of that personality into behavior in its social context.

An Interpretive Stance

The behavioral data gathered through the medium of the TAT can be analyzed, as can any system of data, in a variety of ways. It has been proposed here that certain viewpoints toward personality are productive and facilitating in the interpretation of fantasy. It is recognized that these viewpoints are at times arbitrary and most certainly incomplete. Similarly, it is the author's feeling that there is a particular set of viewpoints toward the process of interpreting, an interpretive

* Modifications of this general principle should be noted in the instance of certain psychotic adjustments in which the confused inner states clearly predominate. Even here, however, the stories reflect the blurred outer world perception. Similarly, in certain neurotic adjustments the stories deal to a predominate degree with the outward characteristics of the pictures or with the perceived characteristics of the generally hostile outer world. Yet, again here, the terrified and cringing inner world is apparent.

stance, that is likewise helpful. The objective in each instance is to facilitate the analysis and understanding of the individual personality. Other objectives are perhaps best approached with somewhat different emphases and methods.

1. The data of the stories represent the individual's rational effort to imagine a plot with order, sequence, and continuity. Whether or not he succeeds, this is the task set by the instructions.

2. The plots and characterizations made represent an externalization and objectification of the subject's habitual response tendencies.

3. Behind the externalized tendencies of the stories lies a pattern of consistency and an organization of need-systems which constitute the individual's effort at self-definition.

4. The manifest content of the stories is symbolic at one of a number of possible levels. At the most general level, manifest plot or character descriptions are specific instances of generalizations about categories of persons and events. These generalizations, "illustrated" in character or plot by the subject, are basic to the description of personality to be derived from the analysis of the stories. In each instance, however, it is normally the underlying generalizations made by the subject that are being sought. The overt character descriptions may be assumed to be only convenient symbolizations of these underlying feelings and hence more subject to change. It is, in part, for this reason that an analysis of the characteristics and attitudes of *all* figures should be made before proposing the tendencies of the subject which they portray.

5. A basic system of interaction to be expected in story content will be the subject's version of the interaction of impulse and control. In this interaction the subject's emotional residues of past experience with inhibition and guidance will be in interplay with his self-expressing and self-defining tendencies.

6. A substantial part of the material will in many instances be a selective reaffirmation of past experiences. This will represent current concerns used in part for curative explanation and in part for role-defining experimentation. In this connection, underplay and overplay are characteristic.

7. The story represents an interaction between subject and picture, the picture representing certain categories of general outer world influence selectively reacted to by the subject. In this connection, it becomes important to see the pictures as miniature reality situations responded to by the subject in ways characteristic of his usual mode of response to similar situations. The definition of similarity of situa-

tions must be made in part by the identification of the picture given
by the subject and in part by the identification known to be general
for subjects of like sex, age, and social experience.

8. Conformity and psychological "usualness" are basic ego-supporting characteristics and should not be neglected on grounds of absence
of idiosyncrasy. Stories of persons from similar groups (at least age,
nationality, social class) should be expected to show many common
features. These common features represent in part the ties of stability
and group-belonging. They are as important a part of the personality
of each individual as are idiosyncratic aspects.

9. It is not necessary to interpret everything in a record. Many
things may seem to have no systematic part in the personality analysis
derived. Granting that they probably do have some connection, it is
hardly necessary to integrate all features of a record into the analysis.
This license to admit that the subject can be in some areas beyond
your grasp is, the writer believes, a necessary corrective for the psychologist's tendency to believe he has explained everything. Unless
these details present some idea that seems contradictory to already
developed analyses, they need not be pursued.

10. Interpretations may be made at a variety of levels of generalization. As is suggested in other chapters, the degree of specification
used should not be greater than the evidence warrants. In general,
it is to be recalled that the TAT data represent generalizations which
the subject has drawn from past experience. Many of these will not
be readily available to him in conscious form. In any event, they will
be somewhat transformed in the construction of his stories. Inferences
made with respect to overt behavior must be made with caution and
must be logically consistent with inferences made regarding covert
drives and with the possibilities of overt action permitted by the
subject's external environment of personal interaction.

CHAPTER 3

The test materials: their description and basic nature

The Thematic Apperception Technique is a method for studying the social and psychological aspects of personality. The technique consists of a series of pictures about which the subject is asked to tell stories. The stories composed by the individual are essentially fantasies, make-believe stories which spring from the imagination of the subject. As contrasted with the free and largely uncontrolled fantasy of the dream or free association, in the TAT the subject is requested to adapt his fantasy to the stimulus content of the picture presented to him. Thus the stories might be called controlled fantasies. They are fantasies in that they are the creative products of the subject's imagination; they are controlled in that each picture presents a topic area to which the story must, in essence, conform. But the control exerted by each picture is of a special kind. It is control only of the topic, of the context of the fantasy. It is not a control of the feelings or of the specific actions which the subject may wish to attribute to to the picture. The context of the fantasy is thus delimited by the stimulus of the picture, but the content and form of the fantasy are unstructured by outside stimuli and are dependent upon the feelings, emotions, and the habitual ways of thinking of the subject himself.

In the effort to imagine a story about the stimuli of the picture presented to him, the subject must call upon the residue of knowledge, impressions, and inner feelings which at the moment occur to him as relevant to the situation. The story so created by the subject partakes of the characteristics earlier described for other forms of outward behavior: *it is a crystallized and symbolic projection of the individual's efforts to formulate his major feelings, anxieties, and satisfactions in the framework of the manner in which he has previously learned to present himself to the outer world.* The story is thus symptomatic of the individual's inner feelings and of his systems of defense and pretense.

In the following pages the pictures will be described. That their nature may become increasingly clear, they will be described in several ways, ways varying in their level of abstractness. First, the TAT pictures will be described in terms of their basic sociopsychological relation to the morality play of ancient times and the theatrical drama of modern times. Second, they will be described in the everyday semantics of object description, those given by Murray. Third, they will be described in terms of certain additional continua of reality description, permitting us to see somewhat more clearly the potential effect of the pictures upon the storyteller, and to note some variables in the pictures suggestive of an approach to the interpretation of the stories.

It was earlier observed that the storyteller does not approach the task of creating a story *de novo.* He approaches it well armed with assumptions and ideas, feelings attached to persons and objects, experienced generally in plots and counterplots. The significance of the fantasies can perhaps best be seen if their kinship to the drama and the morality play is observed. The morality play expressed the feelings and beliefs of its audience by the use of idealized symbols of Good and Evil, of things feared and hoped for. The audience readily identified with both the Devil and God's angels, demanding, however, that the angels triumph and the Devil be punished. Yet it should be observed that the Devil never perishes nor are the angels ever freed of his tantalizing. Both they and the audiences return the next week for a new bout—a bout symbolizing the struggles and anxieties of the audience, out of which they gain confidence and courage. The very exaggeration and overemphases present in these morality plays and in our contemporary secularized versions of them are the key to the satisfaction felt by the audience. The idealized figures of Good are entirely too good to be true, yet by contemplating them, one gains courage; one toys with the potentials of Good. Similarly one tortures oneself, from the safety of an armchair or in the company of friends, with the evils of Evil. While intensely interested, one is never too concerned, since one knows that, in the interplay of Good and Evil, Good will win. Thus we are vindicated in the bet we have placed on Good, while not getting so removed as to miss a touch of brimstone. And those who observe the play, hissing and cheering in turn, know full well that they are neither as good as God's angels in the play nor as evil as the Devil.

The similarity to the "classic human situations" of the TAT lies in the fact that these pictures, too, are of the order of idealized symbols of Good and Evil, and of the many subdivisions possible within their boundaries. As the audience of the morality play identified with the many elements of the play, so does the storyteller identify with the many features of the drama portrayed in the TAT pictures, struggling for clarification through overemphasis, suggesting the presence of a feeling by its vigorous denial, his eyes lighting at the entrance of the Devil and his assistants, sensing the virtue inherent in the happy ending. We should not be led astray by the exaggerations, either of Good or Evil. For as the individual attempts to create a satisfactory plot out of these meaning-laden images, he must select an order, he must make a choice among many possible solutions. In so doing he must distort somewhat both his own feelings and the qualities he attributes to the figures of the drama. As Professor Muller has remarked in a different connection, "an order is necessarily a selection from diverse possibilities, and as such it requires the suppression of other possibilities, has the defects of its virtues, and tends to overemphases—as William James said, without too much we cannot have enough, of anything." *

We may now leave this consideration of the cultural depth of pictures of this sort and describe the test pictures briefly in more ordinary terms. They have been described first in their cultural perspective, since their basic stimulus value is closely connected with this view of the classic situation, a view easily lost sight of in the effort to describe the present physical realities.

The TAT as originally developed consists of thirty pictures, variously designed to be appropriate to the sex and age of the subject. There are eleven pictures (Numbers 1, 2, 4, 5, 10, 11, 14, 15, 16, 19, 20) which

* H. J. Muller, *The Uses of the Past* (New York: Oxford University Press, 1952), 24.

were designed for both sexes and all ages; seven pictures designed for boys under fourteen and males over fourteen (marked BM); seven designed for girls under fourteen and females over fourteen (marked GF); one designed for only boys and girls (marked BG); one for males and females over fourteen (marked MF); and one each suitable for boys (B), for girls (G), for males over fourteen (M), and females over fourteen (F). The selection of pictures for any one subject will consist of the eleven central pictures plus all of those marked with the symbol (B, G, M, F) appropriate to the age and sex of the subject.

The pictures are divided into two series, the pictures of the second series being generally more ambiguous and/or bizarre than those of the first series. Dr. Murray recommends that at least one day intervene between the first and the second session. He emphasizes that in the second session the subject should be particularly encouraged to use his imagination, to "let your imagination have its way, as in a myth, a fairy story, or allegory." The pictures of the series are now described:

1. A young boy is contemplating a violin which rests on a table in front of him.
2. Country scene; in the foreground is a young woman with books in her hand; in the background a man is working in the fields and an older woman is looking on.
3BM. On the floor against a couch is the huddled form of a boy with his head bowed on his right arm. Beside him on the floor is a revolver.
3GF. A young woman is standing with downcast head, her face covered with her right hand. Her left arm is stretched forward against a wooden door.
4. A woman is clutching the shoulders of a man whose face and body are averted as if he were trying to pull away from her.
5. A middle-aged woman is standing on the threshold of a half-opened door looking into a room.
6BM. A short elderly woman stands with her back turned to a tall young man. The latter is looking downward with a perplexed expression.
6GF. A young woman sitting on the edge of a sofa looks back over her shoulder at an older man with a pipe in his mouth who seems to be addressing her.
7BM. A gray-haired man is looking at a younger man who is sullenly staring into space.
7GF. An older woman is sitting on a sofa close beside a girl, speaking or reading to her. The girl, who holds a doll in her lap, is looking away.
8BM. An adolescent boy looks straight out of the picture. The barrel of a rifle is visible at one side, and in the background is the dim scene of a surgical operation, like a reverie-image.

8GF. A young woman sits with her chin in her hand looking off into space.

9BM. Four men in overalls are lying on the grass taking it easy.

9GF. A young woman with a magazine and a purse in her hand looks from behind a tree at another young woman in a party dress running along a beach.

10. A young woman's head against a man's shoulder.

11. A road skirting a deep chasm between high cliffs. On the road in the distance are obscure figures. Protruding from the rocky wall on one side is the long head and neck of a dragon.

12M. A young man is lying on a couch with his eyes closed. Leaning over him is the gaunt form of an elderly man, his hand stretched out above the face of the reclining figure.

12F. The portrait of a young woman. A weird old woman with a shawl over her head is grimacing in the background.

12BG. A rowboat is drawn up on the bank of a woodland stream. There are no human figures in the picture.

13MF. A young man is standing with downcast head buried in his arm. Behind him is the figure of a woman lying in bed.

13B. A little boy is sitting on the doorstep of a log cabin.

13G. A little girl is climbing a winding flight of stairs.

14. The silhouette of a man (or woman) against a bright window. The rest of the picture is totally black.

15. A gaunt man with clenched hands is standing among gravestones.

16. Blank card.

17BM. A naked man is clinging to a rope. He is in the act of climbing up or down.

17GF. A bridge over water. A female figure leans over the railing. In the background are tall buildings and small figures of men.

18BM. A man is clutched from behind by three hands. The figures of his antagonists are invisible.

18GF. A woman has her hands squeezed around the throat of another woman whom she appears to be pushing backwards across the bannister of a stairway.

19. A weird picture of cloud formations overhanging a snow-covered cabin in the country.

20. The dimly illumined figure of a man (or woman) in the dead of night leaning against a lamppost.

These descriptions present to the reader a general image of the pictures, an image sufficiently clear to permit him to visualize the gross features of the picture and to identify the pictures when he sees them. However, such description is sufficient only for this first general level of identification of the stimulus presented to the subject. It tells us only a part of that to which the subject actually reacts when he conforms to our request to identify the picture and tell us a story about it. The more thorough knowledge we have of the total stimulus situation in which the subject finds himself, the better are we able to comprehend the significance of his behavior. For this reason, it becomes necessary to examine in more detail the nature and component parts of the picture stimuli to which the subject responds. It becomes necessary to go beyond the description of the ordinary objects and symbols presented in the picture and to observe some additional ways in which significant variation is to be found. In the following pages, certain additional characteristics of the pictures will be enumerated. Subsequently, the implications of these features for the selection of pictures to be presented to the subject will be discussed. The basic emphasis throughout these descriptions of significant features for the pictures is upon the relevance of these features to the interpretation of the stories told to them, to the understanding of the behavior resulting from the subject's response to the picture stimuli.

Some of the pictures are contextually well structured. In some pictures the basic nature of the situation, the people, and objects represented are well defined by the picture itself. A minimum of ambiguity will be found in these pictures. Thus, in card 1 there is no real ambiguity in determining the basic nature of the stimulus. It is quite clearly a young male in some type of introspective situation involving a clearly seen violin. Similarly, card 2 is without doubt a rural scene in which a young lady, an older woman, and a man are depicted. In these two and other similarly structured pictures (for example, 3MF, 4, 5, 6BM, 7BM, 9GF) there is no real interpretive or imaginative problem involved *in the identification of the major persons or objects represented.* Any deviations from these basic features are to be seen as perceptual distortions or as "misinterpretations" of some special diagnostic significance. It is to be noted, however, that in spite of the relatively structured quality of these pictures, not all features are so structured. First, there are some objects in the pictures that are less clear-cut, often either difficult to define or not always observed by the ordinary storyteller. In 1, for example, the material under the violin lends itself to many possible interpretations: table, music sheets, cloth, etc. Similarly, in 2, the background material is not too readily seen. The second man and horse, the buildings, the "lake," and other less apparent objects are variously interpreted and lend themselves to individual projection. Second, and more important, while the objects, persons, and general situations are sufficiently clear for ready identification, *the relationships between persons, their activities, feelings, and the plot and its outcome are not similarly structured.* It is here that the imagination of the subject is called forth. In these areas, all of the cards, even those where the context is structured, are highly ambiguous and undefined.

Some of the pictures are contextually ambiguous. In contrast to those pictures just described, some pictures are unclear from the point of view of the basic identification of the objects, persons, and basic situation. Card 3BM, for example, shows the huddled figure of a person (called a young boy by Murray) who may be seen either as a boy or girl, young or old. Beside the figure is an object on the floor, variously defined as a gun, knife, keys, toy, or a hole in the floor. The background situation is itself vague, lending itself to varied interpretations as to locus. In cards 10, 11, 19, this contextual ambiguity is even more pronounced. In these pictures the task of the subject becomes more complex. Not only must he propose a story to account for the feelings and interactions between the people and objects, he must also determine the basic situation and the kinds of people and events about which he will construct this plot. This quite simple continuum of ambiguity already suggests a way of estimating some differences in our subjects. It provides a stimulus to which some subjects can respond quite readily. Other persons, however, find themselves at home only with more structured situations and become distracted when presented with the pictures of greater ambiguity.

Some pictures deal with ordinary or usual events and some with events that are unusual. Regardless of their ambiguity, the pictures differ in the extent to which they present ordinary lifelike situations. Picture 7GF, the mother sitting beside a girl, or picture 6BM, an elderly woman standing with her back to a tall young man, both present well-structured pictures representing easily recognizable and ordinary events. Picture 10, while ambiguous and presenting difficulty to many subjects, is still an essentially ordinary event, representative of events well within the experience range of most subjects. On the other hand, while still not approaching the bizarre and distorted, some pictures are most unusual and can be somewhat of a shock to persons not able to cope with the unexpected. Thus 17BM, 18BM, and 19 are out of the ordinary, unexpected events, even though, as in 17BM at least, perfectly identifiable. One would want to present a subject with a variety of picture stimuli such that his ability to deal with both the ordinary and the unusual is tested. The full series consists of two sets of cards. One, up to 10, is designed to be reasonably ordinary and within the subject's experience. The second, from 11 to 20, is designed to be more unusual and to challenge the subject's imagination.

Some pictures are bizarre. Among the pictures of Murray's second series, numbers 11 to 20, are some which are more than merely unusual in the sense just mentioned. These bizarre pictures present an image to the subject in which reality elements are distorted rather than merely seldom encountered—elements which are "unreal." Pictures 12F, 15, 17GF, and 18BM are of this sort. Some are presented in terms of actual persons in weird situations. 12F and 18BM are of this sort. Some, like 15, contain strange figures in bizarre circumstances, while others are of scenes themselves highly unusual and challenging to the imagination, as for example, 11 or 17GF or 19.

Some pictures have no people in them. Most of the TAT series contain either one or more persons in varying situations. Some, however, have only faint suggestions of persons, as in 11, or no persons at all, as 12BG or 19. The basic stimulus value of these pictures varies but a common stimulus of importance is the absence of people.

There is one blank card. Number 16 is blank. The importance of this lies in the extreme challenge which it makes for the subject who must create for himself the entire scene as well as its people, events, and plot development.

Some have simple form and some complex. Independent of the varying complexities of the pictures set by their content, it should be observed that the basic form of the pictures varies. Contrast, for example, picture 1, the boy with the violin, with picture 19, the cloud-formation picture. In 1 the form elements are really only two, the boy and a violin, plus possibly the table upon which the violin rests. The story which the subject tells can be an entirely adequate one if it takes into account only the two central features, two large details, so to speak, the boy and the violin. The form demands made by the picture are thus limited. On the other hand, 19, the swirling, indefinite, ambiguous picture, is quite another matter. The form demands are different in at least two respects: 1. there are no specific readily identified large details to focus upon; 2. the entire image presented is vague and ambiguous. The individual here must attribute form where only vague suggestions of form exist. He must further be satisfied with indefinite forms, clouds, smoke, swirling forces, etc. A further contrast is presented by 2, the farm scene. Here the subject has much large and small form presented to him. Three large details are in the foreground, the three persons. Additional readily apparent details abound—the tree, the books, the horse, the farmlike nature of the picture. Less apparent are many small details—the furrows of the field, the various farm buildings, the pregnancy of the older woman, the second man and horse, the "lake" in the far background. The task and the opportunity presented are more complex here than in 1, or 3BM, or 3GF, or similar pictures of quite simple form. Not only are there more people and potentially more complex human relations to cope with, but a far greater range of form either to take into account or ignore. Similarity of form demand, however, should not lead one to assume the similarity of the stimulus meaning of a picture. Picture 1, the boy with the violin, is in form demand highly similar to 3BM, the crouched figure. Yet here the similarity ends, for the two are quite different in content and meaning. The woman with downcast head, 3GF, is again rather similar in form to the man with three hands, 18BM. Yet the emotions and feelings which they normally elicit and the overt content of stories told to them vary greatly.

Other variations. There are many other ways in which the basic stimuli presented by the cards vary. Those described will perhaps be sufficient to indicate how the variation in the card itself is important both to the problem of card selection and of interpretation. The changes in form demand and stimulus meaning challenge the subject in varying ways, presenting him with differing facets of external reality against which his inner fantasies and personal convictions may be reflected. This is the central reason for knowledge of the characteristics of the card itself—the light it throws upon the precise way in which the subject was stimulated, thus permitting the interpreter to gauge more accurately the significance of the subject's reaction to that stimulation.

Criteria for Selecting Pictures

The preceding analysis of the cards gives us a starting point in the selection of a general set of pictures and some principles for the selection of cards for special purposes. The following criteria are suggested as guides to the selection of pictures from the Murray set and as principles to be used in the design or selection of other special sets.

The criterion of latent stimulus meaning

The most important variable in the selection of pictures is the latent stimulus meaning of the picture itself. While the selection of a picture containing a figure of the sex and approximate age of the subject is undoubtedly of value, it is felt that the analysis of the *emotional issue most usually raised by a given picture* is the prime variable. Thus, for example, the advantage of picture 1, the boy with the violin, lies primarily in the fact that it seems most readily to elicit feeling and stories dealing with authority, with the reactions to authority, and with the degree of initiative and self-directed control which the subject can maintain. The fact that the picture is one of a young boy with a violin is a *convenient symbolization of a person in an ambivalent emotional situation,* but contains little inherent advantage *per se.* If the basic stimulus were the boy and the violin, rather than the emotional issue of authority and control, one would presumably find this picture of limited use with adult subjects or with subjects inexperienced with a violin. Yet this is by no means true. This picture is of considerable value with mature adults, eliciting from them data which readily reveal their experiences with authority and external control and the nature of the assumptions which they make about their own interest in and ability to influence these controlling forces. Given several pictures of similar latent meaning, it would possibly be of considerable advantage, particularly in the case of children, to select the one with a figure representing the age and sex of the subject. But the primary and more vital issue is that of the basic emotional stimuli of the picture.

The criterion of basic interpersonal relation

A number of the pictures selected should represent basic interpersonal relations: a mother-child scene, a father-child scene, a heterosexual scene, a person alone, a group of persons of varying social roles, a scene of two persons of the same sex and age. The analysis of the stories for these pictures provides much basic data for the reconstruction of residual life experiences and gives to the interpreter a picture of the emotional psychic assumptions which the subject makes about the basic interpersonal realities.

To a large extent, we may suggest that the major psychic emotions and dispositions of the subject are organized around specific persons or categories of persons. Thus when the subject reveals in his stories his notions and feelings about a range of categories of persons and interpersonal relations, he also provides us with a statement of his assumptions about life in general and about his basic mechanisms of relating himself to the world as he interprets it.

The criteria of reality representation

The pictures selected should represent varying degrees of objective reality. The advantage of this lies in the challenge to the organized thinking patterns of the subject and in the estimate it provides of his ability to remain stable, logical, and imaginative in the face of unusual or apparently contradictory stimuli. Specifically, four varieties of reality representation should be portrayed:

Clear-cut reality. In a number of cards, the basic content is portrayed in direct, unambiguous fashion. Thus in 1 the boy and the violin are quite clearly portrayed, identification of them as objects requiring only simple skills of observation. In the selection of a variety of interpersonal relations, as in the second criterion, a number of such portrayals of clear-cut reality will unquestionably be found.

Illogical reality arrangement. A special advantage of picture 8BM, the boy and the operating scene, lies in the fact that it presents several quite easily identifiable reality objects, but places them in an arrangement that requires special interpretive skills of the subject. Thus the boy is readily identifiable, as is the "operating scene" in the immediate background. Yet, they are placed, both spatially and in terms of the different art techniques, so as to appear not in the same reality plane. Similarly, the rifle, and to a lesser extent the window or bookcase, are identifiable without exercise of imagination, but are placed in their relation to the boy and the scene in such a manner as to require special attention and explanation. In this picture the point of particular interest is, of course, both the content as well as the manner in which this illogical or unusual arrangement of objects is accounted for. Similarly, picture 18BM, the man with three hands, while it has also a slightly bizarre air, presents a readily identifiable man and three readily identifiable hands. The challenge lies in the arrangement in which there are no other figures present to account for the third hand.

Bizarre or unreal stimuli. Some of the pictures selected for use with all subjects should portray events in a bizarre, startling, or unexpected manner. Such pictures are useful in estimating the facility with which the individual can deal with the unusual and startling as well as in presenting an opportunity for irregular or pathological thought content to be expressed. In general, at least one picture emphasizing some personal scene and one depicting a scene in which people are not dominant should be included. Pictures 17BM, 12F, and 18BM are good examples of the first of these categories. Pictures 11, 17GF, and 19 represent the second.

Ambiguous reality. Some of the pictures chosen should be highly unstructured and ambiguous. Such pictures challenge the imagination of the subject, reflecting the originality of thought content as well as the quality of the personality strength and organization. They are also excellent tests of the individual's habitual ability to deal with new and unfamiliar situations. Picture 19 is the best example of this in the TAT although several pictures in the last half of the set are good substitutes.

The criterion of intensity

Each of the pictures selected should be sufficiently intense in quality as to intrigue the subject and to demand that he propose some sort of solution to it. This intensity may be conveyed to the subject in a variety of ways. Dramatic content, such as 18GF, 12F, and 17BM, is an excellent but by no means the only way to secure such intensity. Picture 12BG, containing no human figures but only a rowboat drawn up to the bank of a woodland stream, is satisfactorily intense to meet this criterion. Possibly the very unusualness of the absence of people, immediately raising the question "where are the people" in the subject's mind, is the element which secures the intensity value. Similarly picture 1, the boy with the violin, is a most undramatic and even drab picture, yet it is more than adequately stimulative. Here the intensity is secured not so much from any drama inherent in the action portrayed as from the conflict which the situation raises in the mind of the ordinary subject.

The criterion of flexibility and ambiguity

The flexibility of a picture has at least two major aspects: the ambiguity of the reality of the object or persons and the ambiguity of the emotions, action, and outcome. The criterion of reality representation emphasized the ambiguity of the reality of objects and persons portrayed. Here the ambiguity of the emotions and actions is in question. Each picture used should permit full freedom of the emotion and the actions which may be attributed to it. The more different the emotions which may be read into the situation and the wider the range of solutions which may be reasonably proposed, the better the picture. Many pictures with clearly identifiable persons, 2 for example, yield as useful data as do pictures that are extremely vague, such as 19. The crucial factor here seems to be the emotion and outcome ambiguity. It further seems advisable to make the initial selection of pictures along the lines of basic interpersonal relations rather than primarily along the lines of selected emotions. Except as one is developing a special set of pictures to explore the dimensions of anger, or of love, or of some other emotional state, the selection of pictures to portray a reasonable range of emotions is probably misleadingly oversimplified. It seems more profitable at this point to select along lines of basic object relationships and reality approximation, designing or selecting each picture so as to permit a wide range of emotions to be attributed to it. In this manner one permits the preferences of the subject to give the prime emotional implications to the picture rather than those of the examiner. This procedure probably places the expression of feeling more readily within its proper context of object relationships. Further, it will reduce the effect of the emotional ties of the examiner, whose prerogative to projection is regrettably equal to that of the subject.

The criterion of culture-appropriate symbols

The pictures selected and the situation portrayed should be appropriate to the culture of the group being studied. The pictures should be so drawn or selected as to employ persons, dress, objects, background that are not thought inappropriate by the persons being studied. It seems overly complicated and probably unnecessary to design pictures for a group using the precise physical features and dress that are used by the group. Rather, they need only be portrayed in a general manner so as to enable the subjects to feel that the persons could be people like them. Thus in dealing with the Hopi of Southwest United States, and with the Navahos of the same region, it seemed unnecessary to design two sets, one recognizable as Hopi and one as Navaho. Rather, a set that is recognizable as "Indian" is adequate. In fact, such a set designed to represent the general category of Southwest Indians * was quite adequate for Dakota plains groups. It is probable that the criterion of culture-appropriateness need imply only appropriateness to the general culture area rather than to any specific subgroup in the culture.

When designing or selecting pictures for a specific culture, one should be cautious not to design the picture in too great detail. One should not include in the picture more specifically recognizable cultural symbols or artifacts than are sufficient to indicate to the subject the general culture pattern involved. The inclusion of such objects helps the subject to identify with the picture. However, too many or too highly specialized objects also tend to inhibit fantasy, calling instead upon the subject to enumerate verbally the objects present or to tell a story highly stereotyped in quality. It is to be recalled that the very quality which makes a certain number of readily identifiable objects useful is the same quality which may inhibit fantasy. That quality, of course,

* Designed by Robert J. Havighurst and Alice Joseph for the Research on Indian Education.

lies in the fact that each cultural object has a pattern of culturally determined meanings which members of the society in question habitually attribute to it. When too specifically identified or too great a quantity of such objects are present, the high amount of culturally defined meanings which they arouse tends to overshadow the individually determined meanings. It is possibly for this reason that, at least in American middle-class society, the "stock" photographs and illustrations from popular magazines are only infrequently useful.

Criteria for pictures for special problems

In the design or selection of pictures for special problems of research or diagnosis, all the criteria given are also applicable. In addition, however, careful advance study of the problem will usually suggest special situations which the examiner will wish to pictorialize. In the case of studies of culture groups, consultation with an anthropologist familiar with the culture is necessary. Emphasis in such consultation should be upon the events, habits, customs, or situations which are hypothesized as relevant to the psychological problem being studied. Undoubtedly many of the basic personal relationships of importance in our own society will, when the pictures are suitably adapted, be useful. Nonetheless, there will also be events or situations of importance that are characteristic of the specific society under study. These, too, should be represented in the pictures. A warning should be made against attempting to portray a particular situation too specifically. There seems to be considerable difficulty in a research person from one culture attempting to put into the symbols of pictures a specific situation from another culture. Pictures should rather be designed to elicit fantasy in the general area of interpersonal relations to which specific importance is attached by the psychologist. The advice of the anthropologist can be of great help here, since he will be familiar with the ways in which such situations are represented in the culture itself.

Pictures for research or diagnosis or special clinical problems should follow the suggestions made here. While opinion varies somewhat in this matter, it is the present writer's preference to use a basic set of pictures for all subjects, relying upon the many varieties of reality representation and types of human situations presented to elicit interpretable fantasy. Should the case being studied present special problems in a specific area—for example, family relations, sexuality, aggression, and control—it would seem appropriate to augment the series of pictures used by additional pictures whose latent content tends to elicit fantasy in the relevant areas. It is felt, however, that it is not advisable to attempt to select a special set for each subject. This is suggested since, first, a general set of ten to fifteen pictures will most likely be sufficient to stimulate the subject's fantasy in relevant problem areas and, second, to select a different set for each case destroys the considerable advantage of comparison inherent in a set which has been used repeatedly with other subjects.

CHAPTER 4

The variables of form

In the analysis of any collection of data, understanding of the patterns of meanings within it may be most suitably derived when the variations of the data themselves are apparent. It is certainly true that insights and valid deductions may be made from TAT data in circumstances where the interpreter is unable to point to the evidence for his conclusions, or in circumstances where the evidence he points to seems equally to suggest an alternative interpretation. These observations, perhaps best called insights, are an important part of the process of thinking which results in interpretations from stories. They should, however, constitute a smaller and smaller part of the total interpretive scheme, giving way gradually to observations about the personality of the subject which are based on describable variations in the actual data of the stories. Yet in stories told to the TAT, it is not always a simple matter to say wherein lie the attributes of the stories which vary significantly with personality. It is, of course, the stories; at the minimum it is the recorded verbalization of the subject during the time interval between the showing of the first picture and the completion of the task set by the examiner. Yet what are the describable attributes of these verbalizations? To give a partial answer to this question is the intent of this and the following chapter. It is proposed to provide a detailed analysis of some of the observed characteristics of stories which may later be shown to vary significantly with personality. It cannot be overemphasized that the focal task of the derivation of personality descriptions lies in the intimate description of the ways in which the subject has gone about the task of telling his stories. In this "way of telling" will lie the key to the habitual structuring of the world which the subject perceives and his habitual response to this structuring. In general, the task of interpretation may be phrased as follows:

1. How does the subject define the stimulus?
2. Given his perception of the stimulus, how does he respond to it?
3. Given his definition of the stimulus, and his chosen mode of response to it, what does this tell us of the subject's personality?

The temptation is always to jump immediately to point 3 and to contemplate directly the attributes of personality. To do this, however, is to describe the sea from the way in which the surface water behaves. It may be correct to observe that the water is rough, the waves are high. It may be a quite proper conclusion to say that in another instance the sea is calm, the water is smooth, the waves are small and regular. Yet does it tell us anything about the sea? What does it tell us of the way in which the sea reacts to its surroundings of earth and air, of the content and composition of the areas below the surface?

One cannot be too cautious in directing attention to the evidence from which personality conclusions are drawn. The data of the stories form the guides to tentative hypothesis formation and the data against which such hypotheses must be checked. One has gone a long way toward deriving a view of the personality when one has described in detail the content and composition of the stories as told, the ways of relating to the surround of images of people and events. This does not mean that the surface characteristics are not important. It is necessary to observe the overt, quickly perceived characteristics. The subject is voluble; he is short or to the point; he is confused and wandering; he is smooth, well organized; he has good perspective and judgment; he is terse, tense, angry—all of these surface observations are an important part of the personality picture. But they are only beginnings and their underlying meanings and motivation must be observed. These can be observed only by probing further into the available data, the stories.

It has been noted in the foregoing that to describe the significant variables of fantasy is no simple task. It is not presumed that the writer has succeeded in describing all of the variables that would subsequently prove to be useful, nor that he has attributed the only and proper meaning to these variables. It will be apparent that some variables are more important than others. Themas are possibly more important than length, outcomes than grammar. Yet, with distressing frequency, short stories give clues to constriction not seen in themas and word choice clues to conflicts not reflected in outcomes. Knowledge of the differential significance of such variables is meager. At this stage one does best by observing all variables that have come to one's attention and deducing from the patternings of those variables meaningful generalizations and trends which characterize the personality.

Form and Content

Form and *Content* are two somewhat overlapping categories within which significant breakdowns of story variables may be made. Two further special categories will be added: *Dynamic Structure of Content* and *Negative Content*. In a sense, of course, these are breakdowns of the over-all category, *Content,* but are, the author believes, sufficiently different to warrant special treatment. *Content* refers to *what* the subject said and *Form* to *how* he said it. *Dynamic Structure of Content,* a category utilizing the spatial characteristics of the order and juxtaposition of content, deals with assumptions of psychic continuity and connectedness of contents which do not appear rationally to be connected or in which the relatedness is other than that which the subject presumes. *Negative Content* will be presented as the concern with *what* the subject did *not* say, in the light of what he might have been expected to say. The determination of what the subject might have said will bring us to normative questions and will be dealt with in terms of a distinction between *Manifest Picture Stimulus* and *Latent Picture Stimulus*. Since to some extent the analysis of negative content also involves the question of what stimulating areas of the pictures normally are responded to, we will deal also with the question of the *form demand* of the pictures.

Form Characteristics

The subject's recounting of a perceived stimulus occurs in a describable form pattern. These form patterns appear to vary markedly from subject to subject and, in fact, vary within a series of stories of a single subject. The rationally oriented narrative is the form for which our instructions ask. The majority of subjects will give us this narrative, though always in some idiosyncratic manner. Variations in form occur in stories of highly similar content, and the same basic plot may be related by one subject in a form quite different from that of another subject. It is proposed that these variations in form reflect variations in the perception and organization of the individual and in the way in which he views and reacts to the stimuli of the world around him and of the world within him.

In the pages that follow, some of the more important form characteristics of stories will be given. They are presented primarily to permit one to focus upon the variations present in the data of stories and to facilitate description of these data. Subsequently, an effort will be made to show how some of these variations in form relate to personality.

Amount and kind of imaginal production

Length of stories. Marked variations will occur in the length of stories produced by a person. General standards for evaluating the basic amount of productivity necessary for fruitful analysis are not at all well formed at this time. It seems clear, however, that useful stories can be produced which are substantially under the word count suggested by Murray in 1943. The story of 300 words was at that time suggested as standard for the adult and 150 words for the ten-year-old child. Certainly stories as short as fifteen words have been analyzed with some success.* It is the author's impression that story length will vary somewhat with personality characteristics, as well as with the overt characteristics of verbality level. It is clear, of course, that subjects can be encouraged to prolong and elaborate their stories and in situations encouraging high verbal productivity all subjects will tend somewhat to longer productions. However, the writer does not feel that the sign of an analyzable story lies primarily in its length. Rather, he would suspect that more to the point would be some evidence that the subject has grappled with the instructions as set for him and has carried these out around the stimuli of the picture shown him. This can be done in few words or in many. The subject who gives us many words indeed tells us something of his word fluency and his vocabulary facility, and these are important personal attributes. It is to be questioned, however, if he thereby tells us more about his personality than a subject who is more succinct

---

* It should not be concluded, however, that such stories represent an optimal length. It seems probable that stories as short as those reported here are unusual and may be specific to the cultures reported and to the test conditions used. Certainly longer stories would have yielded more material. See Henry, Williams E. The Thematic Apperception Test in the Study of Culture-Personality Relations. Genet. Psychol. Monogr., 1947, 35, 3–315.

and economical- in word usage. In fact, it sometimes seems that elaborately lengthy stories present as much of an interpretive hazard as they do extra data. To see the basic values, viewpoints, and plot of the personal interactions involved in a story may, in the case of a lengthy one, require a great deal of shorthand on the part of the interpreter. Length in such instances can be more of a handicap than a benefit. A story which reflects some perception of the stimuli, which presents a plot having some continuity (though not necessarily all three parts as asked in the instructions), which attributes some choice of feeling or action to the figures portrayed, and which has some sort of terminal point is an analyzable story. This can be done in few or many words. If the subject is one who, in addition, gives past, present, and future plot suggestions, who elaborates with statements of feeling and emotion, and who fills his story with dramatic inter-action, then we have more to go on. Such elaborations are desirable, but not necessary, and, in any case, a single story of 300 words would seem to me to verge on the overly verbal. One is not testing the verbality and vocabulary range of the subject; one is sampling his basic viewpoint toward himself and his world.

Amount of introduced content. Closely related to length is the question of the amount of the total story productivity that may be seen as "introduced." By this is meant the quantity of images, figures, events, episodes, descriptions, and elaborations that are added to the basic identification of the details of the picture. Subjects vary greatly in this respect, some filling their stories with associated images and additional figures related to the plot development. Some stick very closely to comments for which there are closely parallel representations in the picture. Certainly some introduced content is necessary to meet the instructions. Some imagination must be utilized to develop a plot, mere enumeration of the details of the picture not being sufficient (though occurring in certain instances, of course). Some judgment of the range of interests, the richness of imagery, and the facility of association can be made from such introduced content.

Kinds of introduced content. Whether great in amount or not, the particular areas within which content is introduced require attention. Does the subject always introduce one particular pattern of imagery, or many? Are there many areas about which he associates freely or few? The relatedness of this quantity judgment to questions of the content of these introduced observations is apparent and will be dis-cussed under considerations of content in Chapter 5.

Vividness and richness of imagery. A rich flow of imagery with vivid illustrations and elaborations clearly differs from a similar quantity of redundant observations or a mere re-enumeration of picture detail. Here the aspects of the dramatic, the picturesque, the gory, the intense, or the casual may be noted and distinguished. Their particular content may also be observed, though discussion of this aspect will be deferred until the sections on content in Chapter 5.

Originality versus commonness of imagery. The originality or popularity of concepts and descriptions has not received as yet the systematic attention which it has in the case of the Rorschach tests. The category is essentially the same, however, and attention should be paid to it even though the determination of originality is now largely a matter of the interpreter's experience and judgment. In considering the originality issue, there is a difference between *original content description* and *original form description*. The former refers to the originality of ideas, feeling-attribution, identification of basic plot or situation, action sequence, and outcome. *Form originality* means the novel utilization of specific form aspects of the picture stimulus, to include both the use of form aspects not generally used (the "lake" in 2), the attribution of special meaning to areas normally otherwise designated (the "clouds" in 19 as waves on the shore), or the novel arrangement of generally observed details of a picture. This area of form originality has been given very little attention and care should be exercised in assuming originality until the more popular form uses have been determined.

It may be well to point out here that the question of originality should be viewed in the light of the question: original for whom? Many concepts, appearing to be original for the ordinary run of middle-class American subjects, may be quite routine for other groups. This does not destroy their novelty for the groups in question, but does place a limitation upon their interpretation. In the absence of statistical evidence on a wide range of social groups, the interpreter should carefully examine his judgments of originality in view of the possibility that the concept is original merely to him, the interpreter.

Rhythm and smoothness. Subjects vary in the ease with which they produce images, events, and action regardless of the basic richness or complexity of their images. To some extent this may be judged by the readiness of flow of words, the absence of pauses, contradictions, and changes of mind.

Interruptions of story production. Hesitations, pauses, side remarks to the tester, remarks intended as criticisms on the pictures or the story as told, all these should be noted as evidence of inconsistency, self-consciousness, and censorship on the part of the subject. Closely related to these "editorial" notations are the clinical observations clinicians are frequently in the habit of making during any interview or test performance. These notations, such as blushing, restlessness, cigarette smoking, twisting of wedding bands, tics, mannerisms, and the like, are generally felt to give added clues to the significance of the formal interview or test activity then in progress.

While the author does not wish to suggest that this procedure be abandoned, it does appear to him that, in instances where meaning is attributed to these by the psychologist, some additional clue to the same interpretation may be found in the data of the stories themselves. Thus if laughter at the beginning of a picture suggests some special embarrassment, it is to be expected that this embarrassment, if indeed present, will find its way into other form or content characteristics of that story or other stories dealing with similar issues. Personally the writer would prefer to rely upon the evidence as found in the stories, feeling them to be more reliable evidences of the interpretive suggestion made from the clinical notations of test performance behavior. Furthermore, it is easier to determine the significance to the subject of these manifestations if they can be traced down in the stories. Thus when a married woman begins to twist her wedding band at the start of picture 4, it is tempting to think of some self-consciousness about the marital relation, or about heterosexual relations in general. Without more substantial evidence, however, it is disturbing to consider the possibility that it is not her marital relations that bother her, but rather a property consciousness which manifests itself in the touching of the diamond in her engagement ring. If either of these suggested attributes is present, they will be found in the stories. It seems best to look for them there, while not ignoring any suggestive clues seen in the test-taking behavior.

Variations in foregoing factors. Any of these features may appear in any or all of the stories told. It is particularly important to note wherein variations in them occur—presence of pauses and hesitation in a particular story in a record otherwise free from these features, presence of rich and vivid imagery in a story in a record otherwise drab. These variations will give clues to pictures of special import to the subject, clues which should be traced down in content and other form characteristics of the stories.

Organizational qualities

The organization which each subject gives to his structuring of the world around him is in part reflected in the organization which he gives to his stories. In the consideration of these organizational qualities, attention is paid to the system and order which the subject puts into his stories and the ways in which various aspects of form are interrelated.

Three basic parts of the story. The instructions to the subject ask him to give a beginning, a middle, and an end to his story. We ask him to say what is now going on in the picture, how this came about or what preceded it, and what the outcome will be. To some extent, the presence of these three requested aspects of the story may be seen as an example of the extent to which the subject complies with instructions. Certainly in some subjects who rigidly adhere to instructions, notions of excessive attention to outside directive stimuli should be considered. More frequently, however, subjects will adhere to these instructions in only approximate form, generally neglecting the past and the future in favor of the present. In this sense the "normal" story tends to be one in which the subject spends more attention upon "what is happening in the picture" and less upon the antecedents or the outcome. Judgments of adequate organization should be tempered in this light. They should be further qualified by recalling the strong tendency, at least in the American middle class (which usually includes the interpreters of projective instruments), to stress sequences of passage of time. Success, mobility, and ambition, strong goals for us all, involve an image of time. As we all lean heavily toward the future, seeing the present as a prelude to it, and the past as best forgotten, we are perhaps inclined to judge too harshly the person who fails to have our own time perspective. We thus can readily mistake attention to the present for sluggishness and fixation, confusing other persons' stability with our own mobility strivings. This viewpoint may also lead us to expect too much by way of outcomes. Our normal judgment of outcome leans heavily to somewhat overly neat proposals of endings which are completions of actions proposed earlier in the description of the present. While it is true that upper middle-class persons, and socially or vocationally mobile persons in general, do use this emphasis in their stories, by no means all normal subjects do. An outcome for many middle-class subjects, which occurs with great frequency, is merely a stopping of the description of "what is happening," including very short future time projections and lacking the somewhat fairy-tale-like endings with which we are more in tune.

In essence, the emphases placed upon the three major time aspects of the story are in themselves diagnostic features and should be analyzed both with a view to the adequacy of story and to t! er-spective which the subject has upon sequence in his own life. Thus emphases upon the past tend to suggest preoccupations with the subject's own past life, whether they are specifically proposed by the subject as descriptions of the antecedents of his story or whether they are past-referent ideas attributed to the figures in the story as characterizations of their present feelings and ideas. Similarly, exaggerated emphases on the future tend to suggest poor reality contact and the subject's tendency to include insufficient present and past data in his future planning. Subjects fearful of their present circumstances often do this. Excessive attention to the present, as well as great emphasis upon the enumeration of physical details of the picture, suggest subjects who are unable to provide perspective in their life and who therefore cling rigidly to the certainties they feel they can see and touch.

If we are to make much of the subject's treatment of these parts of the story, it is wise to be sure that he understands the request for a beginning, middle, and end to a story. This is best done by repeating the instructions briefly following stories 1 and 2, if the subject does not give an ending, and by the usual nondirective promptings toward the completion of stories to these pictures. Since the time distribution is as much a personality characteristic as a matter of compliance with the conditions set by the examiner, one need not insist on the presence of these three parts beyond assuring oneself that the instructions have been comprehended. Subsequent to these reminders, the stories should be allowed to flow as the subject desires, and the emphases which he places on past, present, and future should be analyzed much as any other aspect of the data.

Level of organization. The level of organization of a story should be noted. Roughly such levels may be seen as: 1. enumerative listing of the facts of the picture (that's a boy and that's a violin); 2. the description of the facts of the picture in terms of their meaning and interrelationships (that's a boy looking at a violin); or 3. an imaginative level in which the subject enlivens his description of the picture with his own personal point of view and elaborates his story with imagined details (that's a boy who has been told to play his violin but he doesn't want to).

The first two levels suggested will be found in some subjects of below normal intelligence and from time to time in records of disturbed subjects. Generally a basic imaginative level will be expected from the subject of normal intelligence who co-operates at all with the instructions. The analysis of the organization level of these latter subjects will require more refined data, such as are suggested in the following sections. It may be well, however, to introduce at this time a concept which will be expanded later, that of the *form demand* of the stimulus picture. The concept of the *form demand* calls attention to the fact that the pictures differ in their form complexity. Some, as picture 1, present a fairly simple task and a visually uncomplex picture. On the other hand some, such as 19, present a visually complex task and a wide variety of specific forms to which the subject is asked to respond. Thus in 1, the boy and the violin are in essence the main stimulating forms, though we should not overlook the stimulus possibilities of the bow or of the object upon which the violin lies or of the dark shadowy background in which some subjects can see objects. In 19, in contrast, there is a wide variety of objects: the houselike form, with its two "windows" within which even more may be seen such as curtains and light. In addition, there are the light grays in the front representing "snow," the clouds in the background, the gray forms around the house frequently seen as a variety of animals, spooks, cats, bats, and the like. The point which the author wishes to stress is not that 19 is more ambiguous than 1—it is and this is quite separately of importance—but that the sheer complexity of the stimuli presented varies from picture to picture and that with this variation the subject is confronted with tasks of differing complexities. A judgment of the skill of a given subject's organization level must be made within the context of the fact that we present him with initial tasks of quite differing complexity.*

* I have used the expression *form demand,* rather than a term such as *form complexity* or *level of picture difficulty,* to indicate a certain degree of pressure placed upon the subject by the presentation of these stimuli in a manner requiring organization and structure. These instructions do not readily permit the subject merely to identify selected aspects of the picture and ignore those aspects with which he does not care to deal or avoid the obligation of suggesting a relationship between certain of the forms presented. While a concept of form complexity or form level appears to be an important and sufficient concept for the Rorschach text, the TAT presents a special feature of form in that it requires a statement of *relationship between forms.* Each individual aspect of form may be identified at a simple or complex level, and relationships proposed between these forms at simple or complex levels. It seems to me extremely helpful in analyzing the

Coherence and logic. A further aspect of form closely related to organization level and important in the estimation of intelligence is the degree and kind of logic present in relating the various ideas expressed in the story. Regardless of the level of complexity of the response, attention should be paid to the sequence of objects and ideas presented and a judgment made of their coherence and appropriateness. Such judgments may be made with respect to two systems of coherence: the extent to which the ideas expressed are reasonable in the light of the stimulus presented, and the internal consistency of ideas within the story. Subjects may tell stories of excellent internal consistency but based on entirely false premises. They may also identify correctly the stimuli of the picture but elaborate a story with little internal coherence. In judging the appropriateness of the response to the actual facts of the picture, considerable caution should be taken not to mistake a degree of originality for an error in judgment. In general, the only approach to a correct judgment of the subject's basic identification of the facts of the picture must come through extended knowledge of the stories normally given to the picture.

Inclusive whole concepts. An inclusive whole concept will be found in a story where the central idea used to explain the picture is one which satisfactorily identifies and relates the major aspect of the picture. The number of such whole concepts throughout a full set should also be noted. The judgment of adequate coverage of the major facts of the picture is a difficult one, based in part upon an analysis of the pictures themselves. By way of illustration, it may be suggested that in picture 1, the boy and the violin, an inclusive whole concept is one which takes into account three basic events: 1. the boy, 2. the violin, and 3. some relationship between the two. Thus "a young boy contemplating a violin" is an inclusive whole. We would of course expect a normal subject to continue with what will later be described as elaborations on the central concept. He might add to the previous statement, "which rests on a table in front of him," or "it is an old violin which his grandfather gave him," or perhaps "it is broken," etc. These are all elaborations on the central concept. It is clear that

subject's habits of perceptual and conceptual organization to envision him as responding to this interaction of self and a pattern of form which sets a certain task level for him. I have used the term *form demand* to suggest the presence of pictures with various kinds and numbers of forms, but also to imply that the task set by the instructions places a special obligation on the subject to respond with an effort at stating the relationship between these forms which he proposes at present.

inclusive wholes may themselves vary in quality. Thus "the boy hates to practice" is probably an adequate whole in that it identifies the three major parts of the picture suggested, although it is by no means as well or exactly phrased as the first whole concept suggested and it identifies the violin only by inference (to practice).

In picture 2, to illustrate further, it seems to the author that the major variables of the picture to be taken into account are: 1. the three people, 2. some relationship between them, and 3. the rural nature of the scene. Given this, an identifying response such as "family harvest" is quite adequate, even rather good, and suggests a somewhat more symbolic and abstracting mind than, for example, "a girl with books and her mother and father. The father is plowing while the mother thinks of the work to be done in the house. The girl is coming home from school to help." This eventually gets in all of the basic aspects of the picture, though of course in a more rambling fashion. It is thus worth while noting both the presence or absence of such whole concepts and the manner in which they are derived.

Manner of approach to central concept. It is important to observe the manner in which the central concept explanatory of the picture is derived. Two general possibilities are suggested in the foregoing. They are:

1. Whole concept stated first which may then be broken down in its component details.

2. Details first subsequently built into a whole concept.

The suggestions involve only what are referred to as the *central facts* of the picture. The derivation of certain aspects of the stimuli and others as not *central* will be discussed later. Here, it should be pointed out that attention should obviously also be paid to all aspects of the picture identified by the subject, directly or by inference. To this end special attention should be paid to:

1. The facts of the picture actually taken into account (whether or not those referred to are central).

2. The relationships proposed between the parts actually taken into account.

3. The parts of the picture ignored.

Subjects will vary, of course, in the parts of the stimulus which they actually employ in their plot. The subject who includes all the central, dominant parts of the picture may at least be thought of as able to deal with the normal, usual aspects of his environment and probably of being sufficiently reality-oriented to permit him general group conformity and the ability to deal with the basic concepts of his social group. Beyond the utilization of the central dominant features of the story, subjects will further vary in the additional aspects of the stimulus which they use in their story. These aspects are frequently suggestions either of a general detail-mindedness or of some special preoccupation.

Relationships between the form aspects of the picture noted are generally best seen when considering content features of the plot. However, it is here suggested that not infrequently some basic form split in the stimulus is assumed by the subject which will be indicative of special concerns. Thus the subject who in picture 2, the farm scene, correctly identifies the rural quality as well as the three central persons may do so in such a manner as to suggest that he sees the three persons as part of a total relationship. In this case he will connect the notations of these figures with observations of relatedness and personal contact between them. On the other hand, he may see the picture as split into two groups, one of a young woman with goals directed away from the picture (wants to get away, leaving to go to school, hates the farm, etc.) and a second group consisting of two related persons (friends, husband and wife, mother and loving son). A further possibility is to be noted when detail-conscious persons embellish their stories with many additional references to objects in the picture. The concern here should be with the extent to which the subject is able to make these details a significant part of the central idea he has developed, or, on the other hand, whether he appears to be compelled to note these details but is unable to give them a meaningful place in the basic plot.

Details of the picture ignored may or may not be psychologically relevant. This will depend somewhat upon the form demands which the picture makes and upon the extent to which, in other pictures, the subject normally does or does not emphasize details. It should be recalled that the subject is under no pressure to mention all details of the picture. He would be expected to mention only those sufficient to account for the story he tells, provided in so doing he does not ignore any major details generally seen by subjects or that would contradict the plot he has developed. Thus, in 8BM, the operating scene, it is not basically necessary that the gun be included and many subjects tell quite adequate stories not mentioning it. To ignore the boy in the foreground, or the operating scene in the back, however, is a major lapse. In 3BM, the boy huddled on the floor, there is an object on the floor often referred to as a gun. While this object is frequently identified in other ways, to ignore it altogether would appear to be suggestive of some specific resistance to it, and possibly to its aggressive or sexual implications.

Variations from story to story. Any variations in the aforementioned factors from story to story should be specifically noted. It is apparent, of course, that one does not expect all subjects to be completely consistent in these matters throughout his entire production of stories. However, attention should be paid to what appears to be, for that subject, variations from his own usual manner of organizing his concepts. In both the usual manner and in variations from it lie important features of his mental and personality make-up.

Acuity of concepts, observations, and their integration

Closely related to judgments of organizational level and of intellectual functioning are notations of the keenness of the observations and the ways in which they are integrated. The interpreter must rely heavily on his own judgment here, there being few guides to concepts thought more acute than others. Certainly, however, the observation "that's a boy and his violin," while adequate description, is not particularly perceptive or acute. On the other hand, the observation, "young Yehudi Menuhin contemplating the wonders of music," is undoubtedly better in this respect.

The awareness of the subject of the pointedness of his own observations is also relevant. To what extent does he criticize and modify his own observations, either of detail-identification or of plot development?

Language usage

Many aspects of the use and structure of language will bear special study. Of special use seem to be:
1. Movement and action words.
2. Words which qualify and modify.
3. Descriptive words.
4. Words which indicate emotions.
5. Language usage from a literary and grammatical viewpoint.

The notation of these special features of language sometimes leads to quite basic differentiations in personality description and sometimes merely to less vital changes in emphasis or in notations of the outward manner of the subject. The former is particularly true in the case of movement and action words. These seem to relate closely to the Rorschach large M scoring and to deal with matters of internal motive power and the intellectual grasp of the subject. These movement words are sometimes quite subtle. A young Navaho girl (see Chapter 11) told to a very bleak picture showing waste desert land, cow skulls, and crossed fences the following story:

This fence is going to this corner and then comes through here again. Dead cows' bones here, fire here, and somebody sitting here.

In many respects this may be thought a very bad story: little plot, little notation of feeling or emotion, no basic action, no development of beginning and end. On the other hand, it is of great importance that in a story of this length actually a great deal is going on, a lot is in movement. The fence is "going" and "comes through." It is not merely present, it is in motion. The "fire" is actually in the picture two sets of waving parallel lines frequently identified as a road. However, quite easily and without distortion it can be seen as smoke curling up from a fire. The fire itself is not distinctly indicated. Yet for her it is fire, and further she prefers to notice the "fire," the by far less easily noted event, and to avoid the more static concept which would explain the parallel lines more easily. Needless to say, this same inner spark is seen in her other stories also.

Particular emotional preoccupations become apparent when special emotional phraseology is noted. Thus in one story to the boy-and-violin picture, a male of age twenty-nine (see Chapter 9) points out that the boy is thinking either "in glorification and admiration" of the music or possibly in "boredom and disgust" which a practice session might involve. Two features of importance should be noted from the choice of these words alone. One is, of course, the repetition of the idea in the paired words. The second is the fact that the two sets of possible emotions portrayed are in a sense opposites. Certainly from these structural aspects of the language one could tentatively suggest that: 1. this is a subject of complex emotions; and 2. this is a subject in conflict over his emotions. These observations can be made without too much attention to the strong parallelism which the content of these complex and conflictful statements suggest to the Madonna versus sex confusion.

It seems unwise at this point to place much emphasis upon the literary and grammatical correctness of the language. While notations of well-phrased ideas or bad grammar are relevant and will be of some use in describing the mental approach, great caution should be taken in attributing any special psychodynamic significance to special words, or their absence, unless in substantiation of the interpretive ideas found elsewhere. This applies also to "slips of the tongue" unless it is beyond question that the record is strictly verbatim. This is a hard point to be certain about, considering the many inadvertent minor changes that may occur between the subject's word and the type-written document with which the interpreter usually works. While it is often a temptation for the psychologist to make much of little data, in the author's opinion little is lost if we exercise great caution in respect to these minor language suggestions. If the idea proposed from the "slip" is indeed real, it will appear in more vivid form else-where. If it does not, this writer would place little confidence in the observation. This does not mean that all such small details should not be explored; sometimes quite important observations stem from very small initial clues. But it is suggested that if the small initial clues are all the evidence the entire record presents they should be viewed with skepticism.

CHAPTER 5

The variables of content

The content of TAT stories may be analyzed in a manner partially independent of form. This independence of form and content is obviously an artificial separation created by the interpreter for reasons of convenience and to throw into greater relief the complex of ways in which variations in stories may occur. From future studies it may appear that some of these distinctions of form and content are meaningless, or that some important distinctions have been overlooked. At present, however, those variables described appear useful in interpretation and meaningful in the task of delineating the approach which the subject makes to the definition of the stimulus and to the effort to structure his observations in story form.

As has been suggested in Chapter 4, the discussion of content will be divided into three basic areas: *Positive Content, Dynamic Structure of Content,* and *Negative Content. Positive Content* deals with all the verbalizations made by the subject and the specific attributes and interrelations stated about the persons, events, actions, and emotions posited for each picture. *Dynamic Structure of Content* refers to the notion that the subject, in telling his story, is dominated by his own unconscious chain of associations and suggests that an analysis of these patterns of association will further enlighten us about his personality. *Negative Content* will deal with the things which the subject has not said in the light of the usual responses to specific pictures.

The objective of the analysis of all of these areas of content is, of course, not merely to characterize this sample of the thought content. It is particularly aimed at seeing what underlying assumptions and generalizations the subject makes about himself, the nature of the world of objects and people around him, and the regular principles of interaction between the two.

Positive Content

General emotional tone of stories

The most common use of the content of the stories is to determine the general emotional tone of the subject's language. Here attention is drawn to the general groupings of kinds of content, rather than the content attributed specifically to special characters and action-sequences. This estimate of general tone may often be made in the first general reading of the record, though more detailed analysis should follow in the scrutiny of each story. At least the following four areas of tone may be suggested:

Positive or negative tone of language. Are the stories generally positive and hopeful, or generally negative, depressing, discouraging? Specific words as well as general plot structure should be viewed in making this judgment with particular note of the outcomes and the statements of the initial circumstances of the situation described. More detailed analysis of both of these points should be made in reference to specific plots and pictures. It is helpful, however, in gaining a first over-all impression to sample the basic premises independently. The interpreter may ask himself such questions as: What are the personal and environmental circumstances basically posited for each picture? Are the first identifications generally negative? Initial responses such as the following are certainly noteworthy as suggesting a general pessimistic attitude toward the environment:

Picture 1. There is a boy who has just been punished for not practicing his violin.

Picture 2. This girl hates the farm and is thinking of how to get away from it.

Picture RIE5.* There are fences and bones. There was no food so the cows died.

* Research on Indian Education picture number 5

Picture 3BM. Showing girl in crouched position either broken or drunk, lines and movement too crude, vulgarity too plainly stressed. Lines of ass almost obscene. Right hand showing does not follow expression of rest of body.

Quite independently of the other suggestions in these stories, especially of the negative evaluation of body image in the last story, and the deprivation anxiety in the story to picture RIE5, these parts of story all partake of the quality of discouragement and an assumption of an unpleasing environment. In contrast, the following present views of life events with more optimism and hope, both for the self and as a definition of the environment as more pleasing and helpful.

Picture 1. This boy is contemplating the violin, thinking of the wonders of music and what it can do for him.
Picture 1. He's just come home from school and is studying his lessons. The next time he goes to school, he's going to know them perfectly and he's going to get an A.
Picture RIE1. Two kids back from school ready to make a living. Old man gives them some pointers. He tells them the best way to buy cattle, put them out on the range and by and by increase the cattle.*
Picture RIE4. Little Indian boy praying before he goes to bed. Prays for something to get for his birthday, prays for a home. Next day he wakes and finds his dream come true. After that he prays every night before he goes to bed.

Similar distinctions may be made with respect to the remaining three areas of tone:
Passivity or aggressivity of the language, events, actions.
Expressed or implied conflict or interpersonal animosity.
Expressed or implied interpersonal harmony or affiliative action and thought.

Action core of the story

The basic plot of the story, called by Murray the thema, is of crucial importance. The thema of a story may be seen as composed of the following basic parts:

1. The description of the circumstances attributed to environment of the characters.

2. The personal or emotional state, desires, and needs of the characters.

* In all stories or parts of stories quoted, the original wording and spelling are used. Occasionally words will be inserted by the writer to clarify the continuity or to provide a reference left obscure by quoting only a segment of a story. These will uniformly be placed in parentheses. All remarks which were originally inserted in the story by the examiner will be placed in brackets.

3. The stimulus which the environment places upon the characters.

4. The reaction of the characters to these stimuli.

5. The final outcome of this interaction of situation-motive response.

This series of events, sometimes spelled out clearly and sometimes telescoped, constitutes a basic plot, or what Murray has called a simple thema. It should be recalled that themas do not always follow this simple format. Deviations may occur as elaborations of this plan, or as simplifications and truncations of it. It may happen, for example, that:

1. The needs of the characters described are met by a return stimulus from the environment, which stimulates further response from the characters who in turn react again with the same or different sets of responses.

2. Several outcomes occur, reflecting the subject's indecision or ambivalent feelings on the issue dealt with in the plot.

3. Figures are added whose own pattern of needs and influences upon the plot are introduced.

4. The subject fails to include one or another aspect of the simple thema. This perhaps most frequently occurs when the outcome or the antecedent events are omitted.

These variations on the simple thema occur with great frequency. The interpreter should not be deterred by these failures of orderliness. He should attempt to determine the dynamic structure of the plot regardless of incomplete themas.

The description of a thema may be phrased in any language the interpreter feels appropriate, provided it permits him to see the interplay of emotion, action, internal need, and external press. In this connection the categories of need and press developed by Murray or the modification made by others are extremely useful. The objective in each instance is to see in what way the subject describes the five basic aspects of the plot as outlined in the foregoing. This statement of the thema is, in a sense, a shorthand, a way of getting beneath the specific details provided by the subject and describing the basic plot line. A thema is a statement of the underlying plot line and as such is not dependent upon the actual length of a story. There is, of course, some tendency for a longer story to introduce more complex motive situations and more interactions of need and press. If this is the case, the statement of the thema should reflect them. Frequently, however, length derives merely from elaborate verbalization and detailed description within a plot that is basically quite simple. While the pattern of elaborate verbalization is in itself important, the thema should reflect only the basic motives and actions.

With subjects given to lengthy stories, the main task of the interpreter is normally to cut through the words and get to the plot. The
plot statement is the desired goal. Subjects who state the basic story
with a minimum of elaboration often save the interpreter considerable
time. This is mentioned merely to suggest that there is no premium
to be placed upon length *per se*. The premium is to be placed on
securing a plot line containing as many of the basic elements *as the
subject finds it natural to give*. Forced endings or other aspects of
the story produced through more than generally encouraging and nondirective remarks during the examination are seldom of real use. In
general, endings which are forced by direct questioning should be
given somewhat less importance than endings which appear spontaneously.

The themes represent essentially the assumptions which the subject
makes about himself and the world around him and the dynamic
relationships which he posits as existing between the two. In this
sense the emotions, ideas, and events which he portrays in these
themes reveal the generalizations which he has drawn from his past
experience and which guide him in judging and reacting to new events
as they arise. A listing of the themes of the total set of stories told will
give an over-all view of these generalizations. More refined analysis
is needed, however, to place these in proper context and to evaluate
the relative importance and dynamic significance of particular themes.
To this end the following aspects of the themes should be examined:

Common and uncommon themes. For each picture there will be
a limited series of basic picture identifications and plots which for
any given social group may be thought to be common. A great deal
of individual variation is possible within the details of the recounting
of the plots and, of course, the basic plot itself may vary considerably
from the common ones. It is useful, therefore, to estimate the extent
to which the subject tells stories which are in plot similar or dissimilar
to the stories found frequently in records of that subject's age, sex,
and social group.

The frequency of common themes will reflect the basic social identification of the subject and the extent to which his assumptions about
the nature of events parallel those prevalent in his real environment.
To some extent, a majority of common themes will also reflect an
essential normality of personality. The latter judgment is, however,
only partially possible from a gross observation of common themes.
Not infrequently, pathological subjects may give themes quite in tune
with the basic plots given by others. Only the examination of the

details of the emotions, events, characterizations, and outcomes will show the true stance of the personality and the role which these common assumptions play in it.

Uncommon themes can reflect the complexity of the individual personality, the socially marginal nature of the individual's background, a notable pattern of originality, or a pattern of personality distortion. In any one normal record, the examiner should expect to find a small percentage of unusual themas. These will represent in some sense the idiosyncratic aspects of the individual or particular personal experiences which have been somewhat different from others in his social group. Individuality is, of course, present in the manner of presentation of the quite ordinary themas. These aspects of individuality will be seen through the analysis of the many other variables of form and content.

An uncommon thema in itself, or in fact, a sizable number of them, should not be taken as indications of personality distortion. While they are suggestive of unusual background experience, they may reflect only these unusual experiences and no basic distortion. As has been suggested here, other aspects of form and content should be examined before conclusions of distortion are drawn.

Repeated themas. A common thema is one which occurs frequently within a given group of subjects for a particular card. The uncommon thema is one which is uncommon for subjects of a specific group or uncommon for a particular picture. Special attention should be given to themas which are found to appear repeatedly within the record of a subject. Since the common themas are by no means the same for each card, the repetition of a particular thematic plot, while possibly appropriate for some pictures, will be less common for others. This insistence upon a particular thema requires some slight forcing of plot line for other pictures. These repetitions will usually suggest some strong affective predispositions on the part of the subject and require special attention. Themas may reappear which involve conflicts between desires, or themas of impulse systematically frustrated, or of deprivation leading to disaster, or of narcissistic exhibition leading to magical good outcomes. Such repetitions, or any of the many others possible, will take on special interpretive significance.

It should be re-emphasized that, while the repetition of such themas need not reflect an actual distortion of the content of those pictures to which such a plot is not a usual one, they do suggest that the dynamic content which they portray is a special screen through which the subject interprets reality. The extent to which they permit the realities of the picture to be fitted into them in an adequate manner reflects the flexibility of this special screen. When the thema dominates and the realities of the picture are badly interpreted to conform to the predisposition reflected in the thema, however, the subject is clearly dominated by this emotional preoccupation and is forfeiting his reality observation to the goal of reaffirming his preconceptions. Such preoccupying emotions will appear in other areas of analysis, of course, and may be re-examined in more detail there.

Single themas. Simply because a thema occurs only once in a set of stories is no reason to ignore its possible importance. Its place in the psychic economy of the individual may be less clear than strong and repeated themes, but it should nonetheless be scrutinized for its relationship to the developing image of the personality and for its relationships to other themes and to the picture to which it is a response. While the statistical frequency of themas is important, all themas and their meaningful relationships should be investigated. As Dr. Rapaport has observed,* the interpretation of "strivings, obstacles, thoughts and ideas should not be made on the basis of the statistical frequency of their occurrence in the stories, but rather on the basis of our psychological understanding of the belonging together of different strivings which are genetically or symbolically interrelated and/or interchangeable."

Themas in relation to special characters. Here attention is directed toward a study of themas in relation to the needs, attributes, and environmental circumstances of special characters appearing in the plot. Are stories involving striving persons always set in difficult environment circumstances and do they always have bad endings? What are the plots which characteristically develop around older female figures? Or around older male figures? Are plots of jealousy and rivalry always attached to stories which include two figures of the same age, or always to plots involving same sex figures of different age grades? Are there any general themas which apply to all male figures or to all female figures?

Themas in relation to outcomes. A procedure for categorizing outcomes will be suggested later. Here, however, it should be noted that subjects sometimes assume certain set characteristics of success or failure and attach them to specific themas. This may become especially notable when themas are repeated. Such questions as the following should be asked: Do themas of affiliation and harmony always end well? Do themas of conflict always have bad outcomes? Do those themas in which a choice of alternatives is presented tend to

---

*   Rapaport, David. The clinical application of the Thematic Apperception Test. *Bull. Menninger Clin.,* 1943, 7, 106–113.

have indecisive endings? Do themas representative of the struggle of the individual with opposing environmental press tend to have magical endings in which no relevant skills or knowledge of the characters are utilized?

The sequence of themas. In addition to the interpretive possibilities within a given story, the interrelations between the thema of one story and the thema of the story immediately preceding or following it often prove important. Some subjects create a statement of their emotional problems that carries through for a number of themas. One of the frequent and more obvious sequences is that occurring when a subject is particularly hostile or destructive and then follows this with a story to the subsequent picture which is notably bland or notably intrapunitive. It would be an error to assume, from the first of these stories, that the subject sees hostility as being given permissive expression if in the adjoining fantasy he insists upon punishment. The feature is of special importance if the succeeding thema is a somewhat uncommon one for the picture in question and if the subject therefore must go out of his way to provide a resolution to the hostility expressed in the previous story. In a somewhat different format, preservation of ideas and content may occur from story to story. In this case the preservation from the previous story is probably of greater importance than the analysis of the second story in terms of it as a response to the picture only.

The analysis of the basic thema for a given story and for the pattern of themas for the entire record provides a general orientation to the content of the record and to the emotional predisposition of the subject. Similarly, the initial analysis of the gross form characteristics provides a parallel check of similar attributes with an emphasis upon the subject's perceptual structuring of the stimulus field. To some extent these first views of the form and content of the subject's imaginal productions also provide an estimate of the degree of typicality or deviancy of the personality.

The central figure

It is traditional for the stories with which we are most familiar to have a central figure about whom the basic plot revolves and in whose terms the other characters in the plot become relevant. Such a person is normally the one most involved in the plot, the one about whom the writer tells us the most, and toward whose goals the outcome is directed. When such a figure occurs in a TAT story, it may be called a hero-figure, even though the actions in which he may be involved need be hardly heroic. By no means will all stories present a clear-cut central figure of these characteristics. Subjects whose patterns of identification are such that they symbolize their feelings in forms of persons will tend to develop such hero-figures. The presence of such figures is not a basic feature of the test responses. It is, rather, a personality characteristic, in itself suggestive of a particular orientation to life. It should be recalled that the TAT stories, as well as the myths of more classic dimensions, utilize patterns of hero-figures to symbolize basic human feelings and conflicts. These figures are either composites of several attributes or are overly pure, representative not of a specific person but of an emotional orientation. The effort to identify a hero generally should stop as soon as the data given us by the subject grow vague. When this happens, we do not criticize the examiner for securing incomplete data, but rather inquire in what respects the subject's identification experiences have themselves been vague, incomplete, or contradictory.

It is suggested that the interpreter not concern himself with identifying a hero-figure if such is not readily apparent from the plot. It may superficially appear that it is impossible to describe the personality attributes of the subject without knowing with which figure he experiences identification. To assume this is to assume that the features of the hero are those of the subject and the features of the non-hero-figures are somehow those which the subject attributes to the outer world. It would indeed be convenient if this were true. However, patterns of identification and the expression of covert feelings do not arrange themselves this neatly. Rather, they range widely over the persons and objects of identification familiar to the subject, displaying in their disposition the patterning of affects of the personality and in their structuring, its foci, and firm points. It is thus as important to know that the subject does not structure his life-space in terms of clear-cut identification figures as it is to know upon what occasion and in what circumstances he does.

This point is an important one, having implications for the entire method of analysis, rather than merely for the question of the importance to be placed upon hero-figures. It may be well, therefore, to illustrate it briefly with some stories demonstrating differing degrees of identification with the hero and correspondingly different dispositions of affect.

The first is that of a woman of twenty-six, a waitress:

The expression on the boy's face obviously registers complete disgust. He's supposed to be studying the violin. He doesn't want to. You can understand that. (At this point, the subject said, "I can write it faster than you can," and took the paper and pencil and wrote out the rest of the story.) Aw gee, all the kids are out playing baseball and I'm stuck with this darn thing and just this morning Eddie promised to lend me his new mit, too. Who wants to study on a day like this, violin, too. Nuts!

This woman demarcates clearly the figure of the boy, identifies closely with him, and attributes clear-cut emotions to him. He could undoubtedly be called a hero-figure, and in her other stories she similarly selects one person and centers her entire drama around him. This woman of rigorous but uncomplex emotions finds her identity most aptly portrayed by these close identifications. In so doing she gains a vivid sense of reality, avoids the abstractions she does not care for, and reflects her simplified version of emotional conflicts.

In the following story, that of a business man of forty-five, a somewhat different approach may be seen.

This is a child prodigy dreaming over his violin thinking more of the music than anything else . . . of wonderment that so much music can be in the instrument and in the fingers of his own hand. I would say that possibly he is in reverie about what can be or what he can do with his music in the times that lie ahead. He is dreaming of concert halls, tours, and appreciations of music . . . of the beauty he will be able to express and even now can express with his own talents.

Here the subject quickly presents to us his orientation outward from the central figure, yet maintains a firm grasp on the inner vitality of his hero-figure. As he moves outward into the world of tours, concerts, etc., he shows us his increased span of identification, his ability to depersonalize and abstract from his experiences of reality. Like the waitress, he feels keenly the inner emotion of the boy. In expressing this awareness of inner feeling, however, he extends them whereas she turns them back into the boy. He expands his realm of identification beyond the boy both into broader fields of action and into future speculation.

On the other hand, for another subject, a man of forty in business, the identification is vague, confused, and gains its main source of strength through its reference to a past reality.

The story behind this is that this is a son of a very well known, a very good musician and the father has probably died. The only thing the son has left is this violin which is undoubtedly a very good one and to the son the violin is the father and the son sits there daydreaming of the time that he will understand the music and interpret it on the violin that his father has played.

This story in many respects suggests that the image of greatest vitality for this man is the "father." Even the boy in the picture, the conventional hero, is given identity in terms of the past. He is "a son of a very well known . . . musician." For purposes of analyzing the personality of this man and seeing the pattern of his own sense of identity, it is most important to note that he presents the basic large detail of the stimulus (the boy) as being identified only through an image of a far stronger figure who is no longer present ("father has probably died") as a guiding force. The vitality of the waitress' story is missing, as is the cathexis to events outside the person which is so notable in the story of the business man of forty-five.

A story which is in some respects in an intermediate position with regard to the disposition of foci of affect is that of this woman student of twenty.

A young boy looking at the violin on the table. His expression is one of tiredness and not much interest. It seems to me that he is too young to be forced to take violin lessons, at an age when he would have no love of the instrument or music. It is possible that his mother either believes that it is *good* to have a child "play something" or has visions of his becoming a great violinist. All of this might lead to the child's dislike of the whole thing.*

Here, somewhat in common with the woman of twenty-six, this woman feels keenly the personal emotions, portrays them vigorously in her story. She also empathizes strongly and clearly sees the boy as the hero, the central figure of the drama. It is vital to observe, however, that in this pattern of strong personal identification she is working out a strong personal bias which intrudes from her past experience. Dealing as she does with present reality, she brings into this present drama the residual resentment of her mother and her ambition. In a sense, we may suggest that the first woman shows us her living with the realities of the present; the first man his orientation toward the future; the second man his orienting nostalgia for the past; and this woman, her working out of past emotional issues in present-day events.

One last illustration will suggest a further way of structuring identification-patterns, a way in which the boundaries of inner and outer are vague and in which a sense of inappropriate affect is portrayed. The subject is a woman student of thirty, who, though an active student at the time, soon after experienced a schizophrenic break clearly presaged in this story.

First impression is the staged effect—child does not look at an unfamiliar object so quiescently. The child's facial expression is one of melancholy.

* This story was written out by the subject. The italic and the quotes are thus her own emphases.

The appearance somewhat—remark about questions—the bow is not clean-cut. Emotions as strong as this probably meant to be indicated here not in context with quietness of subject—coloring and delineation of individual and violin.*

The most important cue here, among the many in this story, is her first remark, "first impression is the staged effect." With very little distortion, we may perhaps say that this subject sees the world of reality only vaguely and in impressionistic form, and judges the world to be not real. As she struggles for contact, she can only sketch in lightly and with bold strokes her sense that affects do not match their stimuli. To inquire if the boy in the picture is or is not a hero-figure is to miss the central issue which this subject so clearly presents to us. In a sense, she says that there are no clear-cut people, all is impression, and badly composed and ill-matching at that. In this sense the task of seeing the personality of the subject does not require interpretation at all. Its task is merely to see and believe what the subject tells us so directly.

Other characters described

All attributes of all characters described by the subject should be scrutinized with care. This holds true, of course, for any character that may appear to have a central role in the drama. The author has underplayed the hero-figure problem here, not to the end of denying his existence or importance but rather to stress the analysis of the interplay of emotion and action within the story and their crystallization around any and all characters that play a part. While it appears to be quite true that the attributes of the central figure are more closely related to the dynamics of the subject than are the attributes of subsidiary figures, this does not mean that the attributes of the hero are in any direct way those of the subject. In many ways the best analysis will stem from seeing the interaction of hero and other figures. In any case, there is little to be gained from assuming a direct relation between hero and subject unless other data in the stories suggest that this is the case. Concentration upon the attributes, both physical and emotional, of all the characters and their interrelationships provides a sounder basis for interpretation. It is in reality the general emotional climate within which all characters function that is of highest value. In order to call attention to the many ways in which characters should be viewed, some suggestions are now given.

---

* This story was written out by the subject. The dashes and lack of coherence are hers, not inaccuracies of an examiner or parts lost in recording.

Physical attributes of characters. In the attribution of physical characteristics, the subject may convey much that he may or may not say directly elsewhere. These attributes, sometimes in themselves symbolic of unstated feeling, provide an image of the meanings which the subject attaches, consciously or unconsciously, to persons. For a middle-class subject, the suggestion of a bit of lace at the throat of a woman's dress, attention to the muscularity of the man plowing in picture 2 or of the man in 17BM, a notation of an obscene position of the figure in 3BM, all may suggest an attitude toward the categories these figures represent that will be worth exploration in other features of the stories. Repeated emphases upon the strength or weakness of characters, or upon their physical abilities, will similarly suggest a particular interest.

In the following fragments from the stories of a male shop foreman of twenty-nine, attention to particular physical attributes of characters possibly suggests his basic feelings of disharmony and unbalance.

Picture 1. "Long hair cut like a musician."

2. "There's a distinct similarity between the noses and mouths of these two women, indicating probably a relationship somewhere." "The young woman and man have their shoulders slightly elevated." "She has unnaturally long fingers."

3BM. "I'd say the person's a woman—if there's a question—I mean the angularity of the body and the size of the hand with large bone structure."

14. "The character was a man—because of the presence of a short haircut and the absence of a bustline."

17BM. "He's climbing the rope because of the unequal height of his two legs—right leg's higher than his left leg."

Not only does this man emphasize greatly the anatomical details of the people; he seems further to stress their unmatching or "unnatural" qualities. It is not that he derives necessarily incorrect conclusions from his observations, or that the items he notices are inaccurately observed—there is no bustline in 14 and the right leg of the man in 17BM is indeed higher than the left—but rather that he seems preoccupied with the body, with the clues it gives him to personality traits, and with the disharmonious or irregular aspects of the body.

Many subjects can, in their notations of physical attributes, convey quite different orientations toward the body and life in general. Attitudes of strength and vigor can be conveyed readily in attention to body details, such as these:

A high-ranking military officer:

Picture 17BM. "He is an escapee. He did not want any clothes because they would identify him. He is a hearty, tough boy."

An executive vice president:

Picture 1. "This is a child probably dreaming . . . that so much music can be in the instrument and in the fingers of his own hand."

Many subjects, of course, can give full records without a single reference to a direct physical characteristic or body part. These are subjects who tend more to concentrate on the interplay of action and feeling or upon the ideation of their characters.

Motives, strivings, and general emotional states. To some extent the statement of thema will have focussed attention upon the strivings and motives of the characters. However, it will normally be profitable to examine quite specifically the emotional states of each character in the story. Are they happy or sad, longing or in want? Are they struggling and striving or passive and receptive? Are they quiet and sensitive and calm in the accomplishment of their objectives?

Motives and emotions of specific categories of people. The analysis suggested in the preceding section will be extended to all stories. Once this is done, it becomes possible to categorize the various kinds of people with whom the subject deals and to see to what extent these categories of persons have similar features. Selecting, for example, all the older female figures present in the stimuli of the pictures or in any other way referred to by the subject, a quick tabulation may be made of the physical as well as emotional characteristics attributed to them. Are all older female figures strong, competent, and helpful? Are they all weak, highly emotional, and demanding? Similarly, what patterns of feelings more generally attach to male figures, young and old, to persons in authority, to inferior persons, to children, to people without possessions, to people in trouble, etc.?

To a large extent the categories of people considered will be the categories of characters presented by the subject. In these categories alone, much information may be given. Some may deal with only the basic characters represented in the picture, identifying them in quite direct and usual ways. Others will greatly amplify the list of actual characters, as well as extending greatly the range of feelings and emotions attributed to them. To some extent, the questions to be answered here are: How does the subject see the world of significant persons to be constituted? What are the emotions and strivings which the subject sees as relevant? It should be recalled that certain persons view their world of people as consisting quite simply of good and bad people, the contest between quite uncomplicated representatives of good and evil being their central concern. On the other hand, there are those who envision a rich and complex world of facilitating and counteractive persons, of complex and varied desires and emotions.

Attributes of the environment of characters. A strong and active person in an environment of plenty is quite a different concept than this same character in an environment of want and poverty. Similarly, an environment of helpful and considerate people differs from one of either no people at all or of one in which others are seen as destructive, counteractive, and opposed to the goals of others. Attention should be paid both to the personal and the physical attributes of the environment within which the action takes place. The environment of the subject should also be examined to see to what extent he views this as a lively, social place or a lonely, desolate one.

The following two stories may suggest differences in these respects:

A shop foreman of twenty-nine says of picture 2:

Evidently comparing career girl to the home builder. Woman looks like she's pregnant. That is, I mean the woman on the right. The woman at the left has unnaturally long fingers. She's somewhat younger than the woman at the right. I mean the appearance. (Get a story out of it?) No, unless the girl at the left is the daughter of the woman at the right. No, I think it's just a comparison. I can pick out the details—rocky soil in foreground, water in background. The young woman is probably disgusted with their eking out a living and is leaving them for an education and a career. There's a distinct similarity between the noses and the mouths of the two women, indicating, probably, a relationship somewhere. Both the young woman and the man have their left shoulders slightly elevated.

In this story, the subject portrays the environment as severe: "rocky soil," "eking out a living." He sees this within a social environment of low interaction and few inhabitants.

In contrast, in the following story regarding picture 2, that of a male department head in a large business, the environment is proposed as full and good: "good farm," "well run," "good soil," "successful agricultural enterprise." He further sees action as occurring in a busy, social setting: "most of the people," "the entire group," "*one* of the daughters."

Here we have a farm scene in which the interests of most of the people, not only the people in the picture, but the entire group that is assumed here, is very closely connected with the farm and its prosperity and its problems. The farm means a great deal to the man with the horse and the woman by the tree and other members of the household. It is a good farm. It is well run. Good soil. And it is a very successful agricultural enterprise run by a closely knit, well-integrated group of people. One of the daughters in the family, however, has other ideas—rather disdainful of the farm and farm life and wants to break away to what she would call the "finer things." She has difficulty getting along with the other members of the family because of her feelings. She feels that they are oblivious of the so-called "finer things." They feel that she is a little "uppity" and a little too big for her britches. She expresses her interest in things outside of the house by the kind of reading she wants to do, the kind of clothes she wears, and the things she wants to talk about. She wants to go away to school. She probably wants to study. Probably has in mind wanting to be a writer. She probably makes the break with the family to the considerable pain of both the family and herself. I don't think she will be a successful writer because I think there is too much in her of repudiating the background from which she came. In her aspirations toward the "finer things" she will have separated herself from the elements of strength in her background that her writing will probably be rather ephemeral. Momentary popularity and quickly forgotten. She herself will be left high and dry, unwilling and unable to go back and establish contact and unable to develop any associations and foundations of any permanency and strength.

Reaction of characters to attributes of the environment. The interaction of person and environment, in many ways the central feature of TAT interpretation, is viewed partly through the statement of thema and partly through other previously noted aspects of the story. It will be well, however, to consider specifically how the subject states the reaction of his characters to the environment he describes. How do the characters react to the various kinds of outside influences? Do they react differentially to positive and negative environments? Do they react differently to human environment than to nonhuman? Do they, in fact, see any need to have their characters react? It is often of great importance to observe whether or not a character expresses some action or feeling in response to the environment. It not infrequently happens that one subject, in describing a squalid physical environment, will feel obliged to portray his hero as disgusted at this squalor, or overcome with motives of clean-up and reform. He may, however, suggest no reaction, assuming in a sense that the environment as portrayed is "natural" and requires no particular reaction. The solution which the subject makes of aspects of the environment to which some response is required and the nature of the response are the issues here. If the interpreter can reduce his own bias as to what he thinks the probable responses are to the pictures, he will often find vital clues in the issues which the subject raises or in the assumptions which he appears to be making but which he does not state. Thus the description of an object-rich environment may mean one thing when presented in a "natural" and unemotional fashion and something quite different when presented in a manner suggesting the character's emulation and admiration or his disgust. Again the subject may feel it necessary to imply some special attribute of person-environment interaction, that "they are friends," for example, when the facts of the picture or the rest of the story do not require the decision as to whether they are friends or not. The emotional drive behind the necessity to be disgusted at a squalid environment or to raise the issue of friendship is the point of importance for interpretation.

Empathy with characters. Knowledge of personal motives and of the intricacies of thought of other persons is an aspect of personality about which subjects vary greatly. To some extent this knowledge and the attendant empathy with feeling and motive will be reflected in the way in which the subject portrays feelings of identification with his characters. Some of these points were raised in connection with the discussion of the hero-figure. The points made there are the same. Here it should be stressed that the empathy with all characters, or the differential empathy with certain characters, is of importance in itself as well as being helpful in identifying a central figure. Scrutiny of characters with regard to the evidences of empathy should take account of such features as: the amount of detail portrayed about the lives of the characters, the time given to descriptions of their feelings and emotions, their reactions to the external stimulation, and the emotional evaluations made upon the statement of an outcome satisfactory or unsatisfactory to them. Perceptiveness of motive and the relation of these motives to the goals of story figures will reflect the subject's orientation to internal stimulation and his ability to readily empathize with other persons.

Introduced figures. The introduced figure is one brought into the plot by the subject for which there is no representation in the picture itself. Thus, in picture 1, the boy is the only figure actually present. However, many subjects will refer to a mother who encourages or controls the boy or possibly to a father or uncle who may have given the violin to the boy. These figures, the mother, father, uncle, are introduced figures. In general, the person who utilizes such figures generally may be thought of as one who has a heightened awareness of his human environment. In addition to the sheer frequency with which such figures are introduced, careful attention should be paid to their characteristics and how they are related to the plot. In many ways they may be seen as having an importance equal to other figures, such that they are introduced by the subject in the absence of any stimulus directly suggesting them. They may normally be thought of as representing the subject's need to complete the picture stimulus with figures whom he considers an integral part of the plot as suggested by the actual stimulus picture. Thus the man referred to on page 78 who introduced a competent but dead father tells us in essence that he cannot conceive of independent (boy alone) action and must refer outgoing concepts of action and ambition to some stimulating outside figure. The department head on page 84 similarly introduces many outside figures. He uses them, however, to enliven his actions, to demonstrate his awareness of an active and moving social environment. Subjects who utilize only characters for whom there are direct replicas in the picture are generally more inhibited in their social and emotional contact with the outer world. This may be either a self-sufficient attitude or a direct flight from active social contact. The distinction may be made in terms of the attributes of the themas and characters actually described.

Variations from picture to picture. In all aspects of the content variables of the TAT responses, differential variation with differing stimulus conditions is of the utmost importance. To some extent these variations have been suggested in previous sections. The aspect of these variations which the writer wants to bring into focus here deals with the differential reaction to specific pictures. Some subjects maintain a real consistency in the features which they attribute to different kinds of characters and situations. Normally we would expect that even the highly consistent subject will still adapt himself somewhat to the differing stimulus demands of the picture. That is to say, only a consistency bordering on pathological perseveration would ignore the obvious reality demands of the pictures which require differing situations and casts of characters. Similarly, different moods are often set by pictures to which even the highly consistent subject will adapt. Thus, picture 3BM is generally seen in some sort of negative light— crying, lost, punished, wounded, etc. One should not assume that a positive response to this picture is necessarily a perceptual distortion, however, recalling, for example, the young Navaho boy who claims that this is a boy sleeping and dreaming of the wonderful things his father will give him when he awakes in the morning. Nonetheless, in the general run of normal cases, some responsiveness to the negative mood of this picture will be expected. The subject who does not so respond, or who does not provide an entirely reasonable alternative (as the Navaho boy did), may be suspected of a rigidity of viewpoint which distorts the basic nature of external stimulation. On the other hand, some subjects are either so sensitive to the mood of the stimulus or so detail- and stimulus-bound that they markedly shift their stance on each picture, suggesting their great vulnerability to outside influence and a lack of ego strength.

In considering what aspects of the pictures should be seen as "different" in basic stimulus, the variables suggested in Chapter 3 will be useful. Pictures with many people, pictures with no people; highly structured pictures, ambiguously structured pictures; pictures with male or female figures; pictures with children or adults; all of these will be worth special scrutiny.

These variations may be noted with respect to the various content characteristics suggested here. They should also be noted with respect to the form categories mentioned in the preceding chapter. Thus variations in length, time of reaction, in organization, in quality of affect, etc., will provide clues to the degree of the subject's internal consistency and to his responsiveness to external stimuli.

Interpersonal relations

Having scrutinized the various attributes of the characters, the relationships proposed between characters should be studied. In general all the attributes of the characters are to be studied with respect to their effects upon other characters. Such points as the following will help guide the interpreter in this task.

Action and thought response to various interpersonal situations. Here the author wishes to draw attention to the reactions which the subject proposes to certain special characters or interactions involving them. In the previous sections, for example, it has been suggested that adult female figures be scrutinized to assay the assumptions which the subject makes about them. Here we should look further to note the reaction other figures have in the presence of such figures, however the subject may describe them. Thus adult females may be basically identified as mother-figures and considered kindly but firm. In the presence of such figures, other characters may be childlike and acceptant of this kindly directiveness. Or they may be rebellious and resistant, or as a matter of fact may show no easily identifiable emotion, the subject merely identifying the mother-figure without putting her into interaction with other persons. Conversely, there may be a great deal of intense interaction with all characters without clear statement of the attributes of this figure.

Amount and kind of interplay between characters. To what extent are the figures involved in a great deal of interaction or are they inactive? Does the subject conceive of the environment of persons as static or busy and dynamic? Does this, whether static or dynamic, change with different figures? Are all the interactions static, possibly negative in tone and leading to ambivalence in the interactions with all characters, except perhaps the female characters, or only with the young figures, or the male figures, etc.? These differential interactions will assist the interpreter in defining the subject's perceived world of persons and in assaying his past and present interaction with them. In this task, special attention should be paid to pictures where there is a single figure alone or where, as in 12BG, no human figures are portrayed. Not infrequently subjects will find 14, the lone person in silhouette, a highly intriguing picture, permitting the lone person emotions, feelings, and fantasies which the human environment of other pictures appears to inhibit. Similarly, in 12BG, the rowboat drawn up by a woodland stream, some subjects are dismayed, being unable to allow themselves fantasies of personal action in the absence of human figures to define their action. Or they may sigh with relief at the peaceful noninteraction of 12BG and allow, for the first time, their tender and sensuous emotions to come into view.

Use of emotional basis of interaction. In the examination of language categories and of special characters, the question of empathy and of the use of emotion-laden words was discussed. Here it will be well to examine to what extent these emotions serve as the basis for action. Some subjects are able to load their stories with affect words but do not utilize these notions in developing the plot and outcome. The question to be asked here is: To what extent is the subject familiar with what kinds of emotional states and to what extent does he see these as direct instigators of action? In contrast, of course, is the question: To what extent does the subject fail to see personal emotion and to what extent does he propose all action as being motivated by some situation external to the subject?

In a sense, any examination of the attributes of persons in the stories will lead to a study of these categories of interaction between people. However, it is easy to make the error of assuming that because a given character has many emotions and ambitions then, therefore, these are directly motivating of action for him in other characters. This is not necessarily true and evidence of its truth or falseness in any individual case should be sought through direct examination of the results of these emotions in the subsequent actions of all characters.

Use of objects. The physical objects, other than human figures, in the stories will also bear examination. The tendency of some subjects to use objects in specifically symbolic fashion will be discussed later. Here the writer merely wishes to draw attention to the awareness of the subject to material realities, to the use which he makes of them, and to the affect which he attaches to them. This will in part be a reflection of the subject's range of interests and his ease with the physical world. It will reflect his assumptions about the desirability of physical possessions, the degree of personal identification which he derives from them, and the utilization which he makes of them in interpersonal situations. Is the subject one to whom physical objects are the end point of existence, who sees all goals as involving the accumulation of objects? Is he one to whom objects provide stability and who can quiet his anxieties through counting and admiring them? Is he one who views material possessions as evil, who rejects them as evidence of vanity or worldliness? Does he reject the "slick" objects as evidences of a kind of giving in to society and prefer the simple, homemade, and unadorned objects as suggestion of an assumed "naturalness"? Does the subject reject all notation of objects, dealing only with emotions and their interaction?

Dynamic Structure of Content

This area is separated from the body of content variations to emphasize it as a special area for study, in spite of the artificiality of such separation. Here reference is made not to any particular attributes of content but to the possibility of individual personality factors being suggested by some special order, arrangement, or juxtaposition of content aspects. Two main points may be made: the use of content in terms of symbolic interpretation, and the use of content in terms of association interpretation.

Interpretation of symbolic content

There is no question but what subjects may from time to time use objects in the picture in symbolic fashion, suggesting thereby a feeling which they cannot express directly. The classic object symbolizations of basic maleness and femaleness do occur and interpretation of these along standard lines is certainly justifiable. These object symbols, such as elongated objects as phallic and enclosed spaces as womblike, may lead the interpreter to areas of interpretation which he might otherwise not have noted. However, two special precautions should be observed. First, there must be in the story evidence that the object is for this subject at this time being utilized in symbolic form. The interpreter should keep continually in mind that the violin, for example, while sometimes a phallic symbol, is also a musical instrument. To use the sexual implications of the phallic symbol, however, some evidence must be present that the violin is indeed being used symbolically. Second, the key to the meaning which is attached to the symbolic object should be found in the responses which the subject himself provides.

Association interpretation

It is often useful to emphasize the psychological connection between topics which have no immediate logical connection provided by the subject. Changes in the topic of the plot should be scrutinized not merely for lack of logic and coherence (which may be true enough) but also for their association in connections and meanings. Thus the boy who first talks of war when he views a picture and then describes a mother-figure should not necessarily be accused only of being illogical. Rather the assumption of some unstated connection of hostility and mother should be investigated.

The use made of these areas of analysis should, in the writer's opinion, always be implemented by a more systematic analysis of other form and content characteristics. It is entirely appropriate to base interpretations upon such symbolic and association categories. However, since in these areas the interpreter must bring to the task so much that is outside the data of the case record itself, and since in so doing his own tendency to project may be severely strained, it is best to view such suggestions cautiously and to explore them in other areas of data. The author would place greater value upon these notations if they were carefully screened through the developing complex of personality variables seen in the other form and content areas. If the interpretation of symbolization is correct, the substantiation will be found elsewhere.

With these precautions in mind, some illustrations may be given of these forms of interpretation.

Object symbolism with chain of association support. The story is told to picture 1 by a man of twenty-nine.

A young boy sitting in front of a violin spread out on white table, or white linen. It is not clear in the expression of the face if he thinks in glorification and admiration of that what the violin and music could hold for him or if he is bored and in disgust with the lesson he has to take and doesn't want.

This story is one with minimal plot development, no statement of past and future, and no stated outcome. Yet some very important observations may be made when we view the story as essentially a statement of sexual conflict revolving around his failure to resolve the Madonna versus sex conflict and his preoccupation with and inability to integrate his view of two basic kinds of women. These suggestions derive from several specific sources:

1. "A violin spread out on a white table, or white linen." In his observation the subject goes beyond that required to identify the object and its location, suggesting in his term "spread out" and in the double and indecisive reference to the location of the object some special preoccupation with it. From these, one might suggest some special cathexis to the object, and, considering its possible basic phallic identity, propose that this cathexis is to sexuality. The definition of the meaning which this has for him, however, is not clear until we examine other responses in the light of this assumption.

2. "Glorification and admiration . . . or if he is bored and in disgust." In this complex and overelaborated juxtaposition of opposites, the subject suggests a definition of his preoccupation with sexuality. He asks, in essence, is it magnificent and idealistic or is it disgusting? In his failure to choose or to suggest alternative outcomes, he suggests the idea that for him these are both puzzling aspects of sex which he is unable to consolidate or to escape. Much as we have introduced a realm of theory in saying that the violin may have phallic referents and hence this man is preoccupied with sexuality, it may be well to introduce a further aspect of this body of theory to suggest a possible genesis of this feeling. That is, of course, the Madonna versus sex notion in which the child attempts to resolve for himself the developing awareness that the protective maternal figure can also be a sexual object. In portraying these two seemingly opposite elements (glory versus disgust) this man implies that he has not satisfactorily made this resolution. That is to say, the subject presents us with what may be tentatively seen as a kind of logical parallel to the Madonna versus sex issue. By proceeding on the basis of the theory of which his remarks remind us, this kind of failure at resolution may be suggested.

3. "He has to take and doesn't want." To complete this aspect of the analysis of the story, we should add this partial statement of outcome. It may be noted that for this subject, this is perceived as an "end," the outcome which the instructions asked of him. In it he says quite directly that we must conform to an unpleasant requirement.

If we now take these three ideas, ignore any connections which the subject logically makes or fails to make between them, we might paraphrase this story in terms of its meaning for the subject in this fashion:

1. Sexuality is a preoccupying area.
2. Women are two contradictory kinds of beings.
3. We must conform to this unpleasant reality.

While it is not our purpose to substantiate these minor analyses of single stories, it may be seen from the fuller presentation of this case in Chapter 9 that internal additional evidence is presented by other stories in both symbolic form as well as in the more mundane content and form categories. Some minor evidence may in fact be in this story itself if we note that his perception of this male figure (young boy) permits no task completion. The boy never states his goals, does not further cope with the conflicting emotions presented, and achieves no satisfactory resolution. In sum, he says: women are objects of conflicting identifications, neither of which is satisfactory; man is obliged to conform to expectation, which he does in protest and without satisfaction.

In this example one key to the interpretation lies in the object symbolism and another in the associations which follow it in the subject's story. In a sense, the object symbolism here was only an additional and not the crucial item. It helps to support the conclusion for which the statements of contradictory values are also of importance.

Chain of association analysis with object symbolism support. In the following story, a seemingly illogical break in the plot, a disruption of organization, takes on meaning if we ignore the seeming illogicality and consider that the story contains a chain of association ideas entirely logical in terms of the unconscious feelings of the subject. This is a story to picture 2, the rural family scene, told by a girl of ten.

This family lives on a farm and the mother, she likes to sing songs. She leans against the tree and sang songs, while the father works in the field. Their daughter is eighteen years old and went to school.

The trouble with that story is that it looks like night. It looks dark, and I don't know why. You can't see the house very well.

Oh, and then at night when she comes home and they all sit around the fire and the mother sings songs.

In this story the cherished image of a happy and attentive mother is repeated twice, interrupted by a statement presented as a criticism of the story, not intended to be part of the plot. If we assume, however, that for this girl the chain of associations represents her real feelings, however disruptive of plot continuity it may be, we see a quite different way in which the middle section (typed separately above for sake of convenience) is indeed a criticism. She says, in essence, that the image of the happy home is somehow not true. It looks "dark," it looks "like night." It appears black and unreal to her. Yet she must insist that it is still true, and in compulsive fashion repeats it in the final section. In this, we take the middle section as a direct negation of the idea proposed in the first section, assuming the meaning of "dark" and "night" to be a rejection and a statement of unreality. We may go a little further if we permit ourselves to analyze the associations within this middle section. We then note the connection: it is "dark," "night," "can't see the house." She selects out of many possibilities "the house" and associates it with her ideas of darkness. We may propose that "the home" which you "can't see" is a symbolic representation of the absence of the mother and hence conclude that there is some specific disturbance with respect to the mother. In this light, we would see the repetition of the "sing song" mother in the first and third parts as a reactive attempt at a wistful hoping that the mother were indeed present and very attentive. Since we have in this story very little direct evidence as to the meaning of "house" for this girl— other than its "darkness" association—we are falling back on an area of theory (house-mother) that may or may not be relevant here. It has the virtue of appearing to fit the remainder of the story and subsequent data support the ideas developed from it.

Situation symbolism with object symbolism support. In the story the same girl of ten gave to picture 11, the prehistoric scene, we see a regressive plot which as a total situation may be suggestive of her strong fear of the external world and her desire for maternal protection. The story is as follows:

This little beetle, he was going along real peacefully on his way, going down the cliff. All of a sudden he heard a rumble and jumped out of the path of the rocks. Then he saw this tail-like thing, and he was very worried. Finally he found out that it was a kangaroo, and so he got friends with the kangaroo and they lived on the mountain together. Every time a roar came he would climb into the kangaroo pouch and stay there very safely.

Indeed a happy nostalgic scene of the little beetle retreating to the pouch for comfort in times of trial. The entire situation, rather than any specific detail, suggests her fear of the "rumble" of the outside world and her search for protection. The "pouch" may of course be perceived as a specific reference to the mother. It is perhaps a matter of semantics or of theoretical preference, but the author would avoid in this kind of a story the temptation to interpret this as a desire to return to the mother's womb. As a matter of fact, he would not even consider this a more "dynamic" interpretation or even one of greater "depth." It seems quite sufficient to see this girl as terrified by external events, fearful of her ability to find protection, and reacting to this dilemma with unrealistic wishful fantasies of maternal protection (the pouch retreat). It may not be amiss also to notice the sudden and, if you wish, traumatic way in which the "beetle" finds himself endangered. Things were going peacefully when "all of a sudden" with a rumble rocks came crashing down. That this trauma has not been abreacted may be suggested by her fear that the "roars" will continue, and that every time they do she will run to her fantasy pouch.

Best- and least-liked stories

Not all aspects of the stories to which special meaning may be given are symbolic in the ordinary sense. Certain other features of the stories may take on significance through some feature which lies not in the content itself but rather in some special dynamic relationship attributed to it by the subject. Thus the stories selected by him as best liked or least liked bear some special significance worth study. In general, it may be suggested that the best-liked stories represent for the subject his positive image and constructive defenses. The least-liked stories represent his apprehensions and ego defects. Needless to say, it is the content of the particular stories selected that permits one to propose these specific positive and negative points.

Thus in the record of a successful business man of mobile but stereotyped goals, we note the best-liked choice of 2 and 7BM. His least-liked stories are to 3BM and 14. It may already be noted, without examining the content of 2 and 7BM, that they are both fairly well-structured pictures permitting readily organized and stereotyped stories. Both 3BM and 14, however, are more ambiguous pictures, with single persons in poorly defined situations. This immediately suggests a person who counts heavily upon protocol to carry him through and who fears unstructured situations, particularly when they involve the lone person. Examination of his stories tends to support these ideas. To 2 he tells a short but positive story of a young girl leaving a successful farm to provide herself a "more educated program in life." In indicating his choice, he says this picture: "seems to be emblematic of life itself." In 7BM he suggests further that he sees clear-cut and positive authority relations as one of the keys to success. This is the "cut-and-dried" story of an "eager youth listening" to one who is "administering wisdom by virtue of years of experience." Of this story, in indicating his choice, he says: "You could go on and on about that one. I like it very much." Progress through stable family structure and mobility through education and the wisdom of your elders seem to be his chosen path. It need hardly be mentioned that neither of these stories is notable for its attention to human motive and affect.

It is noteworthy, however, that in his least-liked choices he appears specifically to reject the pictures that remind him of embarrassing human emotions. 3BM is a badly organized story of a "man or a woman" who has committed an unidentified crime and may commit suicide. "Other than that," he finished, "it is fairly empty and void." He further rejects this by saying: "possible repentance, I don't know what it could be . . . it doesn't excite me." His fear of introspection and of the dangers of self-inspection are again rejected in his choice of 14. In this picture about which he says, "don't care much for this," he presents a fellow in an open window where he doesn't "quite understand the light and darkness here." He finishes the story by proposing a number of innocuous endings fleeing away from the usually introspective trend of this picture, completing with the observation that the picture could be a photographic negative. His dependence upon authority and his fears of affect or self-examination are amply suggested by these choice patterns.

A quite different significance may be attributed to a best-liked choice for 2 told by a disgruntled and discouraged man of forty. He tells of a poor and unhappy child who is on the verge of trying a new life by leaving the homestead. His second-liked choice, that of 8BM, has a similar plot in which a young man, without technical training and with only his general education, performs a major surgical operation and saves a life. That these two potential readjustments to unfortunate situations are still not really believed by him is suggested by the indecision and uncertainty that he puts into 2 and by his finally attributing the heroic plot of 8BM to the "imagination" of the boy. If we suggest that 2 and 8BM represent a faint hope that some "new life" will save him, we can perhaps see from his least-liked story his fears and basic evaluations of the situation he feels he is in. To 3BM, one least liked, he portrays a lost boy whose car keys have been stolen. "He has sat down and fallen asleep." In this story of helpless castration, he suggests his real fear that he has indeed given up the battle. In 19, his second choice, he tells us not so much that he dislikes the ambiguity of the unstructured 19, but rather he deals with it quite simply, projecting into it a story of "wonderland" in which a "tremendous cat" creates mischief around a house divided. In this rejected story, he attributes his difficulty to the home and marriage situation.

It is not suggested that the analysis of the choices be different from the analysis of other stories, but merely that some additional significance be explored in the light of the general meaning suggested for best- and least-liked pictures. Meaning may be attributed in part through general knowledge of the nature of the picture itself. More reliably, however, meaning should be derived from the story which the subject himself tells to the picture.

The sequence of stories

While each story will have its own meaning as indicated by the analyses already given, it will be worth while to examine two other special attributes of the stories. The first is the possibility of important connections between individual stories which occur in sequence. The second is the possibility of additional significance to be attached to stories which occur early in the sequence—the first five or six—as contrasted with those that occur later—the last three or four.

In individual instances, stories may take on special meaning if they appear to complete or continue an action initiated in the preceding story. Thus in a story of aggression which is not given a satisfactory ending, it not infrequently occurs that the subsequent story is in actuality the ending to the previous one. Thus the second story may be one of punishment or retribution.

In a subject confused about his own aggressive impulses, such hesitations are not infrequent. The subject appears to want to try out a plot of unpunished aggression and does so in one story. His guilt, however, may be such that he feels obliged to correct what he feels is an imbalance by a story of repentance or retribution to the next picture. While there is some point in suggesting that each story is in a sense stimulated by the previous one and is thus a reaction to it, it does not seem profitable to search for special connections except in instances where some fairly clear-cut sequence appears. Generally speaking, the clues to such sequences may lie in stories which are uncharacteristic for the subject in question. Thus, when a subject who normally tells nicely completed plots tells one in which some act or moral position is left incomplete, it will pay to examine carefully the story following it, expecting that his usual closure tendency will influence this story.

The general difference between the first few and the last few stories may often suggest some differences between the subject's systems of defense and his anxieties. While this is by no means an inevitable pattern, it frequently appears that subjects will gradually allow their defenses to drop as they proceed through a series of pictures. In this case, one may look to the first stories to give us a picture of the functional defense system and to the last ones for an image of the material defended. In subjects who fear ambiguous and unstructured situations —which occur in the last and not the first cards—this sometimes does not operate. These subjects may merely dismiss these last cards with detailed description and avoid giving analyzable content. These rejections will, of course, give one a notion of the subject's fear of lack of structure and his handling of it.

By way of illustration, the case of the male aged twenty-nine referred to earlier may be examined in this light. In his first story he presents a moderately well-organized and in any case vigorous story of a boy in a quandary (see Chapter 9). Here he presents his dilemma and active choice pattern between the two kinds of women whom he envisions. Similarly, in the subsequent few stories, while still giving us a great deal of material, he reports in an organized manner without appearing to lose control or to be reflecting his inner uncertainty. In contrast, his last story, to picture 20, is as follows:

Man leaning against lamppost, winter night. Obviously big city, man suggesting loneliness, being lost, face hidden. . . . Position of man in leaning against lamppost that of a man who is not waiting for date but obviously alone and will be alone.

While the general organizational level of this story is comparable to that of earlier stories, his sense of futility comes through here strongly.

Similarly, in the case of the business man of forty, the difference between his first and last stories again demonstrates this kind of break. His first story is a fairly strong one implying, in its direct content, ambition and emulation. In his last story, however, picture 20, he tells a tale of loneliness and monotony which reflects directly his basic resignation.

This is one of our employees. He lives out in the far suburbs and he is a member of the share-the-ride club and it is about an hour's drive to the plant to go to work. It means that they have to probably start before seven o'clock in order to get here on time. This is a very cold morning and it is snowing and he is standing on the curb under the street light waiting for his ride. Due to the fact that it is very cloudy because of the snow, it is still very dark and the street lights are all lit. He is not thinking much of anything in general and it is pretty cold and he has been waiting for some time wondering if his watch is right or if he got there too late or too early. The sun being obscured by the clouds, he has no way of estimating how close his watch is. He has stood on this same corner waiting for this ride for many years and he has fallen into a habit and just stands there waiting for his ride.

Negative Content

The difference between positive and negative content may be summarized in this way: the analysis of positive content is concerned with what the subject has actually said; the analysis of negative content is concerned with what the subject has not said in the light of what he might have been expected to say. The analysis of negative content is clearly dependent upon detailed knowledge of the stimulus qualities of the pictures and upon the usual reactions to the pictures by subjects of various cultural, age, and sex groups. A brief summary only of the major points relevant to negative content interpretation will be given here.

Any given picture may be thought of as presenting to the subject stimuli of three basic sorts: 1. a stimulus of form, called *stimulus form demand;* 2. a stimulus of content, termed *manifest stimulus demand;* and 3. a stimulus of meaning, called the *latent stimulus demand.* These stimulus-demand qualities of the pictures provide one of the major elements determining the subject's response to the card. They are essential to an understanding of the subject's perception of these pictures and to an interpretation of his story response. It is to be recalled that these are seen to be attributes of the picture, not of the story as told by the subject. The various aspects of the story are those identified earlier as story-form and story-content variables.

The *stimulus form demand* refers to the form complexity of the picture and to the apparent fact that the task as presented to the subject varies in its difficulty in proportion to the level of complexity of the forms presented. Thus, picture 1, the boy with the violin, presents a quite simple form problem. Essentially only two major form details are present, that represented by the boy and that by the violin. Other form elements present, but not generally required for an adequate story, are of course the bow and the table or sheet of music upon which the violin rests. In picture 2, the farm scene, the form stimuli are more complex. There are the three forms represented by the three persons, and the rural or farmlike qualities of the buildings and landscape. Also in this picture are a number of significant small details: the books in the girl's arm, the horse, the "pregnancy" of the older woman.   Beyond these the details of the farm building, the second man and horse, the furrows, the "lake," etc., represent additional small details that may be utilized in story construction.   Another contrast is presented by 13BG, in which only a rowboat, a stream, and woodland are noted, and 19, in which a great variety of amorphous form elements are present.

The *manifest stimulus demand* refers to the usual identifications made of the forms present in the picture and the usual relationships proposed between them.   Here the identification of the two major forms in 1 as "boy" and "violin" is noted.   Further, the content demand of this card calls for some statement of a relationship between these forms: studying, practising, having been given, hating, trying to get away from, and the like.   At least in middle-class American groups, a significant aspect of content demand here includes an introduced figure, normally a mother.   In 2, the farm scene, the content demand is essentially the three persons, some relationship between them, and the farmlike qualities of the scene.   Generally subjects can ignore details beyond these without sacrificing adequate story logic.   In 3BM, the major content demand is that presented by the figures in some sort of reclining position.   It seems probable that the "gun" on the floor is also a major stimulus demand.   The sex and age of the figure are sufficiently unclear so that we should not include any specific sex and age attributes as part of the basic content requirement of this card.   In 1, in contrast, the youngness and the maleness are apparent and hence are part of the definition of stimulus content.

Latent stimulus demand refers not to any specific form or content aspects of the stimulus picture but rather to the emotional problem or focus most generally raised by the picture.   *Latent stimulus* is thus an emotional matter and will be defined for each card in terms of the analysis and interpretation of subject's responses rather than in terms of inspection of the picture itself.   It will vary from group to group somewhat, representing to some extent a definition of the foci of emotional concerns of the group in question.   Thus, in number 1, the boy with the violin, the stimulus meaning for most middle-class American subjects deals with the basic problem of expressiveness versus order and control.   The emotional definition of this picture does not deal with a boy and a violin; it deals with an underlying question, symbolized by these content features, of the relationship between the individual's internal desires and the external world's pressure for conformity.   In picture 2, the latent stimulus may be phrased in terms of the issue of interpersonal relationships: how can three people be related and what is the emotional basis for this relationship. Here a subsidiary issue of importance is that of the old versus the new, the traditional versus the modern, or some other statement of such a value contrast between the settled tradition (the farm) and new ambitions (the girl getting education).

Each of these aspects of the stimulus-demand qualities of the picture becomes relevant for an understanding of the meanings of the subject's response in both its positive form and content aspects. From the viewpoint of negative content, the issue becomes one of the subject's failure to employ some normally utilized form or his "misidentification" of some usually identified content or relationship. Rejection of the whole or parts of pictures may be seen in the light not merely of card refusal but of latent-stimulus refusal. Thus a rejection of card 3BM, the depressive and possibly suicidal aspects of the card, may be suggested as related to this rejection. It suggests merely that these negative emotions are distressing to the subject for reasons probably not directly apparent in the card, but possibly to be found in the analysis of other responses. Of some interest here is the rejection not of the whole card, but only of the "gun" on the floor. There is some reason to assume, from analysis of subjects who do utilize the "gun," that its symbolic significance is in the area of genital sexuality. It appears profitable to conceive a rejection of the "gun" alone as a refusal to deal with this manifestation of genital sexuality. As was mentioned earlier in the discussion of symbolic interpretation, such assumptions as these are made in three contexts: 1. that of evidence of symbolic use; 2. dynamic association of the subject to the symbol; and 3. corroborative evidence from other areas. In this instance, we take the rejection as evidence of symbolic intent and the meaning which we attach to it as projected from the "usual" meaning attached by other subjects. A similar logic will apply to all other areas of negative content analysis. Needless to say, this kind of analysis, while an extremely useful supplement to analysis of more direct data, requires caution and the substantiation of conclusions from other areas of analysis.

CHAPTER 6

A conceptual framework
for
individual case analysis

An analysis of an individual personality may take a variety of forms. The choice to be made between them is essentially a matter of theoretical preference. The outline suggested in this chapter is one which has been found useful in the analysis of many instruments of personality study. It is organized around a notion of life areas, some dealing directly with "internal" events and some with "external" events. At each step of this outline of analysis, effort is made, when it is at all appropriate, to integrate these external and internal frames of reference. Observations on basic intelligence and mental approach are related directly to overt behavior, particularly in the areas of school or work adjustment. The description of the overt behavioral patterns is meaningless and cannot in fact be systematically described without reference to inner dynamics. Similarly, the area of inner adjustment cannot be pictured except as it is related to the mechanisms for perceiving the outer world and for adjusting to it. Some of these concepts appear to be overlapping and other workers may prefer to consolidate a number of them. Undoubtedly, some workers will want to add concepts or to completely discard this system for one with which they can work more readily.

In general, the author strongly favors two viewpoints which may at first seem contradictory. First, he would suggest that some systematically applied single conceptual framework is necessary for the initial explorations with instruments as new and undeveloped as the TAT. Precisely what this framework may be is not of the first importance. What is vital is that the data of the instrument be systematically reflected through a conceptual mesh of known characteristics. The second viewpoint, which he holds to be equally important in the long run, is that the workers in this area should be flexible and imaginative in the concepts which they bring to bear upon the analysis of the TAT. Ultimately, the greatest gain will derive from the use of a wide range of conceptual frameworks designed to fit the scientific problems under scrutiny. An instrument which can be significantly analyzed into only one fixed framework is greatly limited in its broader utility in the investigation of human behavior. It is precisely this flexibility that makes the TAT so attractive in the study of behavior.

In this chapter a proposed outline for the analysis of the individual case record is presented and briefly discussed. Following this, each section of the outline is considered from the point of view of the aspects of form and content which at this stage appear to be relevant to the analysis of the record in each area. Illustrations are given from time to time; they will be recognized as merely suggestive and are given only when one or two stories demonstrate in particularly clear form the attribute under discussion. Some areas, perhaps best exemplified by that of *general adjustment,* can hardly be illustrated appropriately short of the inclusion of a full record. In subsequent chapters, fuller records will be included. Here the author wishes merely to suggest the kinds of story data that appear to relate to the outline.

Outline for Individual Case Analysis

Area 1: Mental approach

In this area an effort should be made to describe and evaluate the approach which the subject takes to the stimuli. Perceiving the task as exclusively as intellectual one, in what manner does the subject solve the problem presented to him? Analysis here should provide both a description of the manner of problem-solving as well as an evaluation of this in intelligence level terms. The following breakdown is suggested.

Level of intellectual capacities. An estimation of the mental ability of the subject in one of six grades:

Very superior—IQ above 130.
Superior—IQ of 110–130.
High average—IQ of 100–110.
Low average—IQ of 90–100.
Dull normal—IQ of 80–90.
Borderline—IQ of 70–80.

Adequacy and efficiency of intellectual functioning. The extent to which performance is up to ability or the extent to which emotional involvement is reducing efficiency. Here specific forms of intellectual impairment or efficiency reducing approaches should be noted: whole-compulsion, detail-compulsion, unrealistic fantasy, perceptual distortions, and the like.

Organization and logic of intellectual approach. The level of organization, coherence, and logic manifested by the subject's responses and the extent and nature of any interferences or facilitations of these by emotional factors. It is also useful here to consider the characteristic mental approach in terms of inclusive whole concepts (W's), large-detail (D) responses, and small-detail (d) responses.*

Intellectual approach to new problems. It is useful to distinguish the subject's mental approach to new and, especially, unstructured stimuli to estimate to what extent his mental flexibility permits him to cope as adequately with new problems as with old. Here also the nature of the emotional investment in unstructured problems should be considered.

Area 2: Imaginative processes

The extent, freedom, and quality of the imaginative processes; the manner in which they are used intellectually; their constructive or escapist qualities.

Imagination. The freedom, fluidity, and amount of imaginal production.

Creativity. The richness and complexity of fantasy and the extent to which it is used constructively or to which it provides reality-escape.

Originality. The novelty and uniqueness of idea and association as opposed to their commonness and popularity. This area bears obvious overlaps with the previous two. It is separated here to take into account the fact that many original observations may be of poor

---

* These concepts and the symbols W, D, and d are of course taken from Rorschach terminology. They are very useful in the analysis of TAT.

or distorted quality and hence not be appropriately judged in terms of imagination constructively and creatively utilized.

Area 3: Family dynamics

The emotional relationships to specific family members and their influence upon the subject.

Relationship to father, mother, and siblings. Overt and covert relationships to the image of father, mother, and siblings; personality of mother and father.

Resolution of primary parental ties. The resolution of the primary attachment to the mother and the present state of emotional dependence or emancipation from mother and father.

Family emotional atmosphere. An estimate of the dominant emotional atmosphere of the home and the interpersonal relations of family members.

Area 4: Inner adjustment

Inner life characteristics and personality adjustment pattern.

Basic emotional attitude. The strength and direction of drive toward the solution of emotional problems. This is an estimate of the basic passivity or assertion of energy toward emotional issues, independent of the success of the solution or the techniques used.

Attitude towards inner life. Acceptance or rejection of impulse life.

Anxiety. Insecurity feelings and anxiety; its adaptive or inhibiting nature; diffuse or specific to special areas.

Ego strengths and defenses. Nature of ego strength and defenses, to include ego sources of comfort and stability.

System of control. The method of personality control and its balance. Three control areas may be distinguished. They are:

1. Conscious control, or the extent to which external guiding factors form a major part of the method of relating the self to the outer world.

2. Inner control, or the extent to which inner feelings, personal desires, and impulse strivings are utilized in the relating of self to outer world.

3. Outer control, or the facility with which the subject controls his overt behavior.

Approach to interpersonal relations. Emotional basis of ties to other people and the quality of these ties.

Maturity. An evaluation of emotional maturity and the balance of control factors with impulse life.

Area 5: Emotional reactivity

Spontaneity and reactiveness to emotional stimulation. Drive towards outer world. The reaction to outer world stimuli as opposed to receptiveness to stimuli from own inner life.

Spontaneity and personal freedom of action. The extent to which the subject reacts to the objective nature of the stimulation and to which his responses are free from emotional preoccupations that warp his objectivity.

Area 6: Sexual adjustment

The maturity, stage, and general adequacy of sexual adjustment.

Adequacy. Age-appropriate sex attitudes.

Anxiety. Anxiety of sexual origin.

Role perception. Age- and sex-appropriate conception of sexuality and overt sex role.

Area 7: Behavioral approach

The patterning of overt behavior and the function of overt roles in the psychic economy.

General overt pattern. A descriptive statement of observable daily behavior in general terms.

Peer relationships. Overt behavior and motivational background of relation to peers: emotional relation to male and female peers and to group. In children and adolescents, the nature of the friendship and group patterns is the central focus. In adults, especially where a work emphasis is required, the focus is best placed upon patterns of co-operativeness versus isolation, resistance versus forced involvement, and the relation of these to both work and social relations.

Authority (adult) relationships. Acceptance or rejection of authority (adult) relationships, nature of emotional ties to authority figures, and ways of dealing with authority relations. In children's cases, this area profitably deals with attitudes towards parental figures. In adult cases, attitudes toward authority figures are the better focus. When a work emphasis is important, the focus is well placed upon attitudes toward superior and subordinate figures, ability to take or give direction, and the like.

School (work) adjustment. Relation to teachers and to schoolwork; acceptance of academic organization and demands; relation of these to foregoing categories and to mental approach. In adults, the emphasis would most frequently be upon work adjustment, in which case attention would be paid to acceptance of the organizational goals; pattern of work cathexes; mobility and accomplishment strivings; executive, work, or professional orientations.

Specific behavioral problems. Concrete symptomatology presenting overt difficulties and its motivational background.

Area 8: Descriptive and integrative summary

The patterning and integration of material in Areas 1 through 7 and an estimation of general adjustment to self and outer world. It will be ovious that if the case analyzed has a specific history of presenting difficulties, this presenting problem should be brought into focus here. Similarly, if the case is one of occupational adjustment, specific strengths and weaknesses may well be discussed here, as well as any predictive statements regarding adjustment to various possible organizational situations.

Form and Content Variables and the Outline of Analysis

It would be a quite impossible task, and indeed presumptuous, for the author to suggest that he could at this time indicate the precise content and form variables which are diagnostic of specific attributes suggested in the outline. At best, he can give some suggestions and ideas, based primarily upon the analysis of nonclinical cases. It might even be better to refer to them as general impressions, as yet not formulated in hypothesis form, of the characteristics of stories that are useful in the description of personality variables. This is all that will be attempted in the remainder of this chapter. One special feature will become apparent in the following pages, but deserves specific mention now. It is the fact that, in spite of the possibility of indicating specific categories which have more significance for one personality variable than for another, the single most important feature of these categories is their multidimensional nature. That is to say, no one category in itself has any unvarying significance and no single interpretation can be made from it without substantiation from a number of other categories. This will perhaps serve as a reminder of the artificiality of the breakdown of form and content variables and act as a precaution against interpretations based on any single element. It should be clear that the writer does not think of this as an entirely desirable situation, but one that at this time represents the state of knowledge with respect to the relation of specific TAT categories to personality variables. It is entirely probable that future work will show us with far greater clarity which of these categories are stable and descriptive of describable personality attributes and which are not.

Area 1: Mental approach

To a larger degree than is probably true of any other area of the outline, the delineation of the mental approach rests upon consideration of the form characteristics of the stories. Consideration of each of the form items in Chapter 4 will readily show that no one is at all reliable in itself in estimating the intelligence level or other mental approach elements. Thus in respect to the amount of introduced content (page 58, Chapter 4) a subject may include in his story sufficient material in addition to a sterile reporting of the facts of the picture to convince the examiner that the subject has a good intellectual grasp of the picture and that he is elaborating his observations in an intelligent fashion. Sheer quantity of content, however, is no indicator in itself since it is obvious that a highly verbal child of low mental ability may give volumes of verbalizations indicative only of an active compulsion and lack of critical ability. Again, evidence for good intellectual capacities hinges upon the inclusion in the stories of a sufficient number of well-organized and keenly elaborated inclusive whole concepts (page 64, Chapter 4). The presence of a large number of inclusive whole concepts solely may be evidence only of compulsive tendencies in the personality, or, if poor in quality and lacking in elaborations, of below normal, highly uncritical mental ability. Originality of content (page 59, Chapter 4) provides evidence for good mental ability to the extent that there are a number of concepts which are original in the sense that they are unusual in the total range of stories told. In addition, however, they must be concepts that are of a high order of quality and are consistent with the core meaning of the picture. Sheer originality, in that the response is unusual or unique, may be of irrational quality and hence evidence more of mental disorientation than of mental acuity.

In general the judgments of level of the intellectual capacities are to be made on the basis of the following elements:

1. Inclusive whole concepts that are of good quality.
2. Well-organized and balanced stories.
3. Stories that are internally consistent and logical.
4. Number of elaborations upon concepts that are consistent with the central concept of the story.
5. Elaborations on central concepts that serve to clarify, modify, or otherwise improve the preciseness of the concepts.

6. An organizational level that (depending upon the age of the subject) goes beyond static enumeration and description.

7. Number of original concepts.

8. Range and variation of content, topics discussed, objects mentioned, and an abundance of introduced content rich in images.

9. Keenness and preciseness of the concepts.

10. Language, vocabulary, and grammatical structure indicative of intellectual grasp of mental abstractions.

11. Story content that suggests that story told has a broader background of thought and experiential content than is actually verbalized.

These characteristics are at least some of the elements upon which an estimate of the intellectual level may be made. Decision as to the specific level will depend upon the extent to which these are present and upon the keenness, acuity, variety, and other qualitative aspects of the content.

The divisions of the outline under mental approach (pages 103–104) are made for purposes of clarifying various aspects of the mental characteristics. In actuality no such division exists, of course. Consideration of the eleven interpretation elements just mentioned in discussing the intellectual level will provide data for the other subdivisions. With respect to Area 1, the divisions on "Adequacy and efficiency of intellectual functioning," and "Organization and logic of intellectual approach," study of the various organizational elements is of special import. Inconsistencies, variations, and disruptions of these elements suggest inefficient functioning. Sudden shifts in the level of organization and changes in the rhythm and smoothness of the stories indicate some disturbance of the mental process. The nature and origin of this disturbance can often be seen by a study of the content of the stories on which these shifts and irregularities occur. And, as Murray has remarked,[129] "Disjunctivity of thema and language and the occurrence in the narrative of incongruities of feeling and action and of bizarre elements—these bespeak mental disorientation."

In Area 1, the division on "Intellectual approach to new problems," decision is based on the foregoing characteristics and upon the variations which occur in the productivity and organizational elements from the beginning to the end of a single story, and on the relation of these same factors as they occur in the first story or two as compared with subsequent stories. In general, one may observe the characteristic approach to new problems in these two factors when one looks for evidence of such variations as, for example, poor organization, indecisive endings, and the like, in the first stories that gradually disappear and are replaced by more definite statements and better organization as later stories are approached and the subject becomes more at home. The differences between subjects who habitually approach problems with reluctance and timidity and those who approach them with challenge and vigor are readily discernible. A third special item is one which combines form and content characteristics. It deals with decisions as to specific emotional problems upon which the subject has difficulty thinking in a rational way and which are consuming much of his available psychic energy. These do not tend to appear in consistent fashion throughout a series of stories but often appear upon the presentation of a specific card that has elements which arouse his anxiety or following his own statement of a particular emotional situation that is anxiety- or guilt-producing. At such points disruptions occur in the usual manner of approach to the storytelling task and these will be reflected in the productivity and organizational characteristics.

Decision as to whether it is the specific picture to which he is responding or the reactions from the preceding card that aroused the anxiety can only be made on a qualitative basis. In general, if it is the preceding picture which has aroused some concern, review of the responses to it will usually locate elements suggestive of greater use of intraception and of greater empathy with the actions and feelings of the characters than is habitual for that subject. In the event that the specific content of this response is aggressive in any way, responses to the following picture that are self-punishing or retaliatory will emphasize the specific importance of the emotional problem aroused by the picture. Responses that are either overly long and elaborate (but usually not equally intraceptive) or unusually short and sterile (for that subject) indicate specific emotional concerns with which the subject is unable to cope.

Deciding the level of intelligence in IQ terms must rely to a great extent upon the examiner's own set of standards for such levels. An examiner with some clinical experience in intelligence testing and experience with TAT records on subjects of known IQ level can usually estimate the IQ to within five points.* The other characteristics of

* A recent study of forty homogeneous cases provides a Pearson r of $+0.85$ between blind TAT estimates and objective intelligence estimates. Other studies provide less positive but basically quite similar results. Cf. Elaine Graham, "A Comparison between Estimates of Intelligence from Projective and Standard Tests" (Unpublished M.A. thesis, Department of Psychology, University of Chicago, 1947).

the mental approach can also be outlined in much the same manner as is done in the Rorschach method.

Two contrasting cases will illustrate some of the gross differences in high and low intellectual levels. The first is that of a girl of fourteen, whose TAT IQ estimate was very superior (140). Her Binet IQ during the same period was 143. Her story to card 1 is as follows:

Right now the boy is looking at the violin. It looks like he might be kind of sad or mad because he has to play.

Before, he might have played ball with the other boys and his mother wouldn't let him. He had to go in and play. Looks like he might practice for a little while and then sneak out.

Short and to the point, this is a good sample of a story produced by a person of superior intellectual abilities. Notice first how clearly it takes into account the basic stimulus demands of the picture—the boy, the violin, and some interaction between the two. Then note how she elaborates upon this central plot with entirely relevant elaborations of good quality—playing ball, mother wouldn't let him, might practice, then sneak out. It should further be noticed that these elaborations are all motion and affect elaborations. They are not static identifications of small details or physical parts of the picture, but rather attribute motive and action to the characters. This inclusion of inner feeling within a solid structure is a further characteristic of the high and well-functioning IQ.

Also notice how well the subject outlines the time sequences. These are even rather complex, referring to two overlapping sequences of time. First, there is an identification of the present (right now he is . . .) followed by an attribution of meaning and motive (he might be . . . sad . . .). Then she returns to the past (Before, he . . .), builds this up again into the present (he played, . . . mother wouldn't let . . . had to go in . . .). She then moves to the future and completes her story (might practice . . . then sneak out).

A highly practical and realistic mind, she observes closely the major details of the picture, then builds them up into an inclusive whole plot. Cautious and considered, she draws no conclusions not supported by some data, and is careful to make her logic clear and her time sequences sensible and explanatory of the plot. Her story is a good example of a superior IQ characterized by a D to W approach, by a practical and cautious efficiency, and by an ability to integrate impulse areas into her intellectual activities. Needless to say, her other stories would be analyzed before an IQ estimate would be made. While subsequent stories would seldom cause one to reduce an IQ estimate, they could well change the picture of the efficiency and the approach or suggest a raise in the IQ estimate.

Picture 5, the woman entering the room, is a good example of the high IQ's ability to handle complex time and space relationships and to integrate several areas of stimuli into a simple coherent plot.

This looks like maybe it's connected with the first picture, the violin—maybe the mother came in and told him to practice. She didn't hear any more sounds. He'd gone. She finds that he has gone out to play with the boys which she didn't want him to do. She brought him in and spanked him, or bawled him out, and made him practice the violin.

The most interesting thing about the story is the spatial relation of the stimulus to the plot. The picture is actually an illustration of a single point in the story, the point where the mother looks into the room. All that follows stems from this stimulus, without further need for stimulus prompting. She does not get lost in this plot that hangs so tenuously to its basic stimulus, but weaves her way well through a rather involved series of events. In many ways the intellectual power of this girl is more apparent here than in number 1, where her ability to move from the stimulus was less apparent. Again, in this story, notice how frequently and consistently she enlivens her observations with relevant inner feeling categories.

Picture 14, the silhouette, will further demonstrate this girl's power to sustain her good structure and intellectual organization in the presence of poorly defined stimuli and to manipulate time sequences with agility.

Well, it's night and this boy is in his bedroom or in the house, looking at the outside things. It looks as though he is kind of sad or wondering what's going on. Maybe this boy has been around this small neighborhood all his life—did not see much—looking at the outside wondering what it's like, wishing he'd go out and see things for himself. He'll go to the city or nearby town and he may get into trouble, bad company. They bring him home and he learned it wasn't so wonderful out alone.

Moving easily away from the readily identified stimulus, this girl ranges far, develops a good plot, and returns to the stimulus. Never deviating from the clues given to her by the stimulus, she is nonetheless able to enliven her observations with imaginative elements of good quality and proportion.

A rather gross contrast is provided by a girl of similar age whose Binet IQ was 75 and whose Wechsler, 68. Her story to card 1, which may be compared to that of the first girl mentioned, is as follows:

He's thinking . . . it's hard to say . . . he's got something on his desk . . . is that a sheet of paper? It's a sheet of paper. That's about all I can say.

It is quite apparent that this story is barely reflective of an awareness of the basic stimulus—she sees "he" and the "paper." In doing so, however, she ignores entirely a major stimulus, the violin, and, in fact, goes deliberately around it in order to query about the "paper" underneath it. There is no plot development, no characterization, no time sequence, no attribution of feelings. There is, however, a strange attribution of meaning—"he's thinking." This first observation brings the story above the level of sheer enumeration. It certainly suggests a girl greatly preoccupied, unable to utilize effectively her limited intelligence.

In picture 5, she proceeds in much the same fashion, identifying details but giving no plot and very little inner feeling.

Here's a lady, got a dress on, and her hair is up. . . . Got a bookcase and dresser with three books on it, a table and a floor lamp, the door she came in and wallpaper—that's about all. [with some prompting she added] She'll go in this room . . . she's sort of afraid . . . maybe somebody's in there . . . a girl or a boy.

In 14, she does a little better, suggesting a very limited kind of interaction and the rudiments of a plot.

Boy looks like he is in his bedroom looking out the window. I guess he sees something. That's about all.

Upon prompting, she added something of interest from the point of view of the form aspects of the story. The content aspects are of course of somewhat greater interest in other connections. She suggested that the boy was "thinking about his mother" who was "probably in Chicago some place." In this forced addendum, she tells us that there is more to her than she can spontaneously give, something she partly suggested in the opening remark to picture 1. She adds here an element of intraception suggesting merely that her operating efficiency is somewhat less than her basic potential. Each time she leads us to the brink of an idea or a plot and then retreats: "he's thinking," but she refuses to say about what; "she's afraid," but she will not suggest why nor what might happen; "he's looking out . . . he sees something," but what she never tells us. It would suggest that her timidity and her generalized apprehension about the outer world have paralyzed her will to self-initiated activity.

It should not be overlooked, however, that in at least the last two of these three stories she does identify the main stimulus and suggests some aspect of the central activity. In 5, she does sense the slight drama of the woman looking into the room and seeing something unexpected. In 14, she does place the boy in a position of fantasy with respect to the world beyond the room he is in. She cannot go on with these or even develop them very closely, but the basic identification is there. This would suggest a basic awareness of the communalities of the stimulus world, but a very limited ability to influence them or even to see their implications. This would imply an IQ in the low average to borderline group. Were she able to give a simple basic plot indicating an identification of the stimulus plus a subsequent action leading to an outcome, one might want to raise the IQ estimate to average. While she does somewhat better on a couple of stories not reproduced here, the stories given represent the form of the majority of her stories. As they stand, they are suggestive of an IQ of 85–90, rather than 75. Her fear of self-initiated action, the high percentage of passive and noninteractional association, and her refusal to give endings all suggest some basic emotional blockings that handicap both her social action and the application of her mental powers and account for the lower standard test IQ's.

The following stories are of a boy of fourteen, with an IQ of about 125, but with very casual interest in its use and generally low ambition. As will be seen in these stories, he approaches a problem practically, directly, and without fanfare. He seems confident in his ability to succeed, but has not felt need to do so. His mental approach is casual, even lazy, observing the major details and putting them together in quite unimaginative fashion. To picture 1, he says:

Looks like the boy's practicing the violin or whatever it is, and when he lies it down, he's dreaming that he'll be a great violin player. Maybe he will turn out some day to be a great person or something.

Certainly a practical and straightforward story, in good perspective, including all the major stimulus details and going well beyond them to propose a developed plot of rather pleasant and childlike ambition.

In picture 5, he again shows his casual but solid approach. He reports:

This woman looks like she is walking in the room. Looks like she's surprised at somebody or something in the room. A person—somebody she hasn't seen for some time. Somebody that's been sick maybe.

Reacting to large details and avoiding the small ones, he reports the central plot without difficulty, relates them to a perfectly adequate whole concept, but without spark or creativity.

His sense of intellectual ease is perhaps even more succinctly conveyed by his story to 14.

Looks like the boy's sitting there in the evening after the day's work, dreaming about tomorrow and about what he had done that day.

While hardly suggestive of intellectual drive, this is nonetheless a superb integration of past, present, and future into an inclusive whole concept. It is done in one sentence, without interruption or irrelevant detail—an excellent example of the superior IQ in operation.

A somewhat different picture and a lower IQ is presented by this girl of fourteen, whose test IQ is 115. She has what might be described as a "heavy" mental approach. She seems burdened down with her own logic, gets stuck observing not too good details, seldom gets good perspective on her own mental observations. Intellectual efficiency would appear not to be up to her abilities. To picture 1, she says:

Well, it looks like a boy is taking violin lessons, maybe about the first or second lesson. He is reading the music. He is puzzled about it, not quite sure what to do. Maybe the violin is too big for him. He is not very enthusiastic. Maybe something else he wants to do and maybe kind of disgusted.

She sees the basic stimuli, puts them together in a sensible fashion. She does not give a finished outcome, however, and her elaborations all deter rather than advance the plot. Her ambition level is not unlike the boy's just described, though she is not at ease with herself nor does she have his mental "idling power."

In 5, she again finds herself overextended and unable to continue. She picks adequate details but not ones that allow her to further the plot.

Well, this woman may have a little baby or something and she heard a noise in the living room and she is opening the door to see what it was. Maybe she thought maybe her baby fell or got into mischief so she had to look. That's all.

Similarly, in 14, she sees the basic stimulus details and proposes an interpretation that is adequate, though uninspired, and again proposes elaborations that deter rather than advance. She reports:

Oh, er—well, it was probably night and this dark spot in here is probably the bedroom. This boy or man had a hard time sleeping, so he—he got up to look out the window—it maybe is hot too—just the man is hot and so he got up by the window to cool off.

These few samples will suggest some of the many differing mental approaches to the stimuli and a range of intellectual levels. Needless to repeat, the remarks about any single story would be checked and if necessary modified by analysis of all the remaining stories. Of particular relevance will be the comparison of the structured with the unstructured stimuli. This will often provide an estimate of the stability of the mental approach seen in structured pictures and an idea of whether fantasy is inhibited or facilitated by ambiguity. Picture 19 is a good unstructured picture for this comparison.

Let us return to the stories of the fourteen-year-old boy, the one with the IQ of 125 and the casual, easy approach, and compare him now with this girl of rather "heavy" and unimaginative approach. Of 19, the boy says:

Looks like a Halloween night. Probably one of those pictures for comic books. Looks like a tree had fallen down, one of these funny comic animals. The dark shape might be a bat—something seems to be peeping over the top. Looks like snow in back.

Here, in comparison with his other stories, his story is poor and lacks organization. With new and ambiguous situations, he loses his good easy organization and falls back on barely adequate observation of details. In contrast, the girl suddenly comes into her own with 19, expressing a freedom of fantasy she had not previously been able to do:

Oh, is this the way it goes? It looks like I'll be here all day if I made a story out of this one. I'd say that this is a witch's cottage and it's Halloween night and the cottage is located by the sea. The witch is looking out her window to see how the sky is for riding the broomstick. Maybe he is pet giant—this is good!—is looking over the back of the house, he is so big that two eyes are sticking up. This is really spooky looking, and she is thinking to herself what a nice night to haunt people.

It should be noted that even here she does not round off her story with an outcome, but rather concentrates mainly upon an identification of the present scene with very short time references to past and future. This she has done in the others, also. However, here both pleasure and active imagination appear. It is as though she is too burdened down by her awareness of reality and can only feel at ease when these reality demands are removed. In contrast, the boy is eminently at ease with the real world and distressed only when the reality demands become vague and ambiguous.

Area 2: Imaginative Processes

Imaginative capacities and their function in personal life are estimated from a combination of form and content elements. The basic question to be asked here is: To what extent is the individual able to enliven and elaborate his perceptions of the TAT cards with content that is expressive of his individual way of experiencing and of his own experiential background? The extent to which this is the case may be conceptualized in at least three areas:

Imagination, to refer to both the quantitative aspects of the amount of imaginative production, as well as the qualitative aspects of the richness, complexity, and originality of these productions.

Constructive creativity, to refer to the subject who is sufficiently imaginative and sufficiently free from inhibiting emotional preoccupations to use his imagination in constructive ways, to assist him in his reality-adjustment, to enliven his perceptions and to cast them in lights that are expressive of his individuality while yet in harmony with the outer reality.

Escapist fantasy, to refer to the use of imaginative energy in repetitive contemplation of emotional preoccupations. In this instance the imaginative processes are directed more upon the concern with personal conflicts than upon the problems of the relation of self to outer reality.

The estimation of these attributes rests rather heavily upon the interpreter's judgment and his conception of the role of creative energies in the personality. Some guidelines are suggested, however, that may help to clarify these concepts and aid in their estimation for the individual case.

Imagination. The estimation of the amount and fluidity of imagination is made on the basis of items dealing merely with the kind and richness of the production: length of stories, range of content utilized, vividness and quality of images, and the ease with which these are given.

The *originality* of the imagination is in part a statistical problem. Decision as to originality versus stereotypy is made on the basis of the interpreter's experience with TAT responses of subjects of similar background.* While it is not customary, due largely to the lack of

---

* Normative studies of responses of known subjects to specific pictures will help to define the range of usual and unusual responses. For more detailed data of this sort, see Chapter 12.

relevant data, to define originals and popular responses in the manner of the frequency counts of Rorschach, the same logic applies.

In judging originality versus stereotypy, study of the content of the responses will provide an estimate of the extent to which a subject's responses are very common, contain some common and some original elements, or are full of unusual, original responses. In making this judgment, one should look both at the central plots developed and the attributes proposed for the various figures. One should look also at the details and elaborations proposed. Not infrequently significant touches of imaginative spark are to be found not in the basic plot, which may be quite popular, but in the details and elaborations added to the plot.

It is not sufficient to judge a record as having many original responses. One must also judge the extent to which the original response is also a plausible response in the light of the stimulus to which it is attributed and the context in which it occurs. These responses, more systematically developed in the various Rorschach concepts of F minus responses, bear careful check to see whether they are not perhaps more suggestive of perceptual distortions of a delusional nature than they are evidence of a constructive creativity.

Constructive creativity. Creativity is a matter concerning the constructive and integrative aspects of the imagination as well as the originality of thought content. The amount of imaginative production is a guarantee neither of originality nor of its constructive utilization. If, however, imagination is used to enliven and vitalize content that deals with the relationship of the individual to the outside world, with the reworking of emotional problems in the light of reality, a constructive and creative use of imagination is being approached.

Escapist fantasy. The distinction between constructive and escapist uses of imagination is an important one, though difficult to document in the analysis of stories. In the instance of escapist fantasy, the imaginative processes are directed more upon the concern with personal conflicts than upon the problems of self-adaptation in an active outer reality. It may help to refer to the notion of the concept- versus picture-dominated responses. Responses which are largely concept-dominated are those which appear to be determined by some unstated inner reality rather than by the demands of the picture stimulus. When this is true to a very large extent, the subject tends to be one utilizing his imagination in an escapist direction. A largely picture-dominated response, in which the stimuli of the picture provide the response to the exclusion of imaginative elements, is suggestive of nonutilization of imaginative energy, a reflection of aggressive resistance, of neurotic anxiety, or of mental retardation. A constructive use represents some middle point on this difficult to define continuum.

Constructive creativity will be reflected in stories where the picture is enlivened by the individual's own point of view but where this is not done to the extent of failing to keep constantly in mind the actual facts of the picture. It also seems probable that a constructively utilized imagination will produce a set of stories marked by the regular use of affect, motivational, and movement categories. The escapist fantasy may similarly utilize affect categories but in circumstances where they are of a preoccupying nature or are not an integral part of the plot development.

The story of low imaginative quality is simple enough to observe. They are of course those with basically popular and stereotyped plots, little use of introduced figures, low response to affect or personal desire, and generally picture-dominated. One extreme is provided by the girl, 14, on page 113. Her story 5 is reproduced here for comparison purposes:

Here's a lady got a dress on, and her hair is up—got a bookcase and dresser with three books on it, a table and a floor lamp—the door she came in and wallpaper, that's about all. [with some prompting she added] She'll go in this room . . . she's sort of afraid . . . maybe somebody's in there—a girl or a boy.

Similarly, the girl of fourteen, page 115, is of quite routine imagination, producing stories of popular structure and without elaborations suggestive of any hidden spark. Her stories 1, 5, and 14 are on pages 115 and 116. In comparison, her story 1 is reproduced here.

Well, it looks like a boy is taking violin lessons, maybe about the first or second lesson, he is reading the music. He is puzzled about it, not quite sure what to do. Maybe the violin is too big for him. He is not very enthusiastic. Maybe something else he wants to do. Maybe kind of disgusted.

In contrast, an active use of imagination in an escapist direction is seen in the following stories of a boy of fourteen. He uses his imagination on a very limited theme, to state his sense of martyrdom and to get even with the neglect he attributes to his parents. To picture 2, he says:

Well, this little girl got these two books. She wants to maybe stay home and help her father and mother. She don't want to go to school. She wants to help. They don't want her to. They don't even look at her. The man's got work to do. The woman looks the other way. The girl will go to school and know she should have gone to school.

Similarly, in story 14, he gives the story an unusual twist, but on the preoccupying issue of number 2. He says:

This looks like a little boy—or maybe a man. He gets outside the window. Maybe he should be in bed. His mother and father want him in bed. They locked the door, but they forgot the window. He's getting out. After a while he gets scared. It's dark, and he's scared, and he gets into bed again.

And to picture 5:

This mother probably locked a boy in the room, or a girl. She's going to see she's asleep and when she's satisfied herself that he's asleep, she closes the door. It doesn't look like a bed in there . . . That's all I can think of.

Further evidence that the imaginative energy of this boy is going exclusively in escapist directions is provided by 19, the least structured of the pictures.

Oh, maybe this house—an old lady and little grandson live in it. One day the grandson went out and threw a big rock at the goblins flying in the air. The goblin or witch got mad, and said he'd wake up in the land of nightmares. He tells the grandmother and she says don't worry about it.

On the other hand, the following girl of fourteen shows an active imagination of excellent quality which she can use constructively in enlivening and coping with her real problems. This is also a good illustration of imaginative powers that are not dramatic or bizarre in quality. To picture 2 she gives an appropriate and balanced story, enlivening it well with statements of feeling and desire, and including a nicely placed original note, that regarding whether or not the "being on a farm" is real or a memory. She says:

Looks like a girl going away to school or has been to school. I don't know whether she is remembering being on a farm or is actually there—she remembers, I think. The man is either her father or brother and she remembers how he used to look. She probably wanted to go to school for a long time and they didn't have the money and maybe she wonders now whether she should have left the farm. She'll probably come back or—and be a teacher, teach there or something. That's about all.

It may also be suggested from this story and from the following one to 5 that to some extent she mistrusts these original twists and prefers at this point not to use her originality more actively. This is in some way connected with her slight hesitancy about permitting affect to appear in direct interpersonal relations. To 5, she says:

Looks like a woman, a mother probably, that's coming into the room, maybe like on her birthday. Sees flowers there—maybe one of her children left them for her, and she looks like she is surprised. But she, there's something about her that don't look happy. Could be that she—well, only thing is she could look unhappy if she wasn't a mother and there's nobody who's left. She looks like a mother but the house don't look too neat—books and everything. Looks more like somebody who might live alone in a city, for instance Chicago, who worked, and maybe she's come home like late at night. . . . I imagine it's night because the light's on . . . and finds the flowers there. That's about all.

The reflection of active and constructive imaginative capacities in terms of movement and action can be illustrated no better than by recalling the story of the Navaho girl of eleven, Betsy, whose story to the bleak desert scene, page 68, carried so much energy. She said:

This fence is going to this corner and then comes through here again. Dead cow's bones here, fire here, and somebody sitting here.

Equal vigor, well integrated in plot, is seen in her story to the first Indian picture, RIE 1, the two boys facing an older man. She says:

This man said to these boys—they had a fight with him—he said: "I'm going to shoot you right now." Looks like he said, "Come on, say something again."

In less belligerent mood, she says to the Indian picture of two adolescents and a man in ceremonial garb, RIE 9:

This man is teaching these boys how to practice their dances, and he's showing them how to motion their hands the way he does.

And to a scene of a mother and baby, facing two children and a turtle, RIE 2:

These two kids said that it is very nice to have a turtle to play with. This woman let them do it and she's going ahead to put the baby asleep.

The ramifications of an active imagination are obviously varied. These examples will illustrate a few of the variations in imaginative capacities as well as a few modalities for relating these capacities to the other goals of the personality.

Area 3: Family dynamics

In this area, the objective is to analyze the feelings and images of significant family figures. These images are residual present images and are generally attributable to specific persons, i.e., the mother, the father, only on certain assumptions and not on direct evidence. In general, it is wise to keep clearly in mind that the attitudes and feelings described here are not specifically attitudes toward the person of *the*

mother or *the father*. They are, rather, certain present residual feelings
which now attach themselves to *motherlike situations* and *fatherlike
situations*. The assumptions made are, of course, that attitudes seen
in present fantasy and expressed toward *motherlike situations* are a
derivative of earlier experiences with the mother or with her surrogate.

By *motherlike situations* is meant situations in which older female
figures are present (cards 2, 6BM, 12F, for example) or in which such
figures are introduced (such as card 1). Another useful interpretation
of the *motherlike* concept refers to the attitudes and events most generally associated with such figures: situations of protection and nurturance, situations of control and inhibition, situations of nonsexual
love and affection. This second interpretation is an assumption, of
course, but, at least in American subjects, appears to be a useful working hypothesis.

The *fatherlike* situation follows a similar logic. It would include
situations involving an older male, especially when combined with
a younger figure. It would also include situations of assertion and
initiative, and situations of outer world oriented activity. In the male
this would particularly include situations of work and attitudes of control over external events. In the female, sexual situations also bear
close examination, particularly as they involve interaction with male
figures.

In general, the following variables of the story should be examined:

1. Attitudes and characteristics implied of, or associated with, adult
female and male figures in the pictures, whether given or introduced.

2. Themas involving children and their interaction with adults.

3. The presence of blocking, refusals, and other disturbed form
elements on pictures generally reflective of attitudes toward parents,
for example, 2, 5, 6BM, 6GF, 7BM, 7GF, 8BM, 12F, 13B.

4. The events and emotionally toned interpersonal situations present
in pictures generally thought to arouse associations to parents.

5. The symbolization in an entire story of typical parent-child
conflicts.

6. The presence of emotionally toned words and situations reflecting
unresolved parent-child events, such as excessive use of situations in
which dependence, submission, or excessive rebellion and restriction-
resistances are present.

It is well to keep constantly in mind that the subject does not always
view older male (or female) figures as direct parent representatives
and that therefore his ideas and associations to them will bear the
distortion and incompleteness that the semiconscious associations to

any area will have. The task is still an interpretive one, and not one merely of assuming that the attitudes expressed toward older female figures are indeed the direct attitudes maintained toward the mother.

The emotional atmosphere in the family group can often be seen from the composite interaction of all the foregoing. In this connection, picture 2 is of particular usefulness. It presents more of a family stimulus than any other picture. In it, the interactions assumed among the various figures are particularly relevant.

T-33, female 14, suggests in her stories an attitude of resistance to a father seen as negative and unsatisfying and to a mother seen as nonfeminine and somewhat punitive. She is a clinging but undemanding bystander in this family. To picture 2, she says:

Picture with people and a road, looks like they live in one of the European countries. He's ploughing the field, the girl looks like she is on her way to school. The woman, she is daydreaming. It must be awfully hot. That's about all.

Here T-33 first places the entire family stimulus away from her (European countries) and fails to propose any interaction at all among the figures. She further indicates her peripheral status by suggesting that the girl is leaving. She proposes no actions or feelings of the girl that relate her to the male or female figures. The mother is passive and noninteractional.

In 3BM, she introduces both an active mother and father, after first assuming an environment of punishment.

Looks like this boy has done something wrong, and he's punished for what he's been doing, sent to his room, or disappointed because he couldn't do what he wanted. [Inquiry: What do you mean?] Well, he's probably— his mother and father told him one thing and he did the other. His mother told him, he sassed her, got punished and sent to his room. [Inquiry: How will it end?] Well, I suppose he'll get away with it because a lot of kids cry about it, and the parents let them have their way.

In 7GF, she again proposes a separation of mother and child:

The girl's mother is reading a book to her. While the mother is reading the girl is probably thinking and letting things take place in her mind.

In 18BM she proposes an older man who might get killed for his money, and in 7BM sees the older man as argumentative and unhappy. To 19, a picture often reflective of the "home" associations, she proposes only cold and no personal interaction. She also rejects this picture as her least-liked one. To it she says:

Looks like a—could be a house in wintertime. There is snow and everything. It's at night and they have lights on in the house. Could be a ship
going through the water.

T-128, a girl of fourteen, sees her family differently. To 3BM, she
also introduces parental figures, but sees them as interactive and potentially understanding. She reports:

Well this is a boy, no, a girl, I guess. Laying here on the bench. Looks
as though it is not outside, looks as though she is sad, maybe crying. Something is on the ground beneath her, something she had to go on an errand
for for her mother. She broke it on the way home. It's lying there, and
she don't know whether to go home or not, maybe it would be better to tell
mother what had happened and maybe they'd understand.

Further reflection of this view of the parents as interactive, though
not without their demands upon her, is seen in her number 14. She
says:

Well, it's a—night and this boy is—in his bedroom or in the house—looking
at the outside things. It looks as though he's kind of sad or wondering
what's going on. Maybe this boy has been around this small neighborhood
all his life—did not see much—looking at the outside wondering what it's
like, wishing he'd go out and see things for himself. He'll go to city or
nearby town and he may get into trouble, bad company. He won't know
how to do things, and has to send for his parents. They bring him home
and he learned it wasn't so wonderful out alone.

Similarly, in 7BM, she proposes that the father is also a reasonable
person, though clearly a firm and strong figure.

It looks as though the old man is talking to son, or relative or just a friend,
and giving him advice. The young man does not want to listen or believe
him, and yet he knows there is some truth in it.

This is hardly an intense or wholly positive tie to the father. It is
rather essentially positive in nature yet realistically aware of the controlling aspects of the father relationship.

In contrast, T-66, a boy marked by a general attitude of reluctance
and distrust, responds to picture 2:

This girl, she looks like she is in a trance—thinking about something and—
is that all you want? [Instructions repeated] He's working in the field
and the mother back there is gazing into the sky. [What else?] She's
thinking back about something that happened. [How will it come out?]
It can't turn out—got to wait until they are dead until you can tell the story.

And to 5:

It looks like this woman is sneaking into a room. That's about all.

Both of these stories present his negative and unsupporting view of the family. In 7BM, the picture often stimulating of father-son ideas, he suggests that the father image is an ineffectual one without either strong positive or negative features. He says:

Looks like a picture of all the old country over there—looks like a sad happening—they look like they are sorry for themselves.

Further probing in this picture produced only a repetition of this evaluation and a suggestion that maybe the sad event had to do with the war.

In 13B, the lone boy on the cabin doorstep, he gives us a further demonstration of the futility with which he views the family situation.

The child's looking—sitting on the doorstep, he looks like he's half starved. The house is made out of logs, looks like it's down south. [How turn out?] Oh, maybe he'll be able to grow up for all I know and be rich.

These few limited examples are obviously selected from full records in which comparison and fuller evidence are provided. As in all areas of analysis, data from one variable in one story must be combined with all other data and the interpretation derived from the totality.

Area 4: Inner adjustment

Within this area may fall a wide variety of concepts useful in the analysis of the inner or self aspects of personality. Their analysis from the TAT stories will depend to a large extent upon the particular formulation which the individual interpreter makes of them. The following are suggested as useful in outlining the inner dynamics of the person and as permitting what appear to be meaningful distinctions between individuals.

Basic emotional attitude. This category deals with the question of the direction of emotional energy and its use in the solution of personal problems and conflicts. The basic issue is one of the assertiveness versus passivity of this energy. No implication is made as to adjustment or conflict state from either end of this continuum. Rather the decision is, regardless of the state of personal adjustment or the individual formulation of personality, with what vigor does the individual channel energy into the mechanism of internal adjustment. Whether successful or not, is he actively working through emotional conflicts and preoccupations? Whether conflict-laden or not, does he allow his emotional concerns to continue unexamined, making no effort to check or redirect them? Data relevant to this area will obviously be found in many places. Particularly useful, however, are the following:

1. The language used implying either forceful assertive action or its opposite.

2. The kind of outcomes and solutions given to various situations, the constructive, forward-looking nature of these versus their succorant and dependent nature.

3. The constructive and self-reliant versus the suppliant and retiring nature of central characters.

Attitude toward impulse life. Acceptance or rejection of impulse life and the various combinations possible here is the issue in this category. Acceptance of one's own inner life implies that impulse life is viewed as good and appropriate. Rejection implies that inner life impulses are bad and must be continually repulsed. Does the individual have an awareness of his own inner motivations and does he find this appropriate?

In general, the inner life acceptance is found in the use of intraceptive language, language that implies feelings and personal motives. This is in contrast to extraceptive language, in which is reflected high awareness of external pressures and standards. The intraceptive language may then be carefully scrutinized both for its presence and for its qualitative nature. Awareness of impulse life is in itself no guarantee of its acceptance. Intraceptive referents which are positive and generally permit successful outcome will suggest both awareness and acceptance. Intraceptive referents that are negative, disturbing of the form qualities, and denied successful completion are suggestive of rejection. Refusal to utilize intraceptive referents at all is similarly suggestive of rejection.

Useful here also is an analysis of the form of the stories. Generally speaking, stories in well-balanced form, with intraceptive referents included and adequately integrated into action and outcome, are signs of adequate impulse acceptance. High positive intraception that disrupts form and is not integrated into a realistic plot suggests high awareness but an inability to utilize inner life functionally.

Anxiety. The evidence of anxiety lies to a large extent in the presence of disruptions in the consistency of the form characteristics, especially in organizational elements, in vacillation from concept- to picture-dominated responses, and in picture refusals. Content characteristics that deal with stories of overt aggression, depression, mental conflicts, or other outstanding emotional states are also relevant.

A useful distinction may be made between generalized, diffuse anxiety and specific anxiety. In the former, the signs of anxiety may be expected to be found in many or all areas of the stories. Any stimulus will be sufficient to activate a chronically and diffusely anxious person. He worries about everything. In contrast, the person with a more specific and delimited anxiety pattern may be expected to show form disruptions in only those situations that relate directly to the source of the anxiety. Persons whose anxiety is aroused only when they are pressed for performance will become upset on cards that (to them at least) suggest these pressures. A specific sex anxiety may appear only in 4 or 12MF, or, if in symbolic form, only in cards presenting conveniently symbolizations, 1, 3BM, or 17BM perhaps. A subject's anxiety may appear only when the demands upon him are lessened and hence the external structuring of his life reduced. Such a subject may be expected to show signs of disturbance on cards that are more ambiguous.

Ego supports. This area is clearly a complex one and will depend upon the formulation of defense mechanisms and ego supports that the interpreter finds meaningful. It requires a relating of material here with material under Area 7 (Behavioral Approach). The basic question is what modes of personality adjustment and behavior does the subject utilize to protect himself from the realization of his own insecurities and to provide himself with functional ego support. It is specifically intended here to call attention to the necessity of seeing mechanisms of personality adjustment in the light of their ego-supporting function and to focus upon them as operating and sustaining mechanisms. This is not to deny or to abandon the view of defense mechanisms. In clinical analyses, however, we frequently forget to see the specific sustaining devices and fail to see the positive supporting aspects of some traditional defense mechanisms. To emphasize only the defensive nature of these mechanisms is not unlike analyzing the methods used to plug leaks in the dike while neglecting to describe the basic structure of the dike itself.

In this area, also, attention should be given to the ways in which the subject comforts and soothes himself in periods of anxiety or exhaustion.

System of control. The basic concepts used in the delineation of the system of control are *outer control, conscious control,* and *inner control.** At that point in life when the individual manages to integrate the rules and prohibitions of the world around him with his more self-directed impulse desires to such a degree that he can function smoothly and without undue conflict, he may be said to have ade-

---

* These concepts are taken directly from Rorschach terminology.

quate *outer control.* It is obvious that no individual can go through life with a satisfactory sense of balance without some use of societal-determined rules to guide him in situations which he cannot integrate directly into his own inner need-systems. The use of these rules and principles may be called *conscious control.* When there is excessive emphasis upon guidance by these rules and a concomitant loss of personal spontaneity, the individual may be called *constricted.* Constriction may take two forms, formalized and unformalized. Formalized constriction is a conscious control in which the preceding elements are outstanding. Unformalized constriction refers to situations where the same underlying need for external control is present but the techniques for acquiring it are inadequate or where the anxiety which the control should allay is still active.

Most persons can to some extent integrate their experiences into their own life, can give them a meaningful place within their own personality without merely covering them up with a system of rationalizations underneath which unintegrated and disturbing forces exist. The process in which the individual implements his own inner feelings and relates outer events to his own inner needs may be called *inner control.*

The estimation of the use of inner control in personal adjustment is made from the study of the imaginative and intraceptive qualities of the stories. In general, a person may be said to have effective inner control if he enriches his stories with reports of personal feelings, emotions, and motives but does so within the context of balanced form qualities. In addition, the content of the stories must lead to the conclusion that the individual is able to accept his own inner life as serious and appropriate.

The use of conscious control is suggested by logical organization in stories, by relevant references to external world demands, and by outcomes in keeping with reality. High degrees of conscious control, constriction, reflect the lack of personal spontaneity. Constriction is seen in stories of high degrees of organization, in a rigid and unvarying manner of approach to the stories, and in content that denies personal feelings and motivations. Such persons have a tendency to concentrate more upon references to control, prohibition, external demands, and conformity. Unformalized constriction partakes of the same qualities, but erratically and with flashes of inner feeling breaking through from time to time. References to conformity and control tend to be inappropriate and mechanisms for integrating the control aspects into inner life markedly inadequate.

Outer control is achieved on the basis of either inner or conscious control, or more exactly, on an integration of the two. It is a statement only of ease of dealing with ordinary daily events. It implies some satisfactory use of inner and conscious control, though adequate social techniques can obviously be developed on the basis of many combinations of personality controls.

Approach to interpersonal relations. In this area one is concerned with the quality of the emotional ties to people. From a study of all content categories, and the form characteristics which accompany them, one may delineate the approach to interpersonal relationships. Such considerations as the following are useful:

1. The amount of interpersonal activity described. Are persons involved in interaction with other persons? Do the actions of persons influence others?

2. The insight into motivation expressed. Do the stories manifest empathy and insight into the motives and goals of persons? Do the motives attributed to one person become intertwined with the desires of others? Do figures respond to the expressed desires of central figures?

3. Introduced figures. Does the subject assume an atmosphere of persons or not? Does he introduce many persons to assist in the story plots developed? Does he utilize only the figures present in the stimulus? What function do the introduced figures play in the plot and what characteristics are attributed to them?

4. General emotional tone of interpersonal events. In what general manner are interpersonal situations discussed—pleasing, rejecting, disgusted, nurturant, demanding? Do certain categories of persons differ in the tone with which they are used? Who is allowed to interfere, to give advice, to be nurturant? What categories of persons are rejected, never given inner feelings? Who is sympathetic? Who exciting and attractive?

Maturity. Maturity is an evaluation difficult to define. It depends to a great extent upon the interpreter's notions and standards. It is used here to reflect the idea that the individual's inner life develops with time and experience, that this development is expected to go in a prescribed direction, and that a judgment of maturity may be made in reference to the age and sex of the subject. Generally speaking, maturity may be defined in relation to the appropriateness of the individual's developmental characteristics. The judgment of appropriateness is essentially a matter of norms, though these norms have at this stage no adequate representation in objective form. It is generally thought to increase up to some point where each of the major personal developmental tasks * have been attempted. This is roughly the late adolescent or early adult period. This seems simple enough until we observe the extremely prolonged psychological adolescence in American middle-class persons and see this in light of what is often called the very early maturity of children in some other societies.

As used here, the estimation of maturity depends upon the balance of the elements of control with the impulse life of the subject. An individual whose system of control is not strong enough to impose an adequate form on his stories (and on his life) and to provide them with content that is logical and in harmony with the facts of the picture is one whose control-impulse system is out of balance and who, hence, is not mature. In such a record will also be found evidences of unstructured impulsiveness, childishness, and the like. The opposite case, the overadjusted person who allows himself no whimsy, who never gives in to his impulsivity, is reflected in the opposite, the control factors overwhelming his impulse life and producing stories high in formal elements, tight and organized, containing little intraceptive material and content characterized by conformity and denial.

Particular attention must be paid to the age- and sex-appropriateness of the affect in making this judgment. It is proposed, though not further developed here, that the stages of psychic development proposed by Erikson † will prove a more fruitful approach to the understanding of the mature or immature emotional life. This is especially true for the stages that are relevant to the adolescent years and beyond —the stages of identity, intimacy, generativity, and integrity.

Area 5: Emotional reactivity

In this area concern is directed towards two aspects of the responsiveness of the individual. First, to what general area of stimulation is he most reactive: stimulation from the outer world contacts, or from his own inner world? Second, in his responsiveness to these stimuli, is he able to react in terms consistent with reality or is his reaction warped and distorted by unresolved conflicts that determine the direction and meaning of his actions? The first is referred to as the drive

* Robert J. Havighurst, *Human Development and Education* (New York: Longmans Green, 1953) and C. M. Tryon and Jesse Lilienthal, III, *Fostering Mental Health in Our Schools* (National Education Association, Association for Supervision and Curriculum Development, 1950).

† Erik H. Erikson, *Childhood and Society* (New York: Norton and Co., 1950).

toward the outer world and the second as spontaneity and personal freedom of action.

Drive toward outer world. The manner in which and the extent to which the subject handles in his stories those things that represent the world of outer reality form the basis for estimating the outer world drive. For this purpose all content that is descriptive of the actions of other people, of facts occurring in everyday life, the familiarity which the subject shows with the world of external stimuli as opposed to his empathy with and use of personal feelings and motives, the degree to which personal motivation is used to explain action upon others rather than merely personal action (where no interaction occurs) are useful. An individual whose experiences have been such as to make him wary and suspicious of the world will tend to retire from it and to give stories high in purely personal motivation and devoid of descriptions of interpersonal interactions, or to give much literary and fairy tale content, or, in the event of the concomitant inhibiting of his inner life, of descriptive and enumerative content devoid of imaginative enrichment.

Spontaneity and personal freedom of action. Personal freedom of action is to a large extent an inference from the total personality picture as it is seen from the TAT. The presence of anxiety signs, of many responses that are clearly concept-dominated, or the presence of symbolic content suggestive of pervasive conflict all go into the estimation of this area.

Area 6: Sexual adjustment

Because of the complexity of the adjustment to sex, the estimation of the adequacy of this adjustment must be made in large part upon the total personality picture and in less part upon the presence of specific signs of sexual maladjustment. In addition to the element of the sexual characteristics and adjustment to be expected from the particular configuration of personality dynamics which the subject presents, several special areas can be utilized in estimating this adjustment.

1. Relation to parental figures as they are described in or deduced from the records (Area 3). On the basis of the fact that the basic orientation to sex is conveyed to the child by his parents, knowledge of the parent-child relationship is essential to determining the individual's sexual adjustment.

2. Relation to same- and opposite-sex peers as described in or deduced from the records. The reaction of the subject to peers of the

same and opposite sex will reveal his attitude toward sex and provide a basis for judging the relationship of his sexual orientation to his overt behavior in sexual situations.

3. Symbolic cues: The use of symbolic representation of sexual objects or relationships is of assistance in this area. The use made of the symbolic interpretation of TAT stories should be done with care and be limited by the examiner's experience and knowledge of symbolism. Many stories, however, and certain parts of stories will be so clearly concept-dominated as to suggest the motivating force of a specific emotional problem. Special study of these areas will often reveal them to be symbolic statements of sexual concerns. In addition, certain pictures will usually prove to be highly selective of content with sexual associations. Blocking or compulsivelike concern for these pictures and areas is of special significance. Which pictures or areas these are can be determined only after experience with a given set of pictures.

Area 7: Behavioral approach

The data on behavioral characteristics derives from three general areas:

1. The attitudes and characteristics which the subject attributes to the characters of his stories and the extent of identification which the subject expresses with them.

2. The presence or absence of form characteristics of the stories suggesting stability and consistency, those that suggest vacillation and inconsistency, and those that suggest indecision, timidity, and lack of force. These aspects are largely determined from such things as the consistency with which any of the form elements are maintained throughout a set of stories, through the ability of the subject to give a well-balanced organization, and through the content aspects of the language used, aggressive, attaching, passive, retiring, succorant, demanding, supplication, etc.

3. The implications for overt behavior of the relation of such characteristics as those just given to the motivational background and the mechanisms of defense observed in Areas 3, 4, 5, and 6. This depends to a large extent upon the clinical acumen and the experiential background of the examiner himself and takes its clues from no particular characteristics of the stories. The greater the familiarity with the psychodynamics of behavior, the more comprehensive and more accurate will be the reconstruction of the overt behavioral pattern. One specific clue may help. The first few stories will in some

cases reflect the mechanisms of defense and the overt behavior more clearly than will the stories given later in the series. Of particular help in this area are the content items, discussed in Chapter 5, in particular the sections dealing with the action core of the story, the central figure, and the attributes which are associated with specific categories of persons, such as boys, girls, adults, figures in authority, etc.

In judging overt behavioral manifestations of personality dynamics, it is useful to assume that each picture is a representation of a reality situation and that the manner in which the subject handles the picture will reflect the way in which he will handle reality.

There is probably some tendency for the attributes of the hero-figure to be more closely akin to those of the subject than those of any other single figure. The nature of their relationship is such, however, that no assumption of a direct counterpart of behavior is justified. It is probably also true that there is some tendency for dominant modes of expression, such as aggression, submission, evasion, to reflect similar behaviors in the subject. The nature of the relationship is, again, limited and no assumption of identity is justified. Both of these principles will serve as ideas to be explored in describing the behavioral mechanisms of the subject.

The most generally useful principle, however, is to assume no direct counterpart of story and subject, but rather to rely upon the analysis of internal dynamics, system of control, and the pattern of ego defenses. To project this analysis into behavior also requires specific attention to the *context* within which this subject in the area of behavior in question will find its overt expression. The manifestation in behavior of self-assertive tendencies combined with guilt will perhaps be one thing in an individual who is a member of a close-knit group of middle-class schoolchildren and another if he should be a member of a lower class gang. The manifestation of high intelligence plus a casual and ambitionless attitude may result in casual and ambitionless behavior and grades if the subject is in a school or work environment which permits this. The child of these qualifications who further resents morality training may find himself resented by the schoolteacher and hence in a situation where he finds failures, low grades, and irresponsible behavior most satisfactory retaliatory devices. Narcissistic tendencies in a child of pleasing appearance and a few basic social skills may be quite successful. He may move to the top ranks of his group in popularity and his feelings of satisfaction increase. This same personality attribute in a subject whose parents have taught him resentment is perhaps more apt to find systematic expression in disharmonious relations.

Even more striking variations with context will be found in predicting adult work behavior. These circumstances are often fairly tightly organized and not oriented toward permitting the expression of individuality. In such circumstances, the ability of the individual to adapt to external events is of crucial importance. Careful analysis should also be made of the areas of life within which the subject can find individuality adequately expressed. The individual with fixed work patterns whose major cathexis is to the work itself may have great difficulty if the work situation does not permit the work pattern he prefers. The individual whose work cathexis is to "getting things done" or to the receiving of monetary or social rewards will often be able to adjust far more readily to a wider variety of actual work conditions. Many persons find great personal reward in being part of a larger work system. In them specific work conditions are often of limited importance, the rewards coming merely from doing as the system dictates. In large modern industries this latter attribute is highly valued. In those who can work readily and can achieve a sense of integrity from this identity with the company's goals, work adjustment can often be easily predicted as satisfactory. In the person who achieves his rewards from more individual-centered pursuits, the characteristics of the work conditions are of more importance and their specific attributes must be predicted in more detail before work adjustment can be analyzed.

In summary, it is to be recalled that the overt behavior of the subject is to some extent *symptomatic of his underlying dynamics*, to some extent *symptomatic of his attempts to express overtly these dynamics*, and to some extent *reflective of his adjustments to external events*. And, in any event, the *individual's overt behavior takes place in the context of other people*, other people with widely varying patterns of desires and behaviors. To a few isolated individuals, this surround of people will be of no moment. To the majority, however, it is crucial to a prediction of the subject's overt behavior.

Area 8: Descriptive and integrative summary

In this area, an integrated summary is called for. The specific foci of this summary will depend upon the purpose of the analysis. If the analysis is of a clinic case with a presenting symptomatology, then the dynamics and genetics of the problem will be stressed. If the purpose relates to some specific research focus, then this will deter-

mine the structure of the summary. If work adjustment and potentialities is the purpose, then not only the summary but other areas of
the outline should reflect this interest.

In a general way, absence of extremes of content (extreme aggression, extreme passivity, constant repetition of the same theme), absence of illogical and bizarre elements, and the presence of stories of
good form enlivened by imaginative details are signs of a subject without specific clinical symptoms. The dynamics of the personality within
the framework of normality, however, are determined only by a detailed study of all the elements suggested here, by analysis of their
interrelationships, and by the application of the interpreter's psychological knowledge and critical intuition.

Part 2

ILLUSTRATIVE
ANALYSES

Comparison
of single stories

In Part 2 a number of individual stories with illustrative analyses are given in Chapter 7 and in the following chapters a number of full records are presented. These records will be accompanied by individual story analyses and by a full write-up originally prepared from the TAT record alone. In two instances records of American Indian adolescents will be presented to illustrate another kind of response to pictures and to suggest the relevance of the method of analysis for data derived from pictures other than the original TAT.

In some instances independently analyzed Rorschach and life history data will be provided for comparison. It should specifically be noted that these independent data from other sources are not intended to suggest that the TAT interpretations are "valid" when they appear to be repeated in the other data. It must be recognized that these additional data provide only other views of the case and that issues of validation must be approached in quite different ways. Certain degrees of correspondence between these data and the blind TAT summaries do indeed appear, but so do contradictions. It cannot be assumed, in this casual presentation of related data, that either of the data sources represent firm external criteria against which the TAT may be judged right or wrong.

In judging the validity of any projective technique interpretation it must be recalled that there are a number of issues—none treated in this volume—which are involved in judging validity. There is, first, the issue of the stability of the basic data. To what extent may we assume that the stories told by an individual represent a true sample of his personality and that this sample is stable over time? There is, second, the most important issue of the constructs utilized as the framework for the interpretation. To what extent is any particular concept, such as those proposed in Chapter 6, sound, psychologically meaningful, and similarly understood by different investigators? There is, third, the direct issue of whether the data are adequately interpreted in the framework of constructs and whether, then, the interpretation derived may be shown to be "true" of the individual in question.

Comparison of Individual Stories

The stories that follow were all told to picture 1, the boy and the violin. They are presented to indicate the manner in which TAT stories differ with different types of people and to illustrate the way in which both individual factors and cultural commonalities are to be seen in fantasy. The first three stories are those of university graduate students of comparable intelligence and education level.°

A man of forty responds:

This is a picture of a young boy contemplating a violin. It is difficult to know where to start to pick out the best relevant details. The boy is certainly concerned with some problem about the violin, but does not seem to be greatly disturbed. Possibly he has wanted to go out and play but has been told that he must spend so much time practicing his violin lesson. He is not interested, however, and is sulking.

A woman of twenty-two:

A young boy looking at the violin on the table. His expression is one of tiredness and not much interest. It seems to me that he is too young to be forced to take violin lessons, at an age that he would have no love of the instrument or music. It is possible that his mother either believes that it is *good* to have a child "play something," or has visions of his becoming

---

° These three stories were written in longhand by the persons themselves during a demonstration class in which all members of the group were asked to write stories. A number of copies of each picture were distributed to the group. Approximately five minutes were allowed for each picture.

a great violinist. All of this might lead to the child's dislike of the whole thing.

A woman of thirty-three:

First impression is the staged effect—child does not look at an unfamiliar object so quiescently. The child's facial expression is one of melancholy. The appearance somewhat—remark about questions—the bow is not clear-cut. Emotions as strong as this probably meant to be indicated here not in context with quietness of subject-coloring and delineation of individual and violin.

These three stories, theoretically from a reasonably homogeneous group, present some important similarities and differences. Let us take each in turn and compare them along a number of lines.

The first man tells a story of fairly standard plot. The boy who is set a task which he resists, wanting to go out and play, is certainly one of the two basic plots to this picture. The thema of the woman of twenty-two is similar. The boy is set a task which he resists. In both stories the outcome is a personal dislike on the part of the boy. Both subjects thus give standard plots with standard characterizations and standard outcomes. Both, in their choice of plot, choose one suggestive of resistance more than of self-ambition, as might be the case had they chosen the second standard plot involving the boy wanting to master the violin and become a great violinist. The third story, the woman of thirty-three, is quite clearly a different matter. In this framework, she refuses to identify a plot, gives no outcome. It should be noticed, however, that the reality of the stimulus is indeed perceived; she sees the boy (child . . . individual) and she sees the violin (violin . . . unfamiliar object). Similarly, she senses the same general negative quality seen by the others. In a somewhat original way, she remarks on the "melancholy" and the inappropriateness (not in context) of the boy's aims and the situation.

To return to the man, let us now examine his own approach to the picture in more detail. It has been noted that he observes all major details of the picture (boy and violin) and that he relates the two in a satisfactory manner. His way of doing so, however, is quite different from that of the two women. His first sentence is perhaps reflective of his characteristic approach. Notice how he actually identifies the basic stimuli but how at the same time he hedges and qualifies. He even insists that it is only a picture, not a real boy. He is, of course, quite correct and one could hardly accuse him of bad observation. However, his approach bespeaks a caution and a hesitancy quite unlike the woman, twenty-two, who moves directly into action. He sees a "picture of a young boy contemplating." She moves directly into "a young boy looking." He is more cautious and pedantic (contemplating), and she more active and direct.

He continues with his pedantic detail observations saying in essence how difficult it is to know what the proper thing, if any, might be— "it is difficult to know where to start to pick out the best relevant detail." This, a completely gratuitous statement, in no way develops the plot. He even must have the "best" relevant details—an attitude highly commendable in a research worker, but hardly the task which is set for him here. The rest of his story shows this same caution and concern with details. It should be noted that his preoccupation with details is not a concern with identifying the stimuli. He actually at no time identifies any objective stimulus detail other than the boy and the violin. Rather, he accepts quite readily the stimuli and worries about the details of the judgment he himself makes. This is quite a different emphasis upon details than the person who carefully identifies the boy's clothing and hair and facial features, the violin's characteristics and strings, the "paper" and "table," etc. In fact, this man does not examine carefully his data, but rather fusses about the conclusion he draws without re-examining the data in this light.

The next sentence is the same, though here he moves cautiously into the area of personal feeling. "The boy is certainly concerned," he reports. Yet he even retreats from this degree of personal identification by insisting that he is not "greatly disturbed." It is perhaps illuminating to suggest that he has already told over four-sevenths of his story (four lines of type out of seven) and has not yet indicated a plot or suggested other than the most pallid of feelings for the boy.

The next sentences continue this caution though he does not propose his plot. A nice note of retreat is seen in his reference to "so much time." He cannot permit himself the abandon of just "practicing" and yet cannot make up his mind to a specific time, whether one hour, two hours, half hour. Rather he selects "a unit of time." The outcome is reflective of the whole story—not interested and sulking. It may be noticed that not only does the boy never come to life in the story but no other figures are introduced. Even though he verges on such a suggestion in his reference to "has been told," he refused to introduce a person to give this directive.

The feelings introduced by this man are certainly casual (concerned) and even this is qualified (not greatly). The plot has no basic action and does not move in time sequences. It is all in reality a description of a static present with similarly static references to the past (has been told).

The woman of twenty-two, on the other hand, moves with vigor into the heart of the matter. In the first two sentences she introduces the basic identification of the stimuli and relates them satisfactorily. She also notices more relevant details than does the man and sees things in better spatial terms (*boy* looking at *violin* on the *table*). She next indicates directly the emotions of the boy (tiredness and not much interest). She sympathizes in active fashion with him and attributes his plight directly to a mother who is similarly real and has strong motivations. It is an interesting note that she has specially marked for us her notion of the social mobility goals of the mother in her underlining of *good* and her quotes around "play something." All of this pressure, she says, might lead to complete rejection (dislike of the whole thing).

Her story is well marked with motive and feeling, her plot lively and showing time sequences. Her basic idea is not too different from the man, but the enthusiasm, vigor, and personal identification which she puts into it distinguish her clearly.

Her resentment of her mother, whose goals are forceful and ambitious, and the girl's intentions to rebel completely are marked. It should be noticed, however, that she does not basically reject the plot as untenable or inappropriate. She merely says it's a bad fit and leads to resentment, but she does not reject the values involved. This is the saga of a young woman resenting her mother's control, rebelling, but laying the groundwork for a return to the middle-class values represented. A quite different and wholehearted rejection of these values is seen in the story of the waitress which will be given later.

It may be of some interest merely to record that the man of forty is generally regarded by his friends and instructors as cautious and potentially a good social science researcher. They complain, however, that he has no enthusiasms, confuses opinions with data, and has no real interest. Even as the hero, he too is sulking.

The woman comes from an upper middle-class suburb and has long resented her mother's desires to turn her into a matron. She developed a "dislike of the whole thing," fled to the university, moved into the Bohemian set, stored her suburban clothes, and for a period made great fun of the solid middle-class virtues represented by her mother. She has since, however, married a most respectable young man and is herself developing the symptoms of respectability.

The last record, the woman of thirty-three, is clearly that of a disturbed personality, though at the time of the test her overt behavior was socially acceptable. In this response, as we have noted, she does sense and respond to the basic stimuli, though most certainly she does so in unique fashion. From the opening phrase on, the question of the form aspects of the story is barely relevant. It is apparent that organizational qualities and time sequences are at a very low level. Her content is rather presented in disjunctive form, a series of firm but logically unconnected associations reflective of a disturbed personality. In these associations, however, she says several things of great importance. In an interpreted form she says:

1. *Reality is fake.* As she first observes the reality sample of picture 1, she rejects it as unreal. Reality is a "staged effect," she says.

2. *Disjunctivity of emotion and stimuli.* While she senses some emotion and inner feeling, she is aware of a sense of misfit between these emotions and their stimuli. At one moment she focusses on the emotion, taking it as a firm reference point (child . . . quiescent) and accuses reality of misfit (unfamiliar object). At another, she claims that reality is the base (color and delineation of individual and violin) and that the emotions are inappropriate. Unable to be sure whether she or the outer world is out of focus, she vacillates, sensing primarily her feeling of inappropriateness and disassociation.

3. *Melancholy.* Her emotional orientation is one of melancholy. She cannot be sure even of this, however, since she sees it both as "quiescent" and "strong." In either state, she is unable to relate it to reality.

It should again be observed that, in spite of these many signs of acute disturbance, she is actively struggling with the fit of inner state and reality; she has not given up nor accepted her inner state as the only reality. Further, her reality observation is still present; she acknowledges the basic content demand of the picture, though she is unable to give it the form and organization required by the instructions.

The week following this test, she was hospitalized following a break of schizophrenic nature. She has subsequently recovered quite well after a period of hospitalization and psychotherapy.*

---

* It is perhaps inappropriate to include this record as part of a "normal" sample. Yet, in fact, she was part of a sample properly so defined at the time of testing. The obviously disturbed nature of the record will perhaps serve to caution us against a tendency to think of the disturbed as *all disturbed* and the normal as *all normal.*

The story that follows presents another treatment of the same stimulus, picture 1. This time, by a waitress, twenty-six, of upper-lower class social position.*

The expression on the boy's face obviously registers complete disgust. He's supposed to be studying the violin. He doesn't want to. You can understand that. (At this point, Bernice said, "I can write it faster than you can," and took the paper away from me. Henceforth the words are exactly as she wrote them. After the third story she said she didn't want me to see what she was writing and covered the page with another page. I was therefore unable to bring up points that might have been omitted.) Aw gee, all the kids are out playing baseball and here I'm stuck with this darn thing and just this morning Eddie promised to lend me his new mit, too—who wants to study on a day like this. Violin, too. Nuts!

It requires little analysis to point to the directness of action and affect reflected in this story. Her rejection of the virtues and social meaning of the violin is direct and unambivalent. Her interpretation of the basic stimulus differs markedly from that of the cases presented above. To her, the situation is an outrage to be reacted against with vigor. Affect is present, strong and empathic. Form level is poor, concentrating primarily on present explosive reactions, with minor past references and no future development.

The following stories are presented as a further demonstration of contrast within highly similar over-all plots. (These stories were given earlier to illustrate different points.) These are given by two men of similar age, working in the same business. The first is that of a chief clerk, age forty-two, who has been in his present position for many years and is considered unpromotable by his superiors. He reports:

The story behind this is that this is a son of a very well-known, a very good musician and the father has probably died. The only thing the son has left is this violin which is undoubtedly a very good one and to the son, the violin is the father and the son sits there daydreaming of the time that he will understand the music and interpret it on the violin that his father has played.

The second is that of a man of forty-five, a department head of major executive standing within the community, well thought of by his superiors and clearly promotable.

* This story is taken from a record presented through the courtesy of William Foote Whyte of Cornell University. It was a record taken during the course of a research reported in Whyte's *Human Relations in the Restaurant Industry* (New York: McGraw-Hill, 1948).

This is a child prodigy dreaming over his violin thinking more of the music than anything else. But of wonderment that so much music can be in the instrument and in the fingers of his own hand. I would say that possibly he is in reverie about what can be or what he can do with his music in the times that lie ahead. He is dreaming of concert halls, tours, and appreciations of music. Music lovers for the beauty he will be able to express and even now can express with his own talents.

The similarities in these two stories are worth noting first. Both select a standard plot, the one dealing with ambition and future accomplishment. They both place it in a context of "dreaming" and "thinking" more than in a context of action. They both ignore entirely the rebellion or resistance aspects prominent in other stories. In a sense it may be suggested that these two men define the basic stimulus in much the same terms. These are the values and assumptions in terms of which they define the task presented to them. They present the virtue of ambition, claim it to require introspection and thoughtful planning, and expect, with some hesitancy, to achieve the rewards in the future. In the same general way, the two students first presented also defined the social problem similarly, but again in a fashion other than that presented by these two business men. In the students, the reality is defined as one of testing the coercive pressures of the authority of the world of significant persons around them. In spite of the many unique differences of their two records, they agree upon these basic social facts: the world is to be treated with resentment but eventually accepted.

The business man of forty-two, the chief clerk, however, differs in some important ways from his executive colleague. It may be noted first that he presents his central figure with an impossible image of identification. He is impossible both because of the social distance created by the attributes given him (very well known . . . very good) and because he is no longer present (has probably died). Already in the first basic observation, this man shows us his preoccupation with excellence and at the same time his inner conviction that to match this example is for him impossible. In contrast, the executive concentrates not upon an impossible object of emulation but upon the acts, the work to be accomplished (thinking more of the music). He then clearly integrates himself into this action system (and in the fingers of his own hand). The chief clerk dreams only of things within himself and in no way indicates a mechanism of carrying out his ambition. The executive clearly dreams of real events, of implementing his intentions. In so doing, he shows his ability to integrate thought with action, to develop a plot with significant time sequences, to relate actions to goals, and inner feelings to future expectations. The chief clerk is unable to move beyond the paralysis created by his emulation.

In many respects, picture 1 is a middle-class picture in that it presents an issue most appropriate to the social definitions made by that large group. The struggle with the conflict of free choice and an imposed task is thus one of the basic common themas to this picture. The aura of ambition is, of course, the second, most generally symbolized by stories of the virtuosity of the boy and the potential future musical success. The stories of most of the persons presented here reflect either or both of these issues. The story of a normal, middle-class girl of fourteen presents the second of these choices, though not without intimations of resentment of the extremely imposed task. She says:

Looks like the little boy's getting tired of his violin. He's been taking lessons and beginning to get tired of playing—let's see . . . He wants to play another instrument—maybe a piano—and his mother wants him to play the violin—so he wants to do what they tell him to do, and when he gets older he becomes a great violinist—I guess that's all.

In spite of this general definition of the boy and violin setting, however, different social orientations permit different interpretations. For example, here are stories of two lower class Negro girls of eleven, both to the violin picture.

First girl:

Trying to learn to play a song. Thinking about going to play. He is trying to play. Maybe he knows how to play a song. Maybe he just got through playing one. That is, after he saw some of his friends and said he was going to play. They enjoyed it. One of them wanted to play, and he let him play. Maybe he had something else to play with. That piece of paper is a song. The family is very poor. He doesn't want to play, but he wants to earn some money. Maybe he is in house by himself and nobody with him. He didn't have anything to eat. His family going to get rich and the little boy is going to marry a fine young girl and live happy ever after, and he took the thing he is playing with him and made some music out of it.

Second girl:

Studying his lesson. Something hard he can't get it right. Look like that was years ago. He got a stand that he put his book on. He is thinking real hard. That is something like these people that are poor in other cities. Some write letters over here to us and Red Cross sends them some clothes. He was starving hunger. His mother didn't have enough money to buy. . . . He have to go from house to house to church because don't have church.

One big room for classes. Brother, sisters have to sleep in one room. Just got two—mother and dad in other. Might have a storm and have flood and won't have enough shelter.

Thus, these two lower class Negro girls of eleven, while not ignoring the task orientation, define the social world of the stimulus in other terms. First, it is a world of deprivation. In the first girl it is a poor world in which magiclike outcomes are possible: the boy will marry the princess. Her hope is further seen in her attention to pleasing her friends. Thus the boy plays a song and his friends enjoy it, an interest seldom seen in middle-class records except in terms of grand tours and concert halls. In this girl, however, it is a close real world of immediate gratification and personal contact. In the second girl, it is also a close real world of personalized events, but they are all bad. Deprivation is common and disaster is imminent. It is of some interest, though not necessarily a general feature of such records, that the first more hopeful girl also has better organization. She develops a real plot with at least fair elaborations, and sees a future as positive, albeit magical. In the second discouraged girl, the world is as chaotic as her story. Elaborations are disjointed and concept-dominated. They follow more from her preoccupation with disaster than from the stimulus or from the logical plot with which she begins the story.

A more general contrast is provided by the records of individuals from cultures other than our own. To this end, the following stories of two Hopi adolescents and a Sioux boy of eleven are presented. The stories are to pictures 1 and 2 of the Indian TAT set. The first, a Hopi boy of fifteen says:

RIE-1. Indians—they are Zuñi—the father is telling the other two to go to the fields . . . and they will go.

RIE-2. Hopi boy is crying—the parents scolded him, he didn't want to go look for the horse. After that he will go.

One loses some of the advantages of comparability by not having these responses to the same card as the previous one. However, some general features may be noticed: first, in both of these stories, the boy adequately identifies the basic parts of the stimulus, attributes logical meaning to them, places them in adequate time sequences, and enlivens his plot with action and references to affect. Future outcomes are given in both instances. Elaborations are few and limited to identifications (Hopi, Indian, Zuñi). While the plots of these stories are tight and overorganized, all essential aspects of the task requested have been completed.

Their basic definition of the social reality represented by both cards (in spite of the potential stimulus difference) is one of obedience to adults, or in the second story threatened disobedience followed by obedience. Role definitions of the adults as in absolute control and the children partially unwilling but obedient are also seen.

In the following two stories of a Hopi girl of fifteen, highly similar plots are presented. She reports:

RIE-1. This man is talking to them. Maybe he is telling them what he has done or maybe he is telling them what they should do. He is their grandfather. They will do what he tells them because they are listening.

RIE-2. The boy is crying. His mother scolded him, that's why. Maybe he did something, maybe he did not go after some wood or something. Then his mother spanked him. He will go then.

These stories are presented as minor variations in the general themes already discussed. They are both quite characteristic of Hopi ado- lescent records. This girl permits herself slightly more imaginative elaboration than the boy, but basically her plots are identical. So is her basic definition of the social reality of the stimulus and the as- sumptions which she makes about the roles of children and adults. There are, of course, some important differences between these two adolescents, but in stories this short it is difficult to go into them with- out the full records. That such short stories provide ample data for individual, as well as cultural, analyses will be shown in the two full cases presented in Chapters 10 and 11.

In the following stories of a Sioux boy of eleven, quite different assumptions about the nature of the universe and quite different inter- pretations of the same stimuli are made. He says:

1. They are talking Indian. They are all Indians. They are talking about catching horses. "Get the ropes and bridles and saddles," the old man says. They go get them. They ride them. They get the cows first. They go buying something, bread and like that.

2. He's praying. He's praying—because he wants them to win the war. At night he's praying and go to bed. Breakfast, he pray for breakfast and eat.

The looseness of plot of these stories is apparent when they are com- pared to the Hopi stories. In neither of these is there the tightly developed plot with its basic identification, time sequence of action and outcome. The identifications made here are adequate and entirely in keeping with the stimulus. However, beyond that the stories are more disjointed, though not irrelevant, observations than they are developed plots. Connections of motive and outcome are made, however (pray . . . eat; pray . . . win war; catch horse . . . ride . . . get cows . . . get bread).

It is most important in the analysis of such stories to view the elements of the story with respect to their balances and proportion within the story actually given. To compare them directly with white middle-class American stories in terms of any specific form or content element is misleading and can provide only comparative statements while not illuminating the basic nature of the personality of the individual or group. It is for this reason that so much importance is attached to the single observation of "fire" (rather than "road" or "smoke") in the record of the Navaho girl presented earlier. In a record so short and sparse, the concentration of energy required to produce this observation is considerable. To note only the shortness, poorly developed plot, and absence of motive-attributions is to miss a central feature of this girl's personality. This is not to say that such comparative judgments are not relevant. They most certainly are and provide us with some important group comparisons. In terms of the analysis of the individual, however, it is perhaps best to see the general comparison as the overt social forms within which an individual must operate and in terms of which he can express whatever uniqueness he may possess.

To return to the Sioux boy's stories, some other differences from the Hopi records should be noted. To repeat, the organization is looser, the assumption of the tight interrelatedness of events is absent. The definition of the social reality of the stimulus in obedience terms is also absent. Rather here there is a definition of the stimulus as one of action: "these men are doing something," in contrast to "these boys are obeying that man." The first story is livelier and the individual is able to see things not specifically ordered—they get horses, cows, bread. The role definitions differ, the man "says," he does not "tell" or "scold," and there is no automatic need for the young to obey. The young may do things, rather than limit themselves to the obedience and social conformity preoccupation.

In the second story, some of the social plight of the Sioux appears. Here the boy appeals for aid—aid in aggression (war) and aid in receiving (breakfast). Again the story is poorly organized and the technique proposed (praying) for solving the problem presented is not related to self-accomplishing possibilities. It is rather a passive supplication without hint of an expectation of success.

Lest the reader conclude from these brief selections that all Indians tell stories of this limited nature, the response of a Mexican Indian boy of ten from Tepoztlan is presented: *

1. One day a father had two sons and he sent them to the fields to take care of his milpa so that the cattle would not enter. They took their shoulder-blankets and their hats and went to the fields to watch the milpa and at night they came back. The father was satisfied and gave them each one peso and told them the next day to take care of it again and so they went. There at the milpa they met a man who was begging; the children told him that they didn't have any money.

2. There was once a girl who was called Carmelita. She lived near a beach. One day she woke up early and went to the beach and tried to climb up the rocks. She fell asleep and a little man came. In the rock there was a little hole and the little man went inside it, throwing some candies. As the girl was hungry she took the candy and ate it. Soon she became very, very tiny and could git into the hole. Once inside she found a pearl there, a diamond and a ruby and she went with the tiny man. The girl started to cry and the tiny man looked at her and scolded her. She told him she was a fairy and that she was going to steal all his treasure. The girl showed him what she had taken and told him that she wanted to see the waves moving and that she was hungry. So the man took some pearls and gave them to the girl and the girl said: "I want these pearls to turn into milk." And they were transformed into milk and she drank it. Then the man gave her some other pearls and she said: "I want those to turn into bread." Then the man gave her some other pearls and told the girl not to tell anybody who had given them to her. Then she went home and slept. Soon her mother shouted at her and said: "I told her that it was late and that she should get up to drink her coffee and she said that she was not hungry anymore." She said she had been on the rocks and that she had met a tiny man who had given her breakfast and some pearls but he had told her not to tell anyone. Then the father said: "I am going to save the pearls for you. When you are grown up you will have much wealth and you will distribute it among your neighbors."

Here the flow of feeling and affect is marked in comparison with the Hopi and Sioux records. The ease of parent-child relation and the ease of relating affect to practicality are also marked in comparison to both the other Indian and the white American records. The mythlike

* This record was collected by Oscar Lewis and is printed here through his courtesy.

fantasy of story 2 also bears these same characteristics. The profoundly different definitions of the stimulus are similarly apparent. Order and system are presumed, but unrelieved melancholy, deprivation, compulsive obedience, and affect depression are not. Rather, fantasy is permitted to range more freely, though not to ignore practical issues.

These selected stories have been presented here to show some of the ways in which individual stories of nonclinical subjects may differ and to suggest ways in which these differences may be highlighted and described. In the following chapters, full records are given, permitting an examination of the interrelations of stories within one record and an image of the way in which a more nearly complete personality picture may be developed.

CHAPTER 8

Joe,

a middle-class boy

of fourteen

T he case of Joe is presented first to show the record of a normal
and healthy middle-class boy. Joe presents no symptoms, no com-
plaints. His record was taken as part of a study of children in a
midwest community. The record was analyzed "blind" and the report
of the original TAT analysis was the one written at that time. The
"blind" nature of the interpretation must be qualified in the light of
certain obvious "knowledge" held by the interpreter. Age and sex
were all the data specifically given, other than the verbatim stories.
However, the interpreter might be thought to have assumed an essentially "normal" record, since he knew that the boy was from a sample
of an average classroom.

The sequence analysis notes are elaborations of the original notes
made at that time. The elaborations were written for this volume.
The sequence notes written at the same time as the original TAT
analysis are entirely too cryptic for presentation here and do not make
explicit a number of points that should be brought out. Subsequent
case material presented is the original material gathered at that time.
The Rorschach analysis is the original and was similarly a blind
analysis.*

* The Rorschach reports on this and the following case were prepared by Hilde
Richard. Miss Richard also took the TAT protocol. The tests were given in a

The full TAT protocol is presented first. The picture numbers refer to the Murray numbers. Reaction time to each story is not recorded here though each story required slightly less than one minute to complete.

TAT Record

Picture 1. The guy is looking at his violin—it looks as if he knows how to do it—he wants to play—hasn't had a chance—someday he is going to be a good violinist.

Inquiry: I: Do you want to add anything to this?
         S: No.

Picture 2. Well, the girl looks like she just came home from school—she is going or coming—lives in the country—and might like school because she got books—she's thinking of something real hard.

Inquiry: I: What is she thinking about?
         S: Maybe about advancing or going to college or something.
         I: How is it going to turn out?
         S: I don't know.

Picture 3BM. I don't know if it is a girl—it looks like she is crying—over something she has done or something.

Inquiry: I: Do you want to tell me something more about it?
         S: Looks something like a gun down there.
         I: What about it?
         S: Maybe she shot somebody. I don't think so, but she might have.
         I: How is it going to turn out?
         S: Crumby—like she's caught or something.

Picture 14. Well, this here picture—looking out at night—looks like a boy—looking out a window at the stars or just looking for fresh air.

Inquiry: I: Do you want to tell me more about it?
         S: No.

Picture 7BM. Ah—looks like the man—that's his son—he's giving him a good heart to heart talk and the man looks worried about the son.

Inquiry: I: What do you mean?
         S: The son doesn't look like he cares much about talking.
         I: How will it come out?
         S: The boy getting into trouble.

special room provided by the school. This record is of a case collected in a research on adolescent personality reported in part in Robert J. Havighurst and Hilda Taba, *Adolescent Character and Personality* (New York: Wiley and Sons, 1949).

Picture 7GF. Well, this picture looks like the lady is reading a book to the girl—the girl doesn't seem very interested—looks like she is wandering off into space.

Inquiry: I: What do you mean?
S: Like she is not paying any attention to what the mother is saying.
I: What is going to happen later?
S: It will probably turn out O.K.

Picture 12BG. That looks like a picture in the spring where there is a boat—looks like out in the country—quite a ways out—probably boys going fishing or something.

Inquiry: I: Anything more you want to tell me about it?
S: It looks peaceful and restful—there probably isn't any school.

Picture 13B. Well, this looks like the little boy—must have been either in the mountains or in the older days because there is a log house. The way he is sitting in the doorway looks like he is thinking awfully hard and he looks puzzled.

Inquiry: I: Want to tell me anything more about it?
S: From what I can see it looks like the house is not very well furnished.
I: What kind of a thing is he puzzled about?
S: Something happened during the day or something like that.

Picture 4. This picture here looks like the lady is trying to keep him back—either a fight or something and—that's about all.

Inquiry: I: Do you want to tell me something more about it? (Pause) Who they are?
S: Maybe there is a fight over a girl or something.
I: Are they a married couple or just friends?
S: I don't think they are married—they are just friends.

Picture 18BM. This here picture—looks like he's either dead and they are carrying him around or taking him and dragging him back.

Inquiry: I: Do you want to tell me anything more about it?
S: (After looking at it closely) More likely he is dead—eyes closed, three hands—there is more than one lifting him.

Picture 19. Looks like a nightmare—you can see outline of a cottage—that's about all.

Inquiry: I: Can you see any more in it now?
S: Looks like smoke or water going along the bottom by the windows.

Story Analysis

Each story will be repeated with sequence analysis notes.

Picture 1. The guy is looking at his violin—it looks as if he knows how to do it—he wants to play—hasn't had a chance—someday he is going to be a good violinist.

Inquiry: I: Do you want to add anything to this?
           S: No.

It should first be observed that this is an essentially "normal" plot. Important to this observation are the following:

1. There are no bizarre or distorted bits of content; it is a "usual," "to be expected" story.

2. The plot as presented is in basic good design, with adequate time structure: a beginning, a middle, and an end.

3. The basic identification of the stimulus is adequate, in fact a little better than that. Note that in the first sentence (the boy is looking at his violin) he notes two of the major stimulus figures (boy . . . violin) and at the same time suggests two relational elements (looking . . . his). This is suggestive of a solid functional intelligence above the average.

4. The elaborations on the basic stimulus identification (it looks as if he knows how . . . he wants . . . hasn't had a chance) are of good quality, all relevant to the initial stimulus identification, and assist in furthering rather than deterring or detouring the plot. It may be worth noting that these elaborations present three different issues, all of them relevant and none repetitive. Further, two of the three are positive (knows how . . . wants to) whereas one is negative (hasn't had a chance). While the author would not always encourage qualitative interpretation so soon, it is of some interest to see these elaborations in a special framework. Let us look upon them as given by the boy somewhat freely, beyond the basic requirements of the plot. If we do so, it may be suggested that these imaginative introductions into the basic plot represent his basic personal orientation toward the world. The requirements of the external world demands (the instructions given to him) he meets in the first and last sentences of his story. The middle section elaborations are his own "free" choice. If so, then we may see his choice of two-thirds positive as reflecting a basically positive philosophy, a philosophy with one hesitant note. He wants to, he knows how, *but* he hasn't really been given a chance. If we

may hold this framework a moment longer, we may perhaps retranslate it a bit to propose that he is a boy with an essentially forward-looking orientation (wants to . . . knows how) who sees any blocks to his spontaneity as being located in the outside world (hasn't had a chance).

5. The ending is *good* in that it: *a.* is an *adequate structural completion* of the issue set by the subject at the beginning of the story; *b.* is in addition a *qualitatively satisfactory solution* to the desire expressed in plot content.

This ending continues the suggestion made about the elaborations. It re-emphasizes his positive hopeful outlook. In this connection the remark "hasn't had a chance" becomes important for another reason. It is a note of realism in a story that could have easily become too positive. It suggests that his orientation, while hopeful, is still reality-tied.

The first analysis of the major elements of the story suggests a normal, healthy boy of above average intelligence, good general intellectual organization, with a positive, though realistic, outlook. It will be obvious that these interpretations are all to be checked and qualified by later stories.

Let us look now at some other features of this story and consider what else we can say about him.

1. The content of his production, while clearly tied to adequate reality identifications, is basically introversion in orientation. That is to say, he stresses "internal" events more than external ones. The boy *looks*, he *knows how*, he *wants*, he is *going to be*. That these are basically soundly anchored in outer world fact is suggested by his sound plot development, and the fact that he relates all of them to outer events—the violin—and that they are all simple and reasonable "inner" reflections relevant to the plot he develops. But they are indeed more introversive than extroversive. He does not here provide us with an equal amount of "external" references. No other people appear in his story, no one listens to him play, no concerts, no critical parents, no competition with others. Even his reference to "hasn't had a chance," while suggestive of some outside event that has not been helpful, still does not identify this outer event. That his introversive orientation is positive in outlook has already been seen. Even the future appears to him to be good and still internally rather than externally relevant. He will become a "good violinist." This "good" suggests a conformity referent of some sort, but he still chooses not to identify the external event. He wants quality, he implies, but still sees this quality as self-defined.

2. Is there possibly some mother-oriented anxiety? This is at best a question to be explored later. It is to be noted, however, that he does not introduce an adult figure, or any figure for that matter. It is hardly mandatory, but there is still a tendency for the middle-class subject to bring an adult into this picture, most frequently a mother. He does not. It is probably not too vital that he fails to introduce a mother-figure, in no way comparable to his having failed to adequately identify the boy or the violin. It is merely suggestive that the mother-relation should bear careful scrutiny in the following stories. However, since it is generally a good idea to have too many hypotheses rather than too few, it may be helpful to examine this lead a little more carefully in this story. In terms of usualness of content, two items are noticeable in this story. The noninclusion of the mother is one. The introduced imaginative and *not-explained* reference to "hasn't had a chance" is the second. It is often profitable to test the proposition that such items are in some way interrelated. If so, may we propose that there is some organization of special feeling about the mother that bears anxiety for him, hence he "blocks" at identifying her. May we further suggest that he sees her as in some way inhibiting; she won't let him have a chance. It should not be forgotten that both of these suggestions are highly tentative and that they occur within the context of positive, well-organized fantasy. Therefore, we do not propose the concept of "hostility" to the mother, nor do we propose that his notion of not having had a chance is reflective of any paranoidlike notion that the world is against him.

3. Does he have friendly and positive relations with his peers? This suggestion stems from one word, "guy." It is, therefore, to be taken with caution. However, this one word may take on a little stronger connotation when we notice a little more about its context. First, it is the only reference to a person given in his story. It is very simple to have introduced many other persons here and, of course, easy to give them any personal attributes one wishes. He, however, only gives this one. Second, the one personal identification that he gives is an unusual one, suggesting some special organization of feeling around it. It is far more frequent to identify the stimulus merely as "boy," "young boy," or "he." Yet this subject selects an unusual identity. Third, the identity he chooses may, in terms of popular parlance, be thought to be a "friendly," informal one. If this logic is correct, it would lead us to suggest that Joe is a friendly and positive member of his peer group. This at least is a good hypothesis to test in subsequent stories. A corollary of this proposition may also be suggested.

It is that he is not also a "leader" in his peer group. While the nature of what constitutes leadership is an important issue not examined here, the corollary would suggest that he does not present the drive and assertiveness seen in the ordinary concept of the leader. Positively oriented, imaginative and friendly, easily accepting of others would form the nucleus of the attitudes which relates him to his peers. These acceptant attitudes, however, are also conventional in nature. His story is a usual one, he strives to be "good." He thus does not challenge his peers with unusual or overly spontaneous positive attitudes.*

4. His motivating drives are internal and self-referent in nature. We have seen his introversive orientation. It will also be profitable to see if there is any special differentiating aspect of this orientation. This will, of course, be examined in each subsequent story. Within this one, however, an important possible differential will bear examination. This is the question of whether his internal reference disposition maintains itself when external action is proposed. Some persons with strong introversive orientations still look to the outside when change and action are proposed. This is especially noted in story endings and in the source of stimulus to the outcome. Thus a person may propose that a satisfactory outcome is achieved only by external intervention: the mother insists, a violin is repaired by the father and therefore the boy practices, success at concerts spurs him on, etc. But for Joe, no such external event is proposed. Rather he is merely "going to be" a good violinist. While he does not clearly propose that entirely internal drive accomplishes this, he is clear that external events do not intercede. One would anticipate a Rorschach M:C balance clearly in favor of M.

5. To re-examine his organizational approach to the stimulus, it should be pointed out that while it is entirely adequate and while his elaborations are of good quality, his approach is still casual and understriving. The details are better than the whole, though he produced the initial inclusive whole (the guy is looking at the violin) with ease. This should be examined later. The suggestion here is that he over-

---

* This discussion, based almost entirely on the choice of the word "guy," should probably be viewed rather skeptically. It is a kind of interpretation that is easy to fall into and is included more as an illustration of a somewhat questionable interpretation. It is based on the assumption that the word "guy" for this boy is indeed specifically a form of "friendliness." It may well be merely the local convention and have no such implications. It is of course no real proof of the "friendliness" assumption that other data may support the conclusion of positive peer relations derived from it.

produces in small details and possibly also in W's of only fair quality. The form of this story is such that it would appear to suggest an IQ in the 120 area, but there is some suggestion of more sloppy organization that may appear later. If it does, it should still be recalled that on this, the first stimulus of a new task, he was able to organize himself readily, construct a quite adequate story, and respond in terms of both adequate reality orientation and inner motivation.

6. Let us now identify the stimulus presented to him in a somewhat different manner and see what light it may throw on him. Let us propose that the basic stimulus of the picture, its *latent meaning*, is one of how the individual relates himself to outer demands and how he copes with the potential individual frustration involved. We have seen in the preceding chapter how two graduate students reacted with resentment and defined the individual as in protest against an encroaching world. Joe, however, does not do this. If the stimulus is a demand for outer conformity, he is prepared to accept it and, in fact, to somewhat outdo it; he will become a "good violinist." If the stimulus presents a possibility of personal frustration, he rejects it and sees rather primarily possible internal reactions. He does suspect that his proper course is to be found within himself and does not expect the outer world to give him much of a "chance," but hostility and resentment, no. The *form demand* and the *manifest demand* of the picture he has met well with his first sentence—recognition of the first large detail (guy), recognition of the second large detail (violin), and recognition of a relationship between them (is looking at).

In the foregoing remarks are a substantial number of hypotheses. Some of them are phrased fairly strongly (suggested IQ about 120), and some of them are phrased quite tentatively (is there some mother-resentment?). But all of them, however, are of the same order, hypotheses to be tested in each subsequent story, to be made firm, modified, or abandoned as subsequent data dictate. New hypotheses, not seen here, will arise, to be similarly criticized in a re-examination of this story as well as all others.

Picture 2. Well, the girl looks like she just came home from school—she is going or coming—lives in the country—and might like school because she got books—she's thinking of something real hard.

Inquiry: I: What is she thinking about?
              S: Maybe about advancing or going to college or something.
              I: How is it going to turn out?
              S: I don't know.

This is again a basically normal plot, with no bizarre or strange ideas. It is, however, one in which he had to be pushed somewhat (inquiry) to produce a full plot, and even then he refused to complete it entirely. The details of the story and some of their implications are suggested now.

1. The basic form demand of the picture is only partially recognized. The man and woman are both ignored. This will be discussed in more detail later with respect to the qualitative implications. However, here it may merely be pointed out that he has produced what might be seen as an incomplete whole, or perhaps better as an incomplete whole made up of a series of connected large details (girl . . . school . . . home, lives in country, books . . . thinking, going to college or something). These identifications are adequate recognition of the stimulus large details. His tendency, however, appears to be to select these and to modify them by small details rather than to integrate them into an inclusive whole. He also neglects two prominent large details— the man and woman. The small-detail emphasis and the possibility of sloppy W's was suggested in story 1. Here he selects further small details to interpret. He recognizes the large D of the "girl" but then selects a series of small clues for his subsequent interpretation. In essence, he structures the picture so that the single large D of the girl is the focus and then moves out from it each time with related small elaborations: *she* has come from home or school, *she* lives in the country, *she* might like school, *she's* thinking. All are reinterpretations of the girl's situation, two of them dealing with her inner life and three with her reality situation.

2. Joe may have some tendency to get lost in intellectual details and to be easily influenced in his performance by interpersonal situations. He prefers to identify this picture as a story of a girl in some quandary as to her status and personal reaction. She is either going or coming and it may be either home or school. In this situation his logic suffers; he ignores the major details, he concludes she might "like school" because she "got books." In any event, in this quandary, she herself is introspective. The only action he spontaneously permits her —ignoring the forced inquiry—is to "like" or to think "real hard." Considering his quite adequate approach to story 1, he seems rather easily distressed by this picture and his organization suffers. In his school-work, is it not possible that he will show similar tendencies to disorganization? This tendency, however, should appear in situations of interpersonal disharmony, rather than merely from heavy work de-

mands. We have already seen in story 1 some suggestion of under-ambition.

3. The *latent demand* of this picture usually presents two issues. One is that of interpersonal action. This is a picture of three people and the reaction to these three is usually suggestive of the subject's orientations in this area. The second possibility is that the subject accept a definition of this picture which emphasizes the adjustment of the individual (usually in the person of the girl) to his life circumstances. The second definition would appear to be the more relevant here, though the first will also require comment. If we take the vantage point of the second, may we not restate this story to present Joe as a boy in some concern about conformity demands and relying primarily upon his own introspection in this quandary? It is clear that he does not propose personal interaction—there is none at all in this story—though his forced partial solution would suggest that the virtues of conformity will triumph. This should bear some relevance for his peer adjustment. It may be suggested that he is saying, when in some personal quandary, don't take it out on others. In the ordinary rough and tumble of adolescent acting-out, he should be unique. Considering the possibility of specific positive peer feeling seen in story 1, he should be a well-liked person who does not greatly strive for peer status nor demand that his individuality be accepted by others. This point is of some importance. Generally we would look to the statements involving interpersonal relations for data on the subject's overt behavioral relations with others. This is, of course, based on the general maxim that the relationships portrayed of the central figure are most generally the relationships characteristic of the subject. There is still much truth in this view. However, this case may suggest one of its many pitfalls.

Do we advance the hypothesis that this subject is a social isolate because in his first two stories no interpersonal actions are proposed? We do not, even assuming that this lack of interaction also characterizes the remaining stories. Rather we remind ourselves that overt behavior is symptomatic of the interaction of underlying motive, defense systems, and situation. The subject whose involvement with external events and their interaction is such that he frequently portrays them in his stories perhaps gives us more direct data and suggests immediately a pattern of overt behavior. With the subject who suggests no such behavior, however, analysis of motive, defense, and its projection into the situation is needed before any behavioral predictions are made.

In the present case, on the basis of the limited data of two stories, we would not propose that the image of interaction he presents in his stories is a direct replica of his own behavior. We would propose that his behavior is not characterized by an active seeking for peer contact, nor by a pattern of assertive leadership. We would propose, further, the pattern suggested earlier, a friendly, warm acceptant attitude that would be sought by others. It is an obvious, though often forgotten, principle that effective interactional patterns can result from active seeking on the part of the individual, or by that individual being actively sought by others. The latter seems more the case here. Elaborations or qualifications will be made on this point as subsequent stories are analyzed.

4. We are faced with a story in which the usually mentioned man and woman are still absent. In the light of the nonintroduction of an adult in story 1, we must examine the hypothesis of some parental resentment that blocks these figures out. The author would say that there is hardly sufficient data to go much beyond this at this time. Two qualifying observations may be made, however. First, it is perhaps possible to ignore the absence of an adult in story 1. Such a figure indeed is not represented in the stimulus. We have seen that this boy is not one to push his intellectual abilities, nor driven to cope actively with the outer world. Hence, for him this omission is perhaps perfectly "natural" and not a sign of a "blocking" due to anxiety on this topic. Second, in story 2, perhaps it is more revealing to say that he concentrates on the girl in an introspective quandary and less pertinent to say that he refuses to see the man and woman. In this story this logic seems only partially useful, since the stimuli for the figures are a clear part of the picture. In any event, this possibility reduces our tendency to propose specific adult blocking and suggests that we look further for evidence on this point.

5. The boy is here still aware of convention and selects the "proper" ending for his story. When a choice presents itself, as here when he initially did not give an outcome, he prefers to let things ride with an introspective statement (thinking . . . real hard). It would appear that the basically introversive orientation suggested above is substantiated here.

Picture 3BM. I don't know if it is a girl—it looks like she is crying—over something she has done or something.

Inquiry: I: Do you want to tell me something more about it?
          S: Looks something like a gun down there.
          I: What about it?

S: Maybe she shot somebody. I don't think so, but she might have.

I: How is it going to turn out?

S: Crumby—like she's caught or something.

1. Joe reacts to this picture with a story generally negative in tone. This is certainly to be expected. A happy and carefree story in the light of the stimulus would have been more unusual. It may be well to analyze this story in the two parts actually given us by the boy. The first part is his spontaneous remarks, ending with "something she has done or something." The second part is that prompted by the examiner's questions. In a sense, these two parts are his spontaneous reaction to the stimuli and his reaction to outside pressure. If this is a useful division of his response, we should then ask what is the essence of the response in each part, with some hope of seeing whether or not he sees these two as different. In the first part, the spontaneous reaction, we see the introversive trend previously noted and we see this phrased in terms of "something" in the outer world. As in the other stories, he does not provide us with much detail of his conception of the outer world except perhaps to say that it requires a conformity he is only grudgingly giving it. Here in the second, "forced," part of his response, he says this more directly. When he is obliged to say what the outer world is like, he says in essence: "I recognize stimuli in the outer world" (looks like a gun down there).

"I can propose action that is appropriate to the outer world stimulus" (maybe she shot somebody).

"I basically don't think much of this outer world" (I don't think so, but she might have. . . . Crumby, like she's caught or something).

This is a story of a boy in inner world–outer world conflict, who, though realistically aware of outer world demands, would prefer to rely on his own introversive interests. Dealings with the outer world will just turn out "crumby."

2. The "gun" on the floor is not always recognized and sometimes reflects anxieties in the assertive or assertive-sexual area. In this instance, the writer proposes neither of these issues as basic ones. He would rather maintain the stance previously proposed and see this section of Joe's story as bearing meaning in terms of the subject's outer world adjustment. If this stance is maintained, the remark about shooting somebody is best seen as a sort of unstimulated assertive outburst. It is "unstimulated" in the sense that it does not appear in any way retaliatory, nor does Joe receive any sense of satisfaction from the act itself. Further, it will turn out "crumby." If it is agreed, as

suggested earlier, that this is basically an introversive boy, that this shooting is unstimulated and unsatisfying, then the author sees it as symptomatic of a kind of random, entirely internally motivated assertive act most frequently seen in the behavior called "tantrums." In sum, the author thinks that Joe from time to time has slight aggressive flares which are not directly responsive to any specific external stimulus, are not disposed to be retaliatory, and that leave him without a feeling of satisfactory catharsis. The writer would reject the notion that these outbursts result in some resentment by his peers—because of their unstimulated and unretaliatory nature, his basically positive orientation, the lack of specificity in his outer world awareness, and his primarily introversive preoccupations. The basic stimulating circumstances for these occasional outbursts would appear to be his own occasional frustration feelings which arise from this inner–outer world struggle. To some extent, these outbursts are also as yet unformulated self-expressive interests. All in all, he is seen by the author as a genuinely introversive boy, struggling with the issue of how much concession he must make to outer world demands. Considering the rather mild fashion in which he objects to the outer world stands (crumby . . . like she's caught or something), the author would not propose any generalized outer world hostility or any reactive flight from it.

3. Anxiety would appear to be present, but neither oppressive in quantity nor disruptive of Joe's basic goals. This story, like the second one, is told unevenly, though quickly. His concerns permit some easy blocking out of stimuli (man and woman in 2), he holds back from pushing his own interests forward (refusal to give details relating to accomplishment in 1, resistance to outcome in 2 and 3BM), he anticipates mild displeasure with the outer world (outcome in 2 and 3BM).

4. It should be noted here that, as with the previous stories, he very adequately identifies the basic stimulus and its meaning, gives it adequate, but not good, structure and adds action and life. While the organization level, here and before, is only fair, this story can be seen as still consistent with a superior intellectual level. The writer would not want to specify an IQ rating at this time though it should be above 110 and below 130.

Picture 14. Well, this here picture—looking out at night—looks like a boy—looking out a window at the stars or just looking for fresh air.

Inquiry: I: Do you want to tell me more about it?
          S: No.

1. It not infrequently happens that the subject himself, in only partially disguised form, presents us with a summary diagnosis. If this boy does, then this is it in this story. He says very succinctly— I am a boy looking for fresh air! He also says that he doesn't propose to be hurried (inquiry) though he has his eyes on meaningful goals (at the stars). We have seen how he readily dismisses issues with which he does not want to deal (man and woman in 2) and the possibility that his rejections are aimed more at clearing the ground for himself than reflective of any strong hostility. This story, usually reflective of the person's inner goals and ambitions, is probably also a good prognosis for this boy. He tells us again that it is his own inner thoughts that he wants to get straightened out and that he would like to do so without too much outer world interference.

2. It is of some interest that this is a picture with only one person. The situation is a very ambiguous one where no inner conflict (as in 3BM) or imposed task (as in 1) is presented. In this circumstance he is entirely willing to leave things alone, to let the "boy" merely be seeking. He does not introduce any of the many possible worries or issues that these unstructured stimuli present: no outer world conformity demands or ambitions, no aggression, no anxiety. This is perhaps good evidence that the "shot" in 3BM is not symptomatic of underlying hostilities, that his anxiety level is not high, and that his drive toward outer world conformity is a realistic one activated primarily by specific stimuli. In this picture where he is not directed by specific external stimuli, it is of interest that his resulting story is calm, friendly, well organized, and at peace with itself.

3. It may be well to summarize some of our conclusions to this point. In general, the subject appears to be a quiet yet readily spontaneous boy, friendly but retiring, introversive yet with active interest, somewhat self-centered but not demanding. His system of control would appear to involve a fairly well differentiated inner control, conscious control low but adequate. His outer behavior is cautious and friendly, tactful and accepting, yet characterized by occasional temper spurts that are not directed against other persons. His anxiety level is not high and appears to center around his general effort to integrate his introversion tendencies with his desire for a pleasant social conformity. The images of parental figures require analysis. So far we have seen only some mild suggestion of block with respect to these issues. Sexuality needs specific study, though it should not be forgotten how comfortably he dealt with the girl in story 2, seeing her as having real goals and inner feelings, and with the girl in 3BM,

similarly seeing her as a real person coping with real events. In a sense, he tells us already that persons of the opposite sex are real people with their own goals and desires. This is a good basis for an adequate heterosexual adjustment.

We have seen that he utilizes his inner feelings readily, and that they are generally appropriate and positive. He has some overgeneralizing tendency coupled with an overemphasis on small details. The author would now propose an IQ of 115 to 125 with the reminder that Joe does not have much intellectual ambition and is a little slipshod in his mental approach.

He has also shown us that, while he is entirely aware of emotional issues and able to deal with them introspectively, he does prefer to ignore many of them and to avoid going into details. He would prefer to mull them over casually rather than analyze them carefully. In this sense, he is not deeply involved continually with either himself or outside events and prefers to leave things alone and have them flow their own way.

In these first four stories he has permitted his figures autonomy for themselves though never neglecting restraints when the circumstances seem to call for them (2 and 3BM). His figures move easily, but without strong affect, and with a minimum of involvement with others (no introduced figures). He is acceptant of the feelings of others (see especially the girl in 2 and 3BM) though not concerned with an active involvement or analysis of those feelings.

Picture 7BM. Ah—looks like the man—that's his son—he's giving him a good heart to heart talk and the man looks worried about the son.

Inquiry: I: What do you mean?
        S: The son doesn't look like he cares much about talking.
        I: How will it come out?
        S: The boy getting into trouble.

1. The plot is a fairly standard one. It may now be suggested that this imagination is generally routine. While he has had one possibly original notion (the boy looking for fresh air), in general his responses picture a quite average imagination. He uses these capacities neither for fantasy escape nor for creative purposes.

2. This picture is the first on which a direct father-image appears. In general it would seem that he sees some closeness (heart to heart talk) but that an atmosphere of minor worry, advice, and control is anticipated. We may recall that there has been no direct father reference earlier and, in fact, that he neglected one potential one in

story 2. As was suggested there, it seems like he is able to ignore the parents when he wishes to focus on some other topic. It does not appear that the parents represent any basic blocking. This seems consistent with this story in which the image of firmness and control is present, but no great worry or terrible trouble. The son may "get into trouble" but it appears rather casual. His major objection actually is not the potential trouble, but merely that the son doesn't care much for "talking." We are perhaps justified at introducing here the fact that Joe selected this picture as one of his least liked. He strongly emphasized that he did so because he "don't like bawling outs—it shouldn't happen. I don't like them." These qualifying remarks suggest that he sees this picture within a "bawling out" context. This would point to the father as the more stern and controlling parent. It is possibly of importance that the father does not really come to the boy's assistance since he finally gets into trouble. The son does not appear to blame the father for the trouble, merely for interrupting the son with "talking."

This image of the father as the firm controlling figure must be modified by the basically easy and not resentful attitude of the boy. He is not preoccupied with parental figures and can easily leave them out of his stories. His relationship to them would appear to be a fairly casual and positive one in which basic firmness and controlling attitudes are recognized but not mistaken for rejection. They are, in a sense, mild nuisances from whom he'd like a "little fresh air."

Picture 7GF. Well, this picture looks like the lady is reading a book to the girl—the girl doesn't seem very interested—looks like she is wandering off into space.

Inquiry: I: What do you mean?
          S: Like she is not paying any attention to what the mother is saying.
          I: What is going to happen later?
          S: It will probably turn out O.K.

1. The image of the parents developed in the foregoing should also take into account this picture. In essence, he says much the same thing. Mother is a controlling person but "O.K."

2. Some grasp of his image of the mother is to be seen in his image of other females. This is based, of course, upon the only partially justifiable assumption that a boy's image of the "female" is reflection of his learning with the mother. If so, we would re-emphasize the generally constructive but realistic view of the female which he has

portrayed in 2 and 3BM. From these and the present story, we would see the mother as firm yet not overly demanding emotionally. It would also appear that the mother is not specifically sex-repressive though she is certainly the superego training figure. Picture 4 to follow will be a relevant stimulus on this point. These points are all important to a consideration of the boy's maturity level. They would suggest that the primary ties to the mother are being satisfactorily replaced with a realistic and basically positive image.

3. In both this and the preceding story, it should be noticed that son and daughter both partially separate themselves from the parent-figure. The son doesn't care much for the talking and the girl is "wandering off in space." Of the two, it may be that the mother is perceived by Joe as the generally most constructive figure. Her advice will "probably turn out O.K." whereas the father's advice may not keep the boy from "getting into trouble." In the light of no specific attack upon the parent-figures and the fact that the final actions proposed for the boy and girl actually do not contradict the ideas of the parents, the author should think of Joe as attempting to establish a healthy psychic distance from his parents rather than feeling hostile and resentful of them to any marked degree. It should be specifically noted that the parents allow and possibly even encourage this to occur. In both 7BM and 7GF, the parents do not interfere beyond the stage of initial advice. The man does not attempt to direct once the son suggests he is not interested in talk and the mother does not object to the lack of interest on the part of the girl. It may be suggested that Joe's family has not led him to assume that all family situations must be intense and tightly interactive. Rather there can be breathing space for all if you look for it.

Picture 12BG. That looks like a picture in the spring where there is a boat—looks like out in the country—quite a ways out—probably boys going fishing or something.

Inquiry: I: Anything more you want to tell me about it?
 S: It looks peaceful and restful—there probably isn't any school.

1. The story is mainly corroborative of some of the trends already seen. Specifically, it may be suggested that it relates to:
 a. The low intellectual ambition.
 b. The ease with inner feelings.
 c. The desire for low outer world contact.
2. This picture is one with no people in it, merely the boat and the rural scene. And Joe appears to feel quite at home with it. He intro-

duces figures, "boys going fishing or something," and expresses pleasure at the peacefulness of the scene. He feels no need to bring in negative or aggressive themes, and no need to give the "boys" more interaction. "Going fishing" is sufficient for him.

3. The thema here is a usual one and, other than the somewhat unusual reference to "peaceful and restful," suggestive of quite average imagination. Elaborations are good, though he still emphasizes small details somewhat (quite a ways out) and is content with adequate but uncritical inclusive wholes.

Picture 13B. Well, this looks like the little boy—must have been either in the mountains or in the older days because there is a log house. The way he is sitting in the doorway looks like he is thinking awfully hard and he looks puzzled.

Inquiry: I: Want to tell me anything more about it?
        S: From what I can see it looks like the house is not very well furnished.
        I: What kind of a thing is he puzzled about?
        S: Something happened during the day or something like that.

1. The outstanding feature of this story lies largely in the absence of the lost, hungry, or abandoned boy thema. Recalling the discussion of 7BM and 7GF, this story would tend to confirm the feeling that the family emotional atmosphere is a positive one, in spite of the "trouble" and "worry" of those stories. Here, he sees rather a boy puzzled—his emotional introversive concern. He is, however, puzzled over a real event (something happened during the day), no fantasied or improbable events for him. It is also to be noted that in this situation he also does not entertain depressive ideas.

2. His observations are still of fair quality. He sees the usual "poor" surroundings. For him, however, they do not connote "poor" personal situations, or hunger, or other deprivation as they do to so many persons. It is important that this boy, in spite of his strong introversive orientation, still observes the external stimuli adequately.

Picture 4. This picture here looks like the lady is trying to keep him back—either a fight or something and—that's about all.

Inquiry: I: Do you want to tell me something more about it? (Pause) Who they are?
        S: Maybe there is a fight over a girl or something.
        I: Are they a married couple or just friends?
        S: I don't think they are married—they are just friends.

1. The basic plot of the restraining woman and the assertive male is a standard one. To this extent he maintains his general approach

seen in other stories. He stresses details of plot (not details of stimulus) and does not complete the story with the usual ending. This is entirely consistent with the description of imagination and intelligence given earlier.

2. The examiner's second question (are they a married couple or just friends) is, of course, bad examining technique, though it is actually of some interest that when presented with this choice he prefers "friends"—the nonfamily solution. This, coupled with the lack of an ending, may point to a further elaboration of his sexual orientation. It was suggested earlier that his feelings in the sexual area were most likely positive. This was thought to follow from the ease and empathy with which he described the girls in earlier pictures. However, an identification with the opposite sex, as this empathy may indeed be called, is not in itself evidence of an adequate sex-appropriate orientation. It could, in fact, imply too clear an empathy and a corresponding failure to see his own male role function. This story, plus his general impulse acceptance, suggests a quite adequate male imagery. He sees the more assertive male role, though he himself does not find assertion easy. To some extent, he nullifies any negative effect of this assertion by his claim that "they are just friends." He sees the interplay of male and female and possibly, if his response to the first inquiry question may be so seen, he conceives some beginning elements of romanticism and its attendant jealousy. The fact that this is not a more straightforward heterosexual story, the fact that he does not see (or possibly only hints at by his reference to "a girl") the second female figure in the background, the fact that there is no outcome, would suggest some entirely age-appropriate hesitancy and uncertainty in his sexual-social adjustment. It is a minimal uncertainty, however, and the author would see him as positively attracted toward girls and popular with them. His general maturity level is at least age appropriate and probably somewhat advanced.

Picture 18BM. This here picture—looks like he's either dead and they are carrying him around or taking him and dragging him back.

Inquiry: I: Do you want to tell me anything more about it?
        S: (After looking at it closely) More likely he is dead—eyes closed, three hands—there is more than one lifting him.

Picture 19. Looks like a nightmare—you can see outline of a cottage—that's about all.

Inquiry: I: Can you see any more in it now?
        S: Looks like smoke or water going along the bottom by the windows.

Stories to 18BM and 19 are given together since they are both short and can be analyzed in much the same fashion.

1. These two stories are to the two most ambiguous and unstructured stimuli and they are the only ones with which he does not do fairly well. He fumbles on 18BM, finding himself unable to construct a plot, merely identifying the basic scene. Even here, though, he sees the stimuli adequately. He accounts for the man and explains the strange pattern of hands. "They" (the three hands) are carrying him (the location of the hands). This general situation is explained by making the man "dead." No basic plot follows, however, and he is unable to tell why this peculiar situation may have occurred. With 19, an even more ambiguous stimulus, he is still more at a loss. He merely identifies the major masses (cottage . . . smoke or water) and indicates some malaise by rejecting the whole thing (looks like a nightmare).

2. In these two stories, often very productive in the more imaginative or more disturbed people, one should not feel obliged to attempt a more detailed analysis. One could wonder about the smoke along the windows of the cottage. Does Joe subconsciously sense some instability (smoke) about his home life (cottage)? In 18BM, does he feel depressed and psychologically weighted down (dead . . . dragging from behind)? Considering his basic general failure to use his fantasy to suggest such possibilities, his general inability to deal with ambiguous stimuli, these psychological possibilities could be ignored. Examination of the full record in the light of the preceding suggestion does not support them. Therefore, one should conclude from the stories only that which stems from the general form analysis. These are points already suggested by other stories:

a. His imagination is indeed routine.

b. He prefers simple, safe circumstances.

c. He does not use fantasy as escape.

d. There are no generally repressed trends that have not been seen before.

Joe was asked to select the two pictures he liked best and the two he liked least.

Pictures liked best:
S: 14.
I: Why did you like this one best?
S: The opening of the window and the fresh air. And 12BG—outdoors and where it takes place—a nice place to be.

Pictures least liked:
S: 3BM—doesn't make any sense—for a person to be crying like that. Looks like she is trying to put on an act or something.
S: 7BM—I don't like bawling outs—it shouldn't happen. *I don't like them!*

He selects two of the least interactive pictures, the single man star-gazing and the "peaceful and restful" outdoor scene. It has already been suggested, and the writer would see these choices as confirming, that Joe sees himself as a calm and simple person, nonassertive and noninteractive. His introversive trends are similarly seconded by these choices.

His "least" choices suggest some of his uneasiness and the things which he attempts to avoid. He is ill at ease when the outer world makes demands, 7BM. And he finds negative emotions and actions unlikely and unreal. It "doesn't make sense" for such situations as 3BM to occur.

His emphasis on 7BM rejecting the "bawling out" is on the story of father and son. As was suggested, his other general parental attitudes seem to suggest that the stimulus for such a response is not a pervasive father-hostility. Rather, it seems to go with 3BM, with which he himself connects it in these choices, as a reaction to outer control and unpleasant emotions.

These analyses of stories have been presented in some detail primarily for the purpose of suggesting the kind of logic which seems to me productive in the interpretation of fantasy. There is no question but what the analysis has been only partially presented and the meaning of some points still remains unclear. It is hoped, however, that this case, and the ones that follow, will serve to demonstrate the interpretive process and to show how the variables of form and content are related to individual case analysis.

In the following pages are presented the original blind TAT analysis and some brief notes from other data to give a general image of the nature of corroboration of the points in the preceding analysis. Evidence of validity of such analysis can hardly be presented in this fashion and such is not the intention here. The original TAT analysis is presented first.

Original TAT Analysis

Social interaction

Peers. Joe should be an accepted and well-liked member of his peer group. He has a spontaneity and an accepting attitude that should make him well integrated into his group. The present writer sees him not as a leader, since he has not the aggression for that, but as a boy thought friendly and spontaneous. He has also a self-centered aspect that may help to consolidate his position. That is, he really does not care much about superego problems and this lack of concern may increase his acceptance. It is probable that he has occasional spots of self-expressive rebellion, temper tantrums, but this will not destroy his position in the group since they are purely self-oriented spurts and not directed against his peers.

Family. His feelings about adults in general and family in particular are essentially that they are nuisances. He sees all adult control figures as bothersome and difficult, but has not developed hostility to them. He is well aware of their controlling aspects and wishes they would leave him alone, let him have a "little fresh air," as he says in one of his stories. The father seems more remote than the mother and is seen more negatively as controlling and not very satisfactory. The mother, somewhat of a superego figure, is also seen as controlling and as getting into his way, but fairly positively and basically accepted.

Characteristics of the self

Mental functioning. Joe is of high average to superior intelligence (115–125) with some tendency to overgeneralize and to relate. He does not have a great deal of intellectual ambition, however, and is not putting much energy into his work. In fact, he may even be a little slipshod in his schoolwork and thus receive only mediocre grades.

Imagination. Imagination is only fair. He has some original twists to his stories, but no great flare in this direction. Creativity is low because he is not primarily interested in construction or in creating at any level. Fantasy is also low and he does not tend to use fantasy as an escape.

Patterns of emotional adjustment

1. *Basic emotional attitude* active but not aggressively so. He seems quite willing to sit and wait until he gets ready before worrying about emotional problems.

2. *Impulse life* is not only accepted but taken as the most important source of dynamics. It is true that there is some superficial restraint, largely mother-originated, and an awareness of outer pressure that somewhat depresses his spontaneity. Acceptance is good, however, and he tends to be quite spontaneous and impulse-directed.

3. *Anxiety* indicators are present in his records—rather hesitant stories, some blocking on sex stories. Most of this anxiety has to do

with his adjustment to outer world demands and is not very oppressive in quantity.

4. *Mechanisms of adjustment.* Low conscious control, active struggle with outer world demands, fairly high and differentiated inner control, jolly, cheerful front, lack of real deep emotional involvement, ignoring many emotional problems.

5. *Emotional reactivity* is low to other people in the sense that his differentiated reactivity to others is low. In general, he reacts to his own inner stimuli. He is generally highly introversive in orientation though with considerable awareness of outer world stimuli to which he does not always care to respond. He has, however, much potentiality for outer response even though he may always remain heavily introversive.

6. *Sexual adjustment* is adequate and in fact he should be regarded quite well by the girls. He has some hesitancy about his role here, but nothing very inhibiting.

Summary

Joe is a well-adjusted adolescent, a cheerful and pleasant member of his social group, not overly aggressive, intelligent, and strongly introversively oriented. He operates mainly on his own self-centered concerns and thinks first of his own pleasure. His most immediate conflict is that of reconciling this fact with the obvious demands of his mother and other controlling agencies.

Summary of Other Data

The observations that follow are a brief summary of a number of other sources of data, primarily the Rorschach, the Sociometric, and Guess-Who data, and interviews with parents and teachers. Intelligence test data are also given.

Social interaction

The majority of the sociometric and observational data on Joe appears in substantial agreement with the TAT analysis. A brief summary of data exclusively from the Sociometric and Guess-Who instruments, also derived independently of other data, reports:

Joe is low in the aggressive-leadership component. However, his high scores on participation in games would offset the apparent lack in his masculine qualities. His security in the affections of the group is outstanding. Both girls and boys choose him as a friend. He also seems to have a capacity to give a lift to the emotional climate through a capacity for cheerfulness and spontaneous enjoyment of social situations. He received high scores for being pleasant to others. He was thought of as outstanding for doing things with others, being nice to everybody, sharing anything he has, liking play, being cheerful, and smiling readily. His scores are lower for going to the trouble to help someone and for working hard for his club or team. The evidence suggests that he flares up more quickly and more often than most of the boys. The data also indicate that he is thought of as sometimes, but not frequently, irresponsible—sometimes has to be urged to finish tasks, lets play interfere. Scores on the character items suggest a certain amount of self-centeredness. Things which interfere with pleasure, he tends to sidestep. This tendency is further substantiated by his tendency to follow his impulses and give expression to anger. On the sociometric choosing, he is also outstanding. He is chosen as best friend by eight boys and five girls. He is also a member of a three-boy mutual choice clique.

Family relationships

The case history material suggests that the father is a quiet, steady, hard-working person, quite interested in his family. The mother is similarly pleasant, home-oriented, realistically dealing with everyday problems. She is seen as supportive and accepting of her children in a variety of situations, including her attitude toward work in school. The mother runs the house but it is clearly a patriarchical household; the father is the code setter and the mother implements the rules. Parents make little attempt to regulate outside activities and are generally nonpunitive, except, according to Joe, for "occasional whippings." The mother points out that "each child is different and requires different handling." Apparently she spanked the older brother, but she reports that the threat of punishment is enough for the others. In general, her training methods appear practical and realistic in terms of the immediate situation. Although there is no evidence of any very complex emotional relationships between the parents, the home appears to be a supporting, accepting, and understanding place, which does not feature much exchange of overt affection. The mother is above average in her acceptance of sexuality.

Mental approach

The intelligence level appears to be essentially that predicted by the TAT. His Binet IQ at the time of TAT testing was 120. His Otis was 119, his Cornell-Coxe was 113. A prior Binet rated him at 118. School grades average C with D in spelling, but have been coming up to more B's recently. School comments are that his normal achievement is not as high as might be expected and that "school grades are definitely below ability."

On the Rorschach, his W% is over, his D% under, and his Dd% extreme over. "There is a strong tendency to produce W's, to grasp situations in terms of general concepts. Dd's are usually of good quality."

Imagination

The only comparable data on imagination is from the Rorschach which reports that Joe "does not allow himself free indulgence in fantasy escape, but probably attempts a fusion between impulses from within and his conscious awareness of reality demands." "He is able to add original twists to otherwise ordinary perceptions."

Inner adjustment

The Rorschach finds much the same pattern as the TAT, although it stresses the conformity elements a little more. Anxiety is found to be "mild" and to consist of some passive FM and inactive M responses, some color shock, overproduction of Dd. Both the TAT and Rorschach suggest the mother as more superego-controlling than the father, although they agree that the mother is not sex-repressive. In the Rorschach the boy is clearly introversive, an M:C ratio of 4:1. Sexual adjustment shows some overt passivity, lack of masculine assertiveness, but shows no "unsolvable conflict. He seems to be making tentative starts in the direction of an adequate social-sex role." The control system on the Rorschach shows well-differentiated inner control with limited use of conscious control. His reactions "are predominantly influenced by introversial tendencies, yet he is amenable to stimulation from without as well as capable of oriented behavior towards the outer world, chiefly in terms of introjection and a feeling of sensitivity to the reactions of others."

The Rorschach summary statement reports: "Joe is altogether in contact with the reality of his social environment. He seems capable of meeting problems and conflicts through rather adequate defense systems, as well as adequate insight into his own feelings and capacities, being able to understand other people via introjection. He is very likely to continue along predominantly introversively oriented lines."

CHAPTER 9

Carl,

age twenty-nine

Carl is a man of twenty-nine who recently came to the United States from Europe. His record is presented to illustrate an older and more complex personality. The record was taken in longhand in interview, the subject speaking an accented but quite fluent English.* No blind test analyses are available for comparison, although the basic story analyses were made prior to the taking of the life history. Selections from a long life history will be given.

TAT Record

Picture 1. A young boy sitting in front of a violin spread out on white table, or white linen. It is not clear in the expression of the face if he thinks in glorification and admiration of that what the violin and music could hold for him or if he is bored and in disgust with the lesson he has to take and doesn't want.

Picture 2. A rural scene showing strong young man plowing a field and a woman, obviously pregnant, leaning against a tree symbolizing the fertility

* This record was taken by Dr. Oliver J. B. Kerner and is reproduced here with his permission. Dr. Kerner also collected the biographical material, extracts from which are presented at the end of this chapter.

of earth and simple living as compared to the left, a girl with a slightly sad sophisticated expression on her face, symbolizing in holding books in her hands, intellectual learning. It's not quite clear which of both is giving the preference. The lines of the first scene are much stronger expressed, the movement—than those of the girl at the left.

Picture 3BM. Showing girl in crouched position either broken or drunk, lines and movements too crude, vulgarity too plainly stressed. Lines ass almost obscene. Right hand showing does not follow expression of rest of body.

Picture 4. Man and woman, man turning away with vague expression on his face. Woman obviously wants to hold him. In background another woman with alluring look and face could be reflection in mirror. The whole very cheap sentimentality expressed as in common magazine illustrations.

Picture 5. Woman opening door to room of rather orderly fashion coming out of the dark, light in her face and body, obviously warm and casted upon her from inside of room, flowers on table, lamp and other rather dull settings. Expression on woman's face not quite satisfying, half tired, half asking. Movement clumsy.

Picture 6BM. Young man, old woman, both obviously at the end of an argument, both with determined face, face of man insistent, face of woman horrified, and turned away. Suggestion of her hands that she is weeping over man in movement of leaving. [How end?] He will leave.

Picture 7BM. Faces of two men, one young, one old. Expression of old man's face tired, and knowing, obviously talked to the young man, young man disgusted and sad, could be a scene between doctor and patient or father and son.

Picture 9BM. Scene of several men sleeping in open fields, could be farmers, . . . resting while harvesting, bodies all heavy suggesting sturdiness and position suggesting previous heavy work; though hands of man in front too fine for hard labor. Man in back has Negro features but seems unlikely he is on account of his physically close position to white man. Otherwise whole picture rather convincing.

Picture 10BM. Man and girl in intimate position, both have eyes closed, very sensual expression in both faces suggesting emotions . . . though eyebrows of man have a rather ugly knowing movement, face of girl especially . . . that eyelid and eye suggesting sort of intimate melting away.

Picture 11. Jesus. This is wonderful! Fantastic scene showing high mountains or rocks, with strange prehistorical beasts, whole scene suggesting prehistoric chaos, to which a rather graceful bridge stands in contradiction. The beast to the left obviously coming out to attack group of men or other beast. Very romantic, cheap drama not convincing, the fantastic note moves along conventional levels as seen in pulp magazines.

Picture 14. Complete blank picture with the exception of light window shade opening against which is silhouetted figure of a human obviously opening the window. Movement of left leg suggesting his getting out of darkness into the light. Face slightly upward turned suggesting joyful new beginning. Conception of whole scene expressed in a fashion, as . . . the early European romanticists did.

Picture 19. Low, one-story house set in winter, storm. Snow very strong movement. Background suggests kinds of strange animals. Stormy, two windows lighted suggesting warmth inside, and home security in contrast to cold and wild movement outside.

Picture 20. Man leaning against lamppost, winter night—obviously big city, man suggesting loneliness, being lost, face hidden only few lines of hat and overcoat accentuated. Background lights of windows which obviously suggest big city and skyscrapers—Position of man in leaning against lamppost that of a man who is not waiting for date but obviously alone and will be alone. . . .

Story Analysis

Picture 1. A young boy sitting in front of a violin spread out on white table, or white linen. It is not clear in the expression of the face if he thinks in glorification and admiration of that what the violin and music could hold for him or if he is bored and in disgust with the lesson he has to take and doesn't want.

Before proceeding to the detailed analysis of the form and content aspects of the story, we will alter the procedure somewhat by going directly to what appears to be the central psychological issue which will serve as hypotheses for later examination. In this instance the author proposes to move quickly into some of this person's personality conflicts and to substantiate them subsequently in the analysis of the story proper. This is done here merely to indicate that the approach to different stories may vary depending upon the certainty with which the interpreter may feel he grasps the meaning lying behind the subject's fantasy. In some instances this meaning becomes clear only after a minute examination of the form and content detail. In some instances, as this one, it strikes the interpreter upon first reading of the story. This does not obviate the necessity for more detailed analysis but does permit one to focus more quickly on the interpretive points.

1. A dominant characteristic of the story is its general form in the continual presentation of alternatives. It is a *table or linen;* it is *glorification or disgust;* the boy *has to take and doesn't want.* These alternatives apply not only to the basic identification of the stimulus but also to the subsequent characterization of the action and its outcome. Before proceeding further, it may be well to suggest that this is a person to whom conflicting alternatives will always be a problem,

whose personality may well be marked by its attraction to opposites.

2. The core of these conflicting alternatives appears to be sexual in nature. This sexual conflict is largely on an idealistic plane, reflecting a pregenital preoccupation with the basic issue of whether woman can be both the Madonna and the sexual object. Integral parts of this basic conflict are several other issues:

a. His male sexual identity: there is considerable confusion on the question of his own masculinity both with regard to his concept of himself as an assertive sexual person and his definition of heterosexual role relationships.

b. His acceptance of his own inner life: he is preoccupied with the definition of his own inner life and confused as to the role it should play in guiding his behavior. This confusion is of a major neurotic quality influencing both his own feelings of personal worth as well as distorting his behavioral relations with the outer world.

3. He has sufficient social awareness to feel he *has to take it.* In other words, he feels impelled to make a formal heterosexual adjustment as well as a conventional social adjustment, even though both are somewhat forced and against his will.

4. There exists for him a strong homosexual attraction. This attraction is disguised from direct awareness in a manner not yet apparent from this story. His behavior, however, is on a heterosexual plane but without ease or satisfaction.

5. The relationship to the mother appears at this point to have been one of considerable coercion but with overt benevolence. This iron-hand-in-velvet-glove relationship has produced no direct maternal hostility, only an inchoate dissatisfaction which now strongly impedes his psychological maturity.

6. The control system of this man is largely an inconsistently organized conscious control. Overt behavior is organized and controlled though strongly symptomatic of the tensions just described. In addition, he has considerable social sophistication in the intellectual bohemian manner.

Let us now return to the data of the story to examine these hypotheses. In this examination it will be apparent that some of these hypotheses flow directly from the data of the story and some are derivatives from the analysis of the hypotheses themselves. To a large extent, the most productive analysis of this story is one which relies heavily upon the dynamic interpretation of content, content associations, and symbolisms. The hypotheses set forth are largely derived in this fashion. Before presenting the logic of these procedures, however, let us examine the more formal and direct aspects of form and content.

7. The plot of the story is incomplete, though the alternatives proposed are usual ones. The basic identification of the stimuli is adequate; the boy and the violin are seen and properly identified and an adequate statement of the relation between them is proposed. These features would suggest a generally adequate ability to deal with reality and a sufficient sense of the common perceptions to permit general social adequacy. Further, he proposes entirely familiar emotional issues, suggesting his familiarity with the commonly held virtues and a preparedness to recognize the usual middle-class dilemmas. These features, plus his ability to present abstract emotions and to propose significant and even rather complex elaborations on his (incomplete) plot, suggest a man of superior intelligence and some advanced education.

8. A special characteristic of his plot is to be found in the many alternatives. Not only is the basic plot formed of two alternatives but so are the details of that plot. In addition, he tends to belabor and emphasize each point: glorification *and* admiration, boredom *and* disgust, has to take *and* doesn't want. It has been suggested that this is a man strongly drawn to conflicting viewpoints. The emphasis which he gives to the alternative parts of these conflicts stresses his preoccupation with them.

9. The entire story might be seen as an incomplete whole response. The fact that he is unable to complete this plot seems related to the accompanying alternatives. He is at home with the statement of problems, not with their resolution. There are many small details, essentially the emphasized elaborations on the details of the plot, which, however, have a very special characteristic. With one exception they are not stimulus-bound details, they are concept-bound details. The ordinary notion of the compulsively detail-conscious person involves an attention to the stimuli details: the strings and bow of the violin, the hair and face and clothes of the boy, etc. However, an equally important approach to detail observation is taken by persons such as Carl whose detail-consciousness is an elaboration of his concepts. Each idea is repeated in a varying form, glorification-admiration, boredom-disgust. This is a quite different frame of mind and suggests a preoccupation with inner states more than a preoccupation with the identification of outer reality. This man, of course, is concerned with both and is also bound to stimulus details. It is of importance, however, that his stimulus-bound details bear a strong pro-

jective selectivity as will be seen in the subsequent analysis of his first sentence and in other stories.

In a sense he uses his stimulus awareness to "prove" his inner preoccupations, giving to his reality perceptions the strong flavor of his inner life. As he perceives this picture, he presents us his view of reality as conflictful, unresolved, and segmented. Outer reality takes on meaning for him more through his projection of inner states than through a system of meaning external to him. As was pointed out, however, this intrusion of his inner states into the orderliness of his perception is not pervasive enough to destroy his identification with the basic stimulus features of reality.

10. A form aspect of his story related to the foregoing remarks is to be seen in his emphasis upon intraception. There is in essence no plot, merely a preoccupation with inner states. He describes no external events and introduces no other figures. He implies a generalized sense of external control (lesson he has to take) but does not personalize or specify any outside events.

11. In spite of the incomplete and fragmental nature of his story, it is not without symmetry; it has a certain internal balance. Even his concluding statement (the lesson he has to take and doesn't want) has a certain succinct harmony. In judging his overt behavior, this ability to give balance to his conflictful emotions should not be overlooked. It is apparent, also, that the phrasing of the problems is presented with some sophistication. This, too, suggests that his behavioral orientation will be influenced by this ability to present issues with some balance and sophistication.

Many of the hypotheses presented in points 1 through 6 are partially evidenced in the discussion of some form characteristics in points 7 through 11. Let us now examine some of the other features of the story.

12. The first sentence of the story is of special interest for two reasons. First, it is a sentence emphasizing entirely the descriptive elements, as opposed to the intraceptive ones in the remainder of the story. With the possible exception of the references to the "expression of the face" and "the violin," it is the only sentence of stimulus description. It is in fact a sentence in which the subject is preoccupied with the detail description. It is done in such a manner as to suggest some particular attraction to the observations made. It is a "sticky" sentence in that the observations are too elaborate for the point made. This suggests a tendency on the part of the subject to project his own feelings readily into external objects and hence to use

objective external events to service his own preoccupations. To a certain extent, this is true of most people, of course. It is suggested here that in this subject the tendency is especially strong and that he will reinterpret and distort outside events, not destroying their reality but always clothing them with the emphasis of his own inner state. This tendency occurs in a more marked fashion in other stories. It is the orientation that lends itself to symbolic statement and symbolic object use.

Second, it is a sentence strongly suggesting a symbolic preoccupation with sexuality. This is an instance of the use of the violin as a sexual symbol. This point has been discussed on pages 91–92.

The point is the same here. Essentially it should be phrased somewhat in this manner. The man is basically preoccupied with some strong emotional issue; hence he utilizes form details in this distorting manner. Given the special attention which he pays to the violin and its setting (spread out on white table or white linen), it seems likely that this symbolizes for him some central problem. The logic from here on depends somewhat upon the sentence following this. However, we may possibly suggest that this problem is most likely of a sexual sort and that the violin is here given phallic implications. The interpretation is on rather filmsy ground, however, unless we can find corroborating evidence. The author would propose that, in this story at least, the evidence is to be found in Carl's concern with the opposed issues of idealization or sexuality phrased in his glorification versus disgust statement. This seems to be a similarly focal issue for him, especially in the light of its central role in the plot and in the double emphasis which he gives to it (glorification *and* admiration, boredom *and* disgust). This is, of course, the Madonna versus sex preoccupation suggested earlier. It provides us with a number of corollary points worth considering.

a. His sexual preoccupation takes the form of basic role preoccupation and reflects an unresolved primary maternal attachment. The logic for this is in part that such a preoccupation usually occurs on a nonsex picture and on one frequently reflecting maternal control concerns.

b. The fact that, on a card generally reflective of some maternal control awareness, he in no way suggests direct hostility to the mother or direct rejection of the imposed task, would eliminate the possibility of direct rejection of the mother. In the light of the idealization formula (glorification-admiration) it seems more likely that a benevolent and protective aura surrounded the mother. That this aura is at

the same time strong and dominant is to be seen both in the awareness of outside control (lesson he has to take) and in the resulting
restraint on his own assertive possibilities. The story is not finished,
the hero shows no active resentment and no action. His phallic assertion is blocked, yet he is sexually preoccupied. This again is a very
important point for predicting his overt behavior in both the social
and sexual areas.

c. The hero of his story is enmeshed in an ideological quandary
most inappropriate to a "young boy." He is inactive, he lacks reasonable assertion. This, in combination with the foregoing, suggests the
male role confusion proposed earlier.

d. It may also be perceived that his internal preoccupation, the intraceptive language, phrases strong personal issues but does so in
rather grand language conceptually removed from direct impulse expression. This issue also never reaches fulfillment. The plot is
blocked, shunted off in the midst of controversy. Straightforward
action is never taken.

e. Yet the story ends with his strong awareness of external control.
In effect, he proposes that the solution is impulse denial and social
conformity. It is of some interest that, in this story so heavily intraceptive, he proposes no assertive, outward-directed impulses. All deal
with the contemplation of the inner states, these being either contradictory or resistive.

We have spent a great deal of time on this single picture. The
objective has been to illustrate a process of interpretation and especially the interrelationships of story element and hypotheses about the
subject. In the following stories, we shall proceed in a less detailed
fashion.

Picture 2. A rural scene showing strong young man plowing a field and
a woman, obviously pregnant, leaning against a tree symbolizing the fertility of earth and simple living as compared to the left, a girl with a
slightly sad sophisticated expression on her face, symbolizing in holding
books in her hands, intellectual learning. It's not quite clear which of both
is giving the preference. The lines of the first scene are much stronger
expressed, the movement—than those of the girl at the left.

1. The sense of a man in active unresolved conflict is again conveyed
in this story. As in the first story, there is no completed plot, no outcome. Within the content given, he sets up alternatives which tend
to opposites.

2. The objective stimuli are described in highly evaluative terms,
showing his strong tendency to permit his inner conflicts to intrude

upon his observation of outer events. In this story, the subject more directly formulates this tendency through his symbolizing references: holding books symbolizes intellectual learning, "pregnant" woman symbolizes fertility of earth. Nothing is simple for this subject. All is surrounded with meaning and personal referents.

3. Yet his observations are of good quality and rather refined in nature. He sees not only the large details of the picture, but a number of small ones as well. He notices "pregnant" woman, the "strong young" man, the "sad sophisticated expression." It would appear, as in number 1, that his preoccupations, while lending a highly personal flavor to his basic observations, do not distort their meaning nor blind him to outer realities. In the identification of his world and in the recognition of his problems, the subject is well skilled. His limitations arise from the obsessive inability to do anything about them.

4. The first observations made by this man are to identify the context (rural scene) and then to equate it with the male which he then describes in highly positive terms. Of importance here is not only the "strong young" description but also that of "plowing." He very seldom suggests a verb that is active and positive. All tend to be intransitive and stressing either conflict or states of being that are passive or conflictful. Yet this man he notices first—before the more generally noticed young woman—and he comments on him positively. This would suggest some positive male attraction and is consistent with the suggestion of male role confusion proposed in 1. It would appear to be the strength and solidity elements of maleness that interest him. It should be noticed, however, that nothing further happens to or with this male figure. He is not involved in further action, he is not related to the other figures. Certainly his experience with older males should be explored in the following stories and the relation to the father studied. At this stage one could propose a strong homosexual attachment that is only partially conscious and generally not carried into overt sex behavior. One would expect a strong but not intimate father experience and some tendency in the subject's life to become attached to older (fatherlike?) males. Considering his symbolizing tendencies and his preference for always attributing special meanings to outer events, it is possible that he also finds himself greatly attracted to social causes, to political groups, and generally to ideologies of social action.

5. The story is essentially an identification of three basic social roles —the strong male, the strong (earth) mother, the sad sophisticated young girl. This selection is an extraordinarily apt one for this sub-

ject, as may be seen from the analysis of story 1 and from subsequent stories. As was proposed in 1, again his conflicts are of basic role-identifications. He experiments and explores these various roles, never daring (no outcome) to carry any one into unequivocal action.

6. The two women presented are again in opposition. For him there appears to be no way of amalgamating the earth with the city, no way of putting sophistication and simple living together. Neither of these women is involved in any action, neither is related to the male figure or to any events outside the stimulus. While he describes the mother-figure somewhat more positively, he is still unable to reject the young woman, making her symbolic of a value (intellectual learning) that he himself holds. Women have disappointed this man, yet have a strong hold on him.

7. The point at which his plot breaks (the lines of the first scene) represents another real problem for him. The question he struggles with is basically this: Will he accept the dominance of the mother-image, which he does not care for, along with the simpler living and peaceful lack of conflict, which he does want? Or will he reject the dominance, lose the peace, and make a same-age heterosexual adjustment—which terrifies him—to the more crackling and sophisticated definition that he makes of same-age women? It would appear that at present he is attempting some artificial amalgamation of these two philosophies.

8. In brief summary of some other features of these two stories, it may be suggested that:

Intelligence is superior.

Intellectual efficiency is hampered by his caution and by the involvement of his inner life in his observations.

Control is primarily a *high conscious* one that does not hide his restlessness. *Inner control* is used experimentally but not effectively. *Outer control* is effective, but forced and marked by his inner preoccupation at the cost of artificiality and depression.

Picture 3BM. Showing girl in crouched position either broken or drunk, lines and movements too crude, vulgarity too plainly stressed. Lines of ass almost obscene. Right hand showing does not follow expression of rest of body.

1. Again the subject presents objective details bearing the high gloss of his preoccupations. In this card, his concerns even more strongly intrude and the evaluations begin to outweigh the objectivity. It would appear that his tendency to project his anxieties into overt

events is somewhat unstable, allowing the occasional break-through of the anxieties themselves. It is thus that his intellectual efficiency would suffer and his overt behavior reflect his biases.

2. The internal stimulus to the break on this picture would appear to be that of pure sexuality, or should we say, impure sexuality. This he presents to us in his analysis of the picture. It is important to note that, while he gains some satisfaction out of describing just how obscene his thoughts are upon perceiving this picture, he clearly rejects it. He also appears to feel ill at ease about the stimulus, calling attention to perceived irregularities in it (arm not follow).

3. The author would see in this response the subject's rejection of direct sexuality and his preference for a somewhat more involved image of sexuality, one possibly more glorified. It is of some interest that the subject becomes involved with sexuality matters on a card more usually reflective of negative, depressed emotions. The connection is perhaps not fortuitous, since certainly his inner life is confused and depressive. It is in fact this intermingling of emotions that confuses him and makes progress so difficult.

4. The observations of overt behavior as being characterized by some social sophistication should again be noted here. His apparent concern with the vulgarity of the picture is a neat twist to the fact that it was his own idea. He is like the man who introduces a joke in questionable taste to an adolescent girl and at the same time attempts to convince her mother that it was really a needed object lesson and thus concludes that the storyteller is a person of great feeling and sensitivity.

5. We have noted his refusal to give regular outcomes. Another phrasing of this tendency is suggested at this point: he prefers not to come to emotional grips with his problems but rather to wallow in them. He examines his emotional problems continually, lives them out daily most likely, but does not proceed from this recognition to any attempt at solution.

Picture 4. Man and woman, man turning away with vague expression on his face. Woman obviously wants to hold him. In background another woman with alluring look and face could be reflection in mirror. The whole very cheap sentimentality expressed as in common magazine illustrations.

1. Here we are presented with the second stimulus of possible heterosexual relations, number 2 being the first. In it, as in 2 and 1, he again tells us of the two kinds of women—the "restraining" but "vague" woman, and the "alluring" but "cheap." He is again unable to make a choice or to reconcile the two.

2. Structurally this is again an incomplete story, but still as a beginning not at all bad. His imagination is unusual though burdensome. There are a number of original touches to his stories, though they are ponderous, even at times pompous. A potentially creatively gifted person, he has been so burdened by his inability to give adequate structure to his inner conflicts that he can only strain, proposing intriguing settings but being unable to implement them and carry them into action.

3. He also suffers from another curse, that of suspecting that his own struggles are not worth while. Here, as in story 3BM, even as he phrases for himself his own dilemma, he feels obliged to reject his own formulation as "cheap sentimentality." His own sophistication defeats him.

Picture 5. Woman opening door to room of rather orderly fashion coming out of the dark, light in her face and body, obviously warm and casted upon her from inside of room, flowers on table, lamp and other rather dull settings. Expression on woman's face not quite satisfying, half tired, half asking. Movement clumsy.

1. The organization of this story is only fair, with no ending and no basic plot development. The identification of the stimulus is highly elaborate, but he appears not to have the conviction to go on with this partially identified mother-image. In a sense, the draw of the mother-figure is so great that it paralyzes him. Even here, though, he must see ambivalence, half asking, half tired, yet "obviously warm." He is unable to deal with this picture, suggesting again the strong retaining mother tie that prohibits him from exploring.

2. It is noteworthy that he sees this woman as "coming out of the dark," a possible reference to the nostalgic past. It suggests again the dependence of this man upon his imagery of the past and his failure to cope with present realities in terms of the present. He lives out his past conflicts seeing always the past as the referent, not the present. This is at least in part the reason for his refusal to give plots with significant futures. His preoccupation is with identifying basic relationships; he has no energy left to imagine or plan for a future. In a sense, he appears to feel that all will be well if he can magically immobilize the past by identifying it.

Picture 6BM. Young man, old woman, both obviously at the end of an argument, both with determined face, face of man insistent, face of woman horrified, and turned away. Suggestion of her hands that she is weeping over man in movement of leaving. [How end?] He will leave.

Picture 7BM. Faces of two men, one young, one old. Expression of old man's face tired, and knowing, obviously talked to the young man, young man disgusted and sad, could be a scene between doctor and patient or father and son. [No end?] No.

1. The two stories are presented together since they appear to reflect a number of significant parental attitudes. Picture 6BM may be seen as another portrayal of the mother-image, and 7BM, the father-image. In 6BM, also, Carl for the first time gives an ending, though under pressure. This can be viewed as a statement of his positive attachment to the mother-image and at the same time a statement of the real emotional distance between them. They are both strong and headed in different directions. In a sense this is a little bravado. He pretends that he leaves home by choice and through a conflict of strong wills. The very fact that he must dismiss this issue—where he is so willing to stay with all others—through the cutoff statement, "He will leave," suggests that he is uncomfortable with it. Normally, endings can be regarded as suggesting that the subject can adequately deal with the issue at hand. In this instance, however, since it is his only ending in the entire series and the other evidence of unresolved maternal ties is so overwhelming, the writer would view this quite differently.

Picture 6BM is in a way a very sad story in which it should be noted he is not facetious. This is real and cannot be dismissed.

2. Picture 7BM shows the father-image. In it he presents the older man as strong and knowing but having no basic tie to the young man. Again he refuses to end the story. He can in a sense replace this image with symbolically related strong masculine imagery. It is suggested that the father was a strong and dominant man to whom the subject wished but was unable to establish a close tie.

3. In this subject one would expect the residual parental imagery to be rather more reflective of actual early relationships than would be true in many other cases. Carl portrays past-oriented events so readily, does not work at changing events to suit his current pleasure —little action, figures do not exert desires and motives, no outcomes. He is so exposed to his nostalgia that the images he presents of father and mother prototypes should be fairly direct.

Picture 9BM. Scene of several men sleeping in open fields, could be farmers, . . . resting while harvesting, bodies all heavy suggesting sturdiness and position suggesting previous heavy work; though hands of man in front too fine for hard labor. Man in back has Negro features but seems unlikely he is on account of his physically close position to white man. Otherwise whole picture rather convincing.

1. This is the only picture for which the subject expresses direct liking. Unfortunately, the subject was not asked for best- and least-liked pictures. We would expect this to be one of his best liked. However, he gives us ample evidence within the story. It is, of course, "on the whole rather convincing," something no other picture except possibly 6BM has been for him. It is also a picture upon which clear positive values emerge; men are doing constructive things, they have some positive virtues, there is some interaction taking place that is described positively and not rejected. He sees different kinds of men: one has fine hands, one could be Negro. He does not approach this with the fixed stereotypes presented on cards of females. This of course suggests some interest and realistic knowledge of the masculine category.

2. The homosexual conflict is again reflected and yet its expression denied. He examines the possibility carefully, in his attention to the physical proximity of the men, and decides against it.

3. This picture suggests an attribute we have not specifically observed before—a tenderness and a softness of emotion which would appear to be possible primarily in connection with males.

Picture 10BM. Man and girl in intimate close position, both have eyes closed, very sensual expression in both faces suggesting emotions . . . though eyebrows of man have a rather ugly knowing movement, face of girl especially . . . that eyelid and eye suggesting sort of intimate melting away.

1. This requires little comment. It is a repetition of his earlier definition of:

a. Sexuality as bad and ugly.

b. Intimacy as sexual.

c. Passivity as having attraction.

2. It does further suggest an intensity of feeling noted earlier, an interest in deeper emotions. It is an interest, however, that is badly mixed up with his own complex emotions.

Picture 11. Jesus. This is wonderful! Fantastic scene showing high mountains or rocks, with strange prehistorical beasts, whole scene suggesting prehistoric chaos, to which a rather graceful bridge stands in contradiction. The beast to the left obviously coming out to attack group of men or other beast. Very romantic, cheap drama not convincing, the fantastic note moves along conventional levels as seen in pulp magazines.

1. This is possibly the second picture, along with 9BM, that he actually likes. It is certainly the only other picture to which he expresses some clear positive affect. It is noteworthy that it is a

picture with no people, on it he can allow some emotion to escape.

2. The ideas that soon arise, however, are aggressive—beasts attacking "men or other beasts." This picture is one often readily arousing unconscious emotions. For him, aggression and attack arise in what the writer would call a masculine context. If this is a feasible hypothesis, it would suggest that the subject perceives his father to have been rough and callous in his treatment of him. This results not in complete rejection but in a kind of fascination with strength and power.

3. This picture, in its enthusiasm for unstimulated (no people) aggression and fantasy, suggests that Carl's drive for outer world contact is low and that he prefers his own fantasy of escape to idealistic protection and warmth. This has been suggested with other pictures by his refusal to put people into action, by dismissing emotions that appear to be connected with the outer world (of magazine illustration), by refusing to deal with future action.

Picture 14. Complete blank picture with the exception of light window shade opening against which is silhouetted figure of a human obviously opening the window. Movement of left leg suggesting his getting out of darkness into the light. Face slightly upward turned suggesting joyful new beginning. Conception of whole scene expressed in a fashion, as . . . the early European romanticists did.

1. He becomes very "corny" in the style of his own rejected "cheap magazine illustration" whenever he deals with a new and hopeful idea. He is interested but ill at ease with the notion of a "joyful new beginning." His approach to it is the same heavy intellectualization seen before.

2. This suggests how he himself can be embarrassed by traditional views of future planning and outer world success, the theme most frequently raised by this picture in middle-class males and one with which he plays embarrassedly.

3. The person coming out of the dark idea has been presented before by him—in 6BM—in the mother context. The content of the two is not greatly different. This is of relevance in that he presents the idea of new beginnings not in its usual context of an assertive, energetic new look at things, accompanied by a determination to overcome all obstacles. Rather for him it is a female thing, characterized by new lights being thrown on him, still passive and inactive. He is in fact not even sure it's a man, it is only a "human" though he uses the masculine pronoun subsequently.

Picture 19. Low, one-story house set in winter, storm. Snow very strong movement. Background suggests kinds of strange animals. Stormy, two windows lighted suggesting warmth inside, and home security in contrast to cold and wild movement outside.

His nostalgia and regressive preoccupation are here more boldly stated. But again still there is no plot, no action, no future, merely identification of an issue. The inside, to which he proposes no entrance, is warm. The outside is not only cold and wild but is full of strange animals, the people with whom he must deal daily and cannot understand. In spite of the warm inside, this is a story of despair. The warm house is over the horizon, out of sight. He is left only with the strong movement of the strange animals.

Picture 20. Man leaning against lamppost, winter night—obviously big city, man suggesting loneliness, being lost, face hidden only few lines of hat and overcoat accentuated. Background lights of windows which obviously suggest big city and skyscrapers—Position of man in leaning against lamppost that of a man who is not waiting for date but obviously alone and will be alone. . . .

This again is its own comment. Here he phrases directly the loneliness apparent throughout his other stories. The lonely and dissatisfied man waiting for the woman who will be to him mother, sex, and father. He knows it is a futile watch. This he does not treat facetiously. It is too close to home.

No additional test data are available on Carl. A several hours' recording of his own life history with some observations on his present life will now be presented briefly. The selections are in part disguised, although the quotations are verbatim.

Selections from Carl's Autobiography

Carl was born of German parents, then living in Austria because of the father's business. This business was sufficiently prosperous to permit them to live in a respectable suburb and employ two servants. He reports that his father was a person of some military importance during World War I and Carl appears to have been impressed with the glamor of his military activities. In reporting on him Carl recalls particularly how successful he was and how busy. His many activities at home and abroad are stressed and there is a mysterious reference to his "espionage" connections. "He wasn't kind, however, but he was smart and he was bright." He was educated in that he "had traveled and been abroad."

"My mother was a lovely woman, pleasant and nice but not educated. I guess their marriage was average. My father probably would have liked it different but it wasn't and he went along with it."

"There was a lot of tension in the home during the war. My father hated my older brother and made it pretty clear. My mother loved him, however. She was a warm and loving person, though not intellectual, and she couldn't keep up with father."

Carl's interest in the humanities always struck his parents, and especially his father, as strange. The fact that Carl's school grades were bad did not help. When Carl graduated from the Gymnasium he wanted to go to a special school for art and literature. But his father objected and wanted him to go to a military academy instead. It appears that "father then didn't want to support me anymore. In fact, he had really told me to get out, get a job, and support myself." Carl got into the special school but was soon expelled from it, which increased his father's resentment.

And this time, Carl stresses the role of his father in throwing him out of the home. "My mother was a very simple and very kind and a very warm person, but of a rather low intellectual level. My position to my father was, of course, that of an enemy. To me he was the man who didn't know me, didn't want to know me, but who punished me occasionally. He thought a man should have a beautiful handwriting and I didn't. He despised me for that and made me do little laborious things I hated to do. I remember at that time I desired the love of my mother and being as I was disappointed because she felt much stronger for my brother, I was a long time suffering from that. To me she was the acme of warmth and kindness. She was the only feminine member of our household, the rest all being masculine and more so because my father played so dominant a role."

Carl was especially fond of his older brother who was "very, very beautiful. He was wonderful to look at and a great social success. . . . My relation to him was always a very complicated one. There were times when I was sincerely in love with him and times when I deeply hated him. For him I was always a charming young man who believed in things. The most complicated time was when we were in love with the same girl. In practice it was that we all three, the girl and we two, were living and loving together and being very active about it. We were all very mixed. At times we were very, very joyful. Then at other times terribly sad."

Carl reports no other sexual affairs with such enthusiasm, saying about it rather that his subsequent relations with women were "rather flimsy with a strong romantic overtone," through reporting that sexual intercourse was always an easy thing to arrange.

Following this he took a number of jobs which he vaguely reports as involving him with many rich and important people. After a period he decided to go "back to nature." "You know, leave the big wicked city and sort of go out where it's simple and everything." To do this he went to a rural part of Austria and got a "job on a farm" from an advertisement he had seen in a newspaper. It turned out to be a large estate, the owner of which wanted an administrative assistant. "Well, it was really something. I was really like a prince. I had a horse all my own and lived in the manor house like a lord. He treated me really like a son, but he always kept his distance. Well, it wasn't really like a son, but it was close enough." Carl describes in more pleasurable detail this episode in his life.

Subsequently Carl reports a series of glamorous events, at least in part true apparently, in which he again mingles with salon society, travels a great deal, and does important tasks. After a similar series of episodes he leaves Europe and comes directly to New York. There he soon locates another landowner who hires him for a task similar to the earlier one in Austria. Here he reports a similar enjoyment and reflects on the joy of the "simple people, farmers and the like." He stayed six months, then returned to New York, and after about a year of odd jobs secured a position which paid him enough to live on. He still holds this position.

At all stages of his career, Carl comments on the "confused state" of his social relations, emphasizing that he knew all kinds of people.

In the past few years, Carl has been notable for his trim young mistresses who do not appear to last very long. He paints as a hobby, primarily landscapes, but occasionally uses his mistresses as models. In these paintings, always dark and gloomy in mood and color, these svelte mistresses appear very buxom and voluptuous. His present social relations are always on the fringe of the bohemian groups within which his easy and sophisticated verbalization is welcomed. He has shown no "progress" in his work, though his position appears stable.

CHAPTER 10

Charlie,

a Dakota Sioux of fourteen

Charlie is a boy of fourteen, a fullblood Dakota Sioux * who told his stories in English to the adaptation of the Thematic Apperception Technique reported by Henry.[120] After Charlie's record and its analysis the original TAT report will be presented, as well as some selected observations from his life history and his Rorschach.

Charlie's record is a short one. However, we should not assume that it is therefore useless. Rather, we should examine closely the same attributes suggested for other stories, attempting to see if the brevity is a result of some special blocking or refusal which may indeed reduce the utility of the record. On the other hand, it may be that the record reflects a tightening and condensation which results in stories still being usable and reflective of individual personality. It is not our purpose here to examine in detail the characteristics of records from other societies. For this the reader is referred to such reports as Henry,[120] Gladwyn and Sarason,[VIE3] and Lessa and Spiegelman.[VIE10] In this chapter the author wishes merely to show how such limited records yield productive material and to suggest that the principles and pro-

* This case was a part of the Research on Indian Education, a joint research of the Committee on Human Development of the University of Chicago and the U. S. Office of Indian Affairs.

cedures of interpretation are not specific to the Murray TAT, nor to stories told in the romantic mold of the elaborated format of beginning-middle-end.

TAT Record

Picture 1. He's telling him something. Not to stole things. Not to do anything they shouldn't. The men don't do anything.

(Picture 2 was not given to this subject.)

Picture 3. He's trading a horse with him. They don't talk. They use their hands to talk. They know what they say each other. It's an Indian horse. Trade with that white man. He want the horse.

Picture 4. Praying. Beside a pueblo wall. He's asking for food, for money.

Picture 5. In Mexico. Desert. There's no food for a cow, so it is dead. That's the people's land and fence.

Picture 6. He's too old so he can't hardly even walk. He sit on a rock. That's in a pueblo house. He's sleepy. He sits there . . . not doing anything but sleeping.

Picture 7. They come from Mexico. Some Indian women going to town. Some cars in the road. One coming. One going. This is broke [points to fact that there is no line between horses and wagon]. The wagon is going but the wheels don't start. That's all.

Picture 8. They are talking to each other. One is a woman, one man. Talks about things coming. A war has happened. They are fighting and they get man like him. That's all I know.

Picture 9. They are dancing. Those other two have apples. The man is a clown. Having a good time. He mark his face. That's all.

Picture 10. Those women making bread with corn. People sitting around watching how they make it. No, they are making soap with soap weed, they don't want that boy to be watching. He sit way down. He is bad boy and he don't do what they tell him. He's lonesome and thinks that he shouldn't do what he do.

Picture 11. He's a pueblo boy of Mexico. He's standing there watching the land. It's desert down there and the cow can't eat food so they die. The Indian boy is watching the cow skulls. He is lonesome he stay there and going home after.

Picture 12. The Indian boy is bad and doesn't like to live with his mother and he sleeps alone and he runs away from home. He is sleeping beside and along with—there's a snake and bat coming, lots of bats trying to eat him and after he was a good boy. He's sleeping there and all the bats and snake try to eat him, so he went home again. He's a good boy when he went home. That's all.

Story Analysis

Picture 1. He's telling him something. Not to stole things. Not to do anything they shouldn't. The men don't do anything.

1. This is a story of the tense control of anticipated aggression. There is no necessary suggestion of aggression in the picture. The picture sets a scene of adult-adolescent relations and, for Charlie, this becomes a scene of potential aggression and negative external sanction. To it, Charlie is "trigger-happy"; he jumps immediately to protect all inner aggression and to decry any possibility of transgression on the part of the adolescents.

2. This story, though brief, does have a plot. There is a "beginning" in an outside inference (He's telling, etc.) followed by a reaction and a statement of "future" (The men don't do anything). His observation of the stimulus is adequate and his treatment of it, while cryptic, nonetheless adequately explains the stimulus as presented. He even provides a number of elaborations, though since they do not basically advance the plot nor add anything new, the author thinks them only sufficient to justify a suggestion of average intelligence (IQ of 95–105).

3. The elaborations, it is to be noted, are basically the second and third short phrases (not to stole things, not to do anything they shouldn't). This story may be one representation of reality as seen by Charlie. Notice that three-fourths of this segment are concerned with admonitions which define the outer world as prohibitive and restraining and one-fourth is concerned with the denial of any internal personal involvement with this outer world (the men don't do anything).

4. Certainly one may suggest that the social world is for him a difficult one, since he sees it as so generally negative, and that controlling his own antisocial aggression is a constant problem. A point for further exploration is the question of the basic assertion or passivity of this boy. While aggression seems the more likely overt social problem, it should again be observed that the first three-fourths of this story is an attempt to get the outer world to define structures for him. It appears to define it through denial, which perhaps has its own implications for Charlie's reactive aggression, but Charlie is nonetheless looking for structure outside of himself.

5. This is a picture of two adolescents and hence may be expected to suggest some peer attitude on the part of a fourteen-year-old. In

Charlie's case, it is difficult to know whether peer attitudes are relevant here or not. They appear to be overwhelmed by his general adult world apprehension. Probably all we can say at this time is that no special attributes are suggested for the adolescents; they merely "don't do anything." There is no interaction between them—interaction is all between the man and the adolescents acting as a single unit (they). One would not expect basically good peer relations, though data for this point are only suggestive.

6. In general, this story brings up some other points to be checked. Given his inner restlessness and the dominance of his anticipation of the need for control, aggressive impulsive outbursts may be a regular problem for him. It is also possible that this very "trigger-happy" quality may suggest that Charlie is very vulnerable to emotional trauma and that his defenses are inadequate.

7. It may also be noted that he identifies only "the men," and this only once, calling the characters at other times merely "he" and "him" and "they." Such refusals to make more specific role-identifications often reflect marked social unease and personal unrest. This would, of course, seem consistent with the other suggestions about his peer relations and possible assertive outbursts.

Picture 3. He's trading a horse with him. They don't talk. They use their hands to talk. They know what they say each other. It's an Indian horse. Trade with that white man. He want the horse.

1. This story is of special interest for a number of reasons having to do with unusual details of content. The first of importance is that of his remarks about "they don't talk. They use their hands to talk. They know what they say each other." This is a most unusual detail, unusual for this group of records. Such unique details generally suggest some special focus of attention on the part of the subject. It is to be noted, however, that the observation is not "wrong." It is an entirely possible and logical observation. Two special features of the remarks warrant comment. The first is to question the personal logic behind the choice of talking in unusual ways. It suggests some sort of preoccupation with talking. The direct association to some physical attribute (they use their hands) may suggest that the inability to talk (they don't talk) has for the subject some physical connection. It is, of course, a temptation to propose some sort of speech handicap. This is a probable guess though there are undoubtedly other situations that might produce this kind of preoccupation with communication.

The second aspect of these remarks to be noted is the reference to "they know what they say." Here, as in the foregoing instance, the objective should be to try and deduce the logic of mind that would prompt this concern with being understood. To some extent it is a part of the concern with talking. In addition, however, the author would propose that Charlie feels somewhat unappreciated and looked down upon by his immediate associates. It would seem he is trying to say that, in spite of being a little "different," he really is like other people—he, too, can understand. It may be that he is thought of by others as rather independent, yet he feels lonely in his autonomy.

2. The notation of using the hands for sign language, in spite of its idiosyncratic aspects, is also a rather keen observation. A feature of special interest is that he uses this observation to describe relationships between people. This may suggest to us that Charlie is a rather acute and observant boy. It is clear, however, that he has inhibited his expressive and affiliative interests, most likely for specific emotional reasons.

3. This story is one of some action, containing the same generally tense feeling as story number 1. The specific contents referred to suggest that at least part of his anxiety stems from definite interpersonal difficulties and possibly some speech disturbance.

Picture 4. Praying. Beside a pueblo wall. He's asking for food, for money.

1. This response is at best an incomplete story—the portrayal of a boy deprived of affection (food) and social support (money); certainly an image of some underlying passivity with an overlay of reactive hostility is suggested here.

2. The outer world, seen here only by implication, is perceived by Charlie as depriving and disorderly. As has been suggested, the "asking for food" could be taken as a reflection of a basic affect deprivation. Similarly, the "for money" may suggest not so much deprivation as a lack of order and system in his life. Both of these are consistent with the previous pictures.

3. The observation "pueblo wall" is of interest here. It occurs elsewhere in his stories. The writer is unable to propose any specific meaning for these observations, and feels that the data from the stories are sufficiently explained without them. However, if he were to hazard an interpretation, always dangerous with limited data, he would select the "foreign" aspect of Charlie's references to "pueblo" and "Mexico," and suggest that this is one way for Charlie to reject both some of his inner feelings of deprivation (picture 3BM) and, in

pictures 5 and 7, his profound dissatisfaction with the social world about him. If this is at all reasonable, another facet of this technique should be noted. It is, in a sense, a displacement at a rather crude level. In this case, may it not be suggested that Charlie similarly displaces other aspects of his behavior. This would suggest, for example, that his early preoccupation with aggression may be similarly handled, i.e., he displays his anger erratically and often in inappropriate contexts. This possibility further extends the earlier feeling of Charlie as a person of rather unstable emotional reactions, given to erratic and inconsistent overt behavior.

4. It should not be overlooked that this story rather implements the hypothesis earlier phrased regarding Charlie's basically dependent orientation.

Picture 5. In Mexico. Desert. There's no food for a cow, so it is dead. That's the people's land and fence.

1. Charlie again places his story in "foreign" territory which he has never visited. He then proposes basically the same definition of the surrounding world as he did previously: it is depriving, "dead," and without support.

2. This story is also of interest for its reflection of his intellectual approach. It is basically a response of identification without much plot development. Yet the identity which he chooses to give is an emotionally loaded one. His reference to the dead cow and to the connection of this with "no food" is logical but also reflective of his strong deprivation anxieties. It may be suggested that his intellectual pursuits, most probably reflected in schoolwork, are powerfully driven by his anxiety. In the light of the generally constricted tenor of his stories, we would presume some strong compulsive elements in his intellectual and work relations.

3. The references to "no food for a cow" will bear further observation. As in his earlier detail regarding the "talking," this observation is correct enough logically yet seems strongly idiosyncratic in some way. Its special importance seems to lie not so much in its deprivation aspects already observed but in the implications of sensitive awareness of action sequences with personal referents. In a sense, it requires a fairly marked sense of inner awareness to project this sequence of food absence in a picture so devoid of action. (Recall that the "cow" is merely a skull.) It may well be that this boy has rather vivid fantasy which he inhibits.

4. In brief summary of some of the structural aspects of his personality, it would appear that:

a. His control system strongly emphasizes unformalized constriction.
b. His outer control is poor and erratic.
c. His inner control is overly active but ineffective

The total result of such a pattern would be a boy intensely preoccupied with inner issues, strongly trying to control all personal expression, but finding himself unable to keep either his overt behavior or his anxiety satisfactorily under control.

Picture 6. He's too old so he can't hardly even walk. He sit on a rock. That's in a pueblo house. He's sleepy. He sits there . . . not doing anything but sleeping.

1. This story again emphasizes the nonactive elements. It is also a story marked by a strong interest in the repetition of the nonaction features of the stimulus: he can't walk, he sits, he's sleepy, not doing anything. In a sense, Charlie finds this very attractive and clings to it. Again this emphasizes the strongly emotionally driven flight into constriction. It is in a sense an action paralysis which only partly conceals his restless agitation.

2. The definition of age is also worth noting here. To some extent, this reflects Charlie's definition of the outer world as depriving and without basic order. He now presents us with a picture of old age in which the primary virtue appears to be the noninteraction. It seems a rather hopeless image for an Indian boy to have, that of the older generation as lifeless and inactive. If this is a reasonable suggestion, then there may well be somewhat of a self-destructive quality in his deprivation concerns. In any event, it would seem that the adult world holds very little positive imagery for Charlie and can do little to make him hope that his problems will be solved by "growing up."

Picture 7. They come from Mexico. Some Indian women are going to town. Some cars in the road. One coming. One going. This is broke (points to fact that there is no line between horses and wagon). The wagon is going but the wheels don't start. That's all.

1. The two small details of observation strike one first here. He first points to a place in the drawing where the equipment is "broke." This is in fact "true" since the line drawing actually is incomplete at this point. He is, however, the only person to have noticed it. He is again bothered that the "wheles don't start." Both of these further

strengthen the impression of Charlie's constriction, his compulsive defense system, and his strong underlying unrest.

2. Certainly his intellectual efficiency is poor, being too readily influenced by his compulsive fears.

3. Basic stimulus identification is adequate, except that no plot or time sequence develops. There is an awareness of movement, but no translating of this into the passage of time. It is of interest that in such a story Charlie should observe the wheels that "don't start." This is most likely a feeling that Charlie has; he is in movement but somehow getting nowhere. This suggestion of the possible qualitative meaning of the "don't start" observation should not obscure the fact that it is not at all a bad observation. The line drawing indeed is not good at this point, not adequately conveying movement in the wheels. Charlie is again, however, the only subject to notice it, the only subject who is unable to accept easily the illusion of movement implied by other aspects of the picture. This awareness of blockage and incompleteness is part of his feeling of unrest.

4. Some special attribute toward women is partially suggested by Charlie's reference to "some Indian women." This appears to suggest some special attitude formation for two reasons: first, it is the only category of person, among several logically possible ones, that he mentions; and second, having selected them, he refuses to carry on the plot with them. It is possibly not irrelevant that on this card which he identifies with "women going" he also sees so much disorder and incompleteness—broken whippletree, wheels not starting. This clearly requires exploration in cards where more direct discussion of women takes place.

Picture 8. They are talking to each other. One is a woman, one man. Talks about things coming. A war has happened. They are fighting and they get man like him. That's all I know.

1. This is a fairly active story; things go on, time passes. It is also the first story which he has chosen to stop in this fashion. Others merely end, this one he stops deliberately with the "that's all I know" reference. This suggests the story is of some special importance to him. The story is not only active, it is also a "war" and "fighting" story.

2. The basic stimulus identification is of some special interest. The card presents two figures. The first is a woman. She is the taller and more prominent part of the picture. In these Indian groups, she is

frequently seen either as a mother or at least as an older women behaving in a "motherly" way. The second figure is a male, clearly subordinate physically in the picture and more generally seen as a "son" or "boy." Yet Charlie insists upon equating them. They are talking, he reports, a statement of equality. Further they are "one woman, one man." Charlie is perfectly able to distinguish "man" from "boy" and does so in other stories. But here, directly confronted with what is usually taken as a mother-son picture, he promotes the son and insists upon equality.

It may be that the relationship to his mother is a difficult one for him and one marked by some open uneasiness and resentment. It is again no accident that the mother-son card should be the one Charlie selects to tell a "war and fighting" story.

Picture 9. They are dancing. Those other two have apples. The man is a clown. Having a good time. He mark his face. That's all.

1. The story has no basic plot, unless we would accept "having a good time" as sufficient. Yet this is still a fairly active story, with full identification of the characters in a way that implies movement—dancing, good time, a clown, mark his face. Yet he is still not indicating interaction between them. This attitude, which we have also seen in other stories, seems to imply a lack of easy and spontaneous social interaction yet also suggests some ready emotionality. He is emotionally labile, yet not at ease in social interaction, either with his peers or adults.

2. "The man is a clown" requires some attention. It is one of the few statements about an older male that would give us a picture of Charlie's image of his father. In 1 he presented us with the strong and stern adult male, in 6 with an old and inactive male, and now here with a busy clown. In picture 3 there are indeed two men, but since the basic issue here for Charlie appears not to be the adult interaction, the author would prefer to treat it as secondary in developing a picture of the father-image. Given these data (and more should be available from card 10) it would seem likely that the relationships to the father are compounded of three elements:

a. Some positive affect that is more beneficial than the attitude toward the mother.

b. Some confusion as to whether the father is a firm person or not—a mixture of authority and clown?

c. Some general feeling, also attributed to society at large, that the father is a man without plans and system and hence a person who can provide no effective guidelines to adult life.

3. Charlie's reference to the many external attributes of these figures, noticeable also in 7 and 8, would suggest that his general drive toward outer world contact is fairly high. His inability to put his characters in interaction and his failure at plot development would imply that this drive is inhibited. To a large extent this inhibition would appear to be due not merely to his confused emotional state but also to a real absence of a sense of direction and purpose.

Picture 10. Those women making bread with corn. People sitting around watching how they make it. No, they are making soap with soap weed, they don't want that boy to be watching. He sit way down. He is bad boy and he don't do what they tell him. He's lonesome and thinks that he shouldn't do what he do.

1. This family scene is perceived by Charlie to revolve basically around a busy family and a rejected boy. Individual figures within the family become blurred for Charlie when this topic is discussed. He presents us here directly with an important part of the picture of him already developed—the part of him that is lonely, guilty, and feeling rejected. It is important here that no one in the group is seen by him as helpful or in any other way related to him. This would tend to substantiate the image of the mother as negative. It should be noted that the father, of whom there is an adequate representation in the picture, is also not singled out. This would tend to corroborate the feeling that the father is not entirely helpful and not perceived basically as a strong figure.

2. This is his longest and most involved story so far and it is a story of home and family. It may suggest that the home is for him the most stable place. Considering his parental images and the feeling of rejection he attaches to the home, this is not much refuge.

3. The guilt which this "bad boy" feels may in part explain the suggested tendency to aggressive outbursts. He is a lonely and impulsive boy whose defenses tend to reactive aggression.

Picture 11. He's a pueblo boy of Mexico. He's standing there watching the land. It's desert down there and the cow can't eat food so they die. The Indian boy is watching the cow skulls. He is lonesome. He stay there and going home after.

1. Here the picture of the lone boy in a deserted world appears to strike home. It has sufficient meaning for Charlie so that he actually tells a story, with a form approximating the requested beginning-

middle-end format. And in it his real plight is apparent. He is, as he himself says, a lonely boy watching an outer world that offers him nothing. In this circumstance, he is lonely and will go home. But home is really only a place.

2. Charlie's second reference to the absence of food and subsequent death re-enforces our earlier feeling that he is prone to have self-destructive fantasies.

Picture 12. The Indian boy is bad and doesn't like to live with his mother and he sleeps alone and he runs away from home. He is sleeping beside and along with—there's a snake and bat coming, lots of bats trying to eat him and after he was a good boy. He's sleeping there and all the bats and snake try to eat him, so he went home again. He's a good boy when he went home. That's all.

1. This ambiguous picture becomes for Charlie a statement of many of his basic underlying fears—the fear of being destroyed and the hopelessness of his single refuge, the home.

2. Sexual anxiety seems also to be suggested here. It would appear to take the form of fear of his own sexuality and his confusion about the meaning of maleness. It seems to be related to his inability to accept his mother and at present takes the form of teasing attacks on girls.

TAT Analysis Summary

Mental approach

Level. Charlie's intellectual level is average to high average (95–105).

Efficiency. His efficiency is poor and intellectual performance is upset by his emotional instability. He has a tendency to be a bit labored and artificial in his intellectual performance which will reduce the general level of his output. He tends to notice details which hamper his observation of the whole.

Creativity

His creativity is not more than average though it is difficult to estimate because of his rather vivid fantasy life. The author would say that not only does his escapist fantasy life become confused with his creativity but whatever tendencies toward creativity and originality may exist are denied overt expression.

Behavioral approach

General. Charlie's overt behavioral pattern is rather confused in the TAT. He is quite aggressive in dealing with his peers and is generally thought of as an aggressive and difficult boy to handle. This aggression is somewhat impulsive and is largely reactive in origin. Charlie is having a pretty difficult time getting along with people in his immediate environment and has almost no real contact with them.

Peers. Peer relationships are very poor. Not only does he have very few friends but probably has trouble keeping them. His relationship to girls is a specific problem at present. This is confused with his own sexual anxiety and probably finds expression in avoidance of girls and/or, considering his tendency toward reactive aggression, in aggression somewhat impulsively directed against them.

Adults. Adult relationships is the one possible area of human contacts which gives Charlie any relief, though this is a pretty meager one. He does not seem to be rebelling against their control and perhaps recognizes their general support as his only safety. He seems to be looking to the adults in a rather immature way for protection though he is very suspicious of the affection that goes along with it.

School. School adjustment is not apparent from the TAT. The author would anticipate that his intellectual work could not be very good, both because of his poor efficiency and because of the fact that the majority of his energy is directed into his overt behavior difficulties.

Family dynamics

Relation to parents. The relationship to the mother is similar to that already mentioned for adult relationships in general. He seems to look to her, as an adult, for some protection, but is unsure of her affection. The writer would propound that she is not an overly dominant person though very incautious in her treatment of Charlie. She has offended Charlie and he cannot accept her as a mother, though he has no hostility toward her. The father relationship seems to be a little better though not much worth counting on. He is felt as dominant and as the authority of the family.

Family atmosphere. Home seems to be Charlie's only refuge in what is for him a pretty difficult world. This implies that the home is the lesser of two evils rather than that it is a very wholesome or satisfying place. One doubts if either the mother or the father are model parents in any sense of the term, and while they may appear fairly adequate on the surface are doing a pretty poor job of dealing with Charlie. They seem to be riding roughshod over him continually and perhaps unknowingly pricking at his tender spots. Charlie is both too sensitive and too afraid of his own aggression to be able to emotionally handle too strict or aggressive parents. He needs far more succorance and protection than either parent is able to genuinely give.

Inner adjustment

Basic emotional attitude. Charlie's basic emotional attitude seems to be slightly passive and somewhat regressive, in spite of his impulsivity and overt aggression.

Impulse life. He has a fairly free and vital inner life which he has not yet denied although it finds expression only in his impulsiveness and aggression.

System of control. High inner control of poor quality and poor outer control giving rise to impulsiveness; conscious control is of a poor quality but seems to be used almost to the extent of constriction.

Anxiety. There is both diffuse anxiety and specific sexual anxiety present in his TAT record. (See also "Sexual anxiety.")

Adjustment mechanism. Reactive aggression, regressive fantasies and actions, self-destruction fantasies, and constriction represent the rather poorly organized nature of Charlie's defenses.

Emotional reactivity. Charlie's interpersonal relations are nonexistent. He is afraid of people and is unable to make any sort of sound emotional ties with them. He seems never to have had any really satisfactory relations with adults or with his peers over a long enough time to give him any confidence in that kind of relationship.

Maturity. His whole personality pattern is on a very immature level: his impulsiveness, his regressive tendencies, and his poor system of control are all evidence of this.

Emotional reactivity

Drive to outer world. Charlie's drive toward the outer world is quite strong and, while he is very sensitive to outer world stimuli and other people, he is inhibiting any direct expression of it. He is unspontaneous, markedly limited in personal freedom of action.

Sexual anxiety

There is specific sexual anxiety which is greatly confused in Charlie's mind with his own feelings of aggression and attack.

Summary

Charlie is an adolescent boy whose past emotional history has given him very little feeling of security or personal freedom of action to attack his current emotional problems. He is a fairly observant boy whose insecurity has forced him to rigorously inhibit any expression of his spontaneous or affiliative tendencies. He is a very lonely and anxious boy who has no real emotional ties to lend him support; he feels unappreciated and unloved by the world, yet wants very much to be loved and reassured. There is a specific suggestion that his speech difficulty has been an acute source of disturbance to him. Charlie seems to be an aggressive, impulsive, immature, and poorly organized boy who will always be a problem in social groups.

In spite of the rather depressing analysis of Charlie's record, the prognosis need not be equally depressing. He has several good features and the fact that his constriction and anxiety have not given rise to denial and rigidity in his inner life is suggestive of possible future improvement. Adequate supportive therapy would, of course, greatly enhance this and there would be a good chance of moderate success. Charlie is at a very unstable period in his development and his problems are now intensified by his physical maturation. It is possible that following his adolescent spurt he will quiet down sufficiently to get a better grasp on reality and his own problems than he now has.

In order to provide some general comparison for this blind analysis, the original Rorschach analysis is now given; this analysis was prepared by Royal B. Hassrick. Following this we shall present some segments from his life history based upon observation and interviews with parents, teachers, and acquaintances.

Rorschach Analysis

Mental approach

a. Average (95).

b. Inefficient and low production; prefers fantasy. Persistence increased by drive to excel.

c. Poor organization and logic; poor conscious control. Capable of good routine work.

d. Childishly encompassing—naive. Handicapped by known inadequacy. Intellectually ambitious.

Creativity, extent and nature

No practical creative capacities, but overemphasis upon fantasy.

Behavioral approach

a. Constriction. Incapable of free rapport—stilted in all social situations. Probably disliked.

b. Co-operative under sympathetic treatment. Not frank, but consciously cautious. If not objectively handled, can be very difficult to manage.

c. Antagonizes at direct domination, possibly cantankerous and sulky.

Family dynamics

No observations provided.

Inner adjustment and defense mechanisms

a. Passive and resigned, yet ambitious (see "Descriptive summary").

b. When possible, accepts inner life; incapable of adjusting to external. Cannot have adequate inner consultation because of insecurity.

c. Generalized insecurity both toward self and outer world. Specific anxiety over inadequacy.

d. Stilted behavior.

e. Constriction of serious nature. Poor, immature inner control, seldom conscious. No outer control *per se*.

f. Superficial and unsatisfactory relations with others. Incapable of emotional rapport, though sensitive through constriction. Cannot react normally.

g. Immaturity prevails.

Emotional reactivity

a. Weak drive for external worldly achievement; overambitious inward drive.

b. Warped and stilted action. Sensitive but unable to digest social situations.

Sexual adjustment

Undefined to him; anxiety present.

Descriptive and interpretative summary

Overcontrol and insecurity permeate this record. Only through his inner self does he find adjustment, but it is here that he suffers from feelings of inadequacy. He has no rapport with his environment, and is oblivious to it. All his relationships are thus warped. Inwardly his overambitiousness seems a compensation for his inadequacy—a result of psychogenic inhibition (constriction). His basic emotional passiveness does not prohibit frequent reactive aggressions to frustration. His apparent overt aggressiveness might be in direct proportion to his domination and his sensitiveness, since his social antagonisms may be fostered by poor rapport and lack of a good inner life.

Prognosis

Encourage respect for inner life, overcoming inadequacy. Develop more satisfactory mechanisms for social rapport. Reduce overambitious qualities by supplying work and pseudo responsibilities. Crystallize role.

Life History *

Charlie is a fourteen-year-old fullblood boy with a round and merry face, who lives in a dilapidated log cabin on the outskirts of a small town. The family consists of father, mother, and older brother and sister. About five years ago Charlie lost a brother a year younger than himself.

The Charging Bulls came to their present home only a few years ago. Before the drought of the 1930's they had a small but well-stocked farm; when crops failed, the father abandoned it to work on reservation relief projects and then as a farm laborer. Thus the family has moved about considerably. In none of the places they have lived have they had close relatives or a neighborhood with which they had blood ties. They now live among miscellaneous Indian families, who remain in the community only as long as there is work or a need to send their children to school. There are also a few resident traders, a hotelkeeper, and white employee families.

Charlie's father is a large, bowlegged man, who associates with very few people in the community. He is usually quiet but is known to have an uncertain temper, threatening to fight or kill when he is sharply crossed or when he thinks any one of his family has been abused. The community fears what he may do. He appears to be a companion to his two boys, frequently riding over the range with them. However, reports of neighbors and the behavior of the children indicate that he

---

* This life history was prepared from interviews and observations with Charlie, his parents, schoolteachers, and others on the reservation. It is quoted, with permission, from Macgregor, Gordon, Warriors Without Weapons, Chicago: University of Chicago Press, 1944, p. 151.

is domineering and scolding in the home. He has made his family, especially Charlie, very much afraid of him. He teases Charlie and tells him stories that worry him.

Charlie's mother is a tall, thin, and seemingly carefree woman, who also teases him. She does not directly threaten her children, although she occasionally makes remarks to them such as, "If you weren't my son, I'd pound you," or "You sure make me mad." She is more amused than antagonized by Charlie and frequently remarked to interviewers in describing his behavior, "He sure is funny" and "That sure tickled me." She is similarly amused by her young daughter, who is something of a tomboy and a rough playmate of her brothers. When Charlie was little, the mother disciplined him with the traditional Sioux child-frighteners, but this ended when one day he said about a spirit she described as living in the creek, "Mommer, that's your imagination. You ain't got no sense." The mother now attempts to discipline Charlie by keeping him out of school when teachers complain of his behavior, but privately regards many of his pranks as great jokes. Like her husband, she is not loath to rush to the defense of her children and has, on a few occasions, threatened to fight other women. The mother says, however, that disciplining the boys is the father's business and that she has enough to do to look after her daughter.

The father and mother come from different communities; neither has relatives near the present home. The mother went to boarding school, where she had a reputation as a troublemaker and leader of gangs against unpopular individuals. In her present community she has more friends than does her husband, but she also is considered to be a very slovenly housewife by other Indian women.

Charlie, her second child, was a fat, dark baby. His umbilical cord was not tied well by the midwife and bled for six days. His mother ascribes this as the cause of his occasional fainting when he was a little boy. He remained fat but weak. When his weight broke his baby "walker," his mother sat him up in a horse collar on the floor. She kept his hair in long braids until he was six. He was weaned at about thirteen months but was given oatmeal and gravy when he was nine months old. At fourteen months he began to walk. He learned his toilet training from watching others, but, until he had achieved this, he used the floor or went out of doors.

Charlie had a speech difficulty during his infancy and early child-hood, and he refused to talk like other children until he was about eight years old. Until this time he had a few words of his own making, by which he made known his wants. When he started to talk, speaking only in English, he was already attending play school. About this time his younger brother died. Charlie still lisps a bit and stammers when he becomes overexcited. He usually speaks in English now, even replying in this language when addressed in Siouan by his bilingual parents. He skips many words and is said to do this also when speaking in Siouan.

Charlie now teases his mother in return for her jibes. He says the bacon looks like bad potatoes and, if asked to do something, often says, "If you can't do it, I think I'll just let it go." He does not have any such joking relations with his father. His older brother, Jerry, is his usual companion outside school hours. They support each other when attacked, and Jerry boasted about Charlie when he competed successfully against him; but they have had several fights and are quite constantly arguing. Yet, when Jerry left for the Navy in 1943, Charlie went along with him and tried to enter also. Charlie plays with his older sister, Lucy, at home; but, as there is some difference in their ages, she is not a real companion. Lucy shows a masculine identification by her behavior in her rough-and-tumble family and, when she speaks Siouan, she uses the masculine endings, as if she were a boy.

At school, Charlie has the reputation of being "bright." He works rapidly but not thoroughly. He was promoted twice in the past year, because he seemed so far ahead of his class and also to keep him busy and thus prevent him from annoying other students. He has been temporarily expelled several times for causing trouble. Charlie has been very annoying to one teacher, whom he can easily force to lose her temper. He picks on little boys and girls and has the reputation of being bullying and mean. One teacher reported he had "a cruel streak." Charlie is usually involved in any fighting or destruction of school property. In spite of this, he gets along well with the one male teacher and works well for him. He has few playmates outside his family and, when he does find one, soon loses him because of fighting or hurting him.

Charlie has an IQ of 101 by the Arthur test and 121 by the Goodenough. He is not the brilliant or exceptional student that his school record might imply. He seems to show no real intellectual accomplishment but a quick and artificial display which impresses his teachers and wins their praise. He is unable to organize his work well, and this may keep him from making a better record. He has creativity and originality, but anxiety about himself and his relation to others keeps him from giving any real expression to his inner life. He appears to use it as a retreat and escape, daydreaming and building fantasies that have little relation to reality.

Charlie's personality appears to be built around his fundamental insecurity and anxiety. The quarreling, hitting, destructive behavior he exhibits is reaction to aggression, or fear of aggression, from others. He is afraid to strike back at elders and bigger children but picks on smaller ones. He throws rocks at the school and destroys property to express his antagonisms. This reaction is impulsive and only half-hearted; figuratively, he appears as if he were thrashing his arms about fiercely and crying in fear at the same time. Fundamentally, he would like to be passive, to be treated kindly and affectionately, but the world continues to prick him, and he does not know what to do with himself or how to build up friendly relationships.

His aggressions toward girls are based partly on his impulsively reactive lashing-back at weaker individuals but seem also due to sexual anxiety. He is uncertain of himself in this sphere and unable to be more direct.

Charlie appears to be a young adolescent unsure of his family ties and with no loyal relatives to support him in the community. He tries to build up favor and attention for himself by good performance in schoolwork, but this is only a show that does not win him the satisfaction or security he desires. He appears to be anxious and floating in a social milieu that affords him no moorings.

CHAPTER 11

Betsy,
a Navaho girl of eleven

Betsy is a Navaho girl of eleven from a community on the Navaho reservation.* Her record presents a contrast to that of Charlie, not only because it is of a quite different culture but also because Betsy herself presents a hearty and energetically well-adjusted personality. Well adjusted to her environment and imaginative in her demands upon it, Betsy presents a picture of a richly developed inner life and a constructive, gregarious outer adjustment. Betsy's full record will first be presented, followed by an analysis of individual stories. The full TAT summary analysis given subsequently is the one originally written and based on the blind analysis of this record. This is followed by the Rorschach analysis prepared by Mr. Royal Hassrick and a summary life history prepared by Dr. Dorothea Leighton.

TAT Record

Picture 1. This man said to these boys—they had a fight with him—he said, "I'm going to shoot you right now." Looks like he said, "Come on, say something again."

* Betsy is one of the subjects from the Research on Indian Education and presented more fully in Leighton, Dorothea C., and Kluckhohn, Clyde. Children of the people. Cambridge: Harvard University Press, 1949. Pp. xi, 277.

Picture 2. These two kids said that it is very nice to have a turtle to play with. This woman let them do it and she's going ahead to put the baby asleep.

Picture 3. [Laughs] They are doing some trading horses—this horse belongs to this white man, and this man is showing a ring to the white man, and the white man wanted the ring and finally they made a trade of the ring for the horse.

Picture 4. That's a bed and he's got a nightgown. Instead of going to sleep he's crying—instead of making a prayer he's crying (?) 'cause he is punished by his mother. Really pictures of somebody?

Picture 5. This fence goes to this corner and then comes through here again. Dead cows' bones here, fire here and somebody sitting here (ditch) looks like a German.

Picture 6. A blind man sitting down here, thinking away about when his death will come in the future.

Picture 7. This fellow is coming back from the store—Frank—and these folks are going to the store—his wife, Annie, Mrs. Joe Pirio, and me.

Picture 8. This woman is telling this girl to go to the store and get two loaves of bread and two bottles of jam.

Picture 9. This man is teaching these boys how to practice their dances, and he's showing them how to motion their hands the way he does.

Picture 10. This boy's name is Haskiba and he's just thinking of a way of getting married. This woman is making some of that dried yucca fruit Annie showed you, and these men are saying how many times after they used to make it that way.

Picture 11. This boy is standing on a hill and looking the place over and it's a beautiful place, and he's singing. He's thinking he's going to ask his mother to move their camp over here.

Picture 12. Here's a snake and somebody lying there—looks like this boy went astray and he just went asleep. And these bats came around and they're going after his ears.

Story Analysis

Picture 1. This man said to these boys—they had a fight with him—he said, "I'm going to shoot you right now." Looks like he said, "Come on, say something again."

1. This story has a developed plot, movement, and interaction. Emotions are expressed, action is taken. Most of the material is also

at an imaginative level. She adequately identifies the stimulus, but moves right on to imaginative elaborations which have the characteristics just stated.

In presenting a story of good stimulus identification, imaginative elaborations with action and movement content, Betsy portrays herself as a girl of above average, possibly superior, intelligence. In emphasizing the motion and feeling categories of her response, she portrays her inner vitality and her active contact with outer world stimuli.

2. The content is essentially assertive in nature (they had a fight) (I'm going to shoot you). Betsy seems rather to enjoy this active interaction. Her last sentence (say something again) seems to suggest a good-humored enthusiasm. The author would therefore see this as more appropriately called active and assertive rather than aggressive. Spontaneity is an appropriate word, as would be the implication of Betsy as an active and aware person. To say that she is aggressive, implying a hostile attacking attitude, seems to be an exaggeration. Subsequent stories will, of course, have to be checked for this point.

3. It is of some interest that, while she involves the "boys" actively in the plot, it is the older man to whom she attributes the proposed immediate aggression (I'm going to shoot you right now). In the light of the suggestion that this is the story of an active and spontaneous girl rather than a hostile aggressive one, the author proposes that this formulation represents her active sexual awareness, but an awareness not without some hesitation, the hesitation being in her transferring the aggressive action to the (safe?) older man. This may also imply that she feels sufficiently comfortable with the older male category to use him in this fashion. If so, we should look elsewhere for the data on the father, hypothesizing a basically strong and positive father-image.

4. Fantasy and imaginative ideas come freely to this girl. It should be noticed that her story begins in the middle, so to speak, i.e., in the first phrase she combines the active plot with the identification of the stimulus. This seldom happens in IQ's below high average. It is as though she had gone quickly through the basic steps of stimulus identification, proposing a relationship between the stimuli, and then adding meaning to that relationship. When she starts to speak, she has already encompassed three steps and verbalizes only the end result.

Picture 2. These two kids said that it is very nice to have a turtle to play with. This woman let them do it and she's going ahead to put the baby asleep.

1. This story also has an adequate stimulus identification and a developed plot. Into this story she puts not her assertive forceful feelings (which she identifies as male in story 1) but rather her tender, permissive, constructive feelings. Already her ability to present these two feeling areas suggests her as a girl of some personal complexity and personality elaboration.

2. The same spontaneity of story 1 is also here. She seems generally quite confident with adult figures. Here she seems able to attribute both order and positive feeling to the mother-context, but is not really impressed with either.

3. It may be noticed that there is no interaction between the "women" and the "kids" other than the giving of permission. It is also to be noted that the somewhat more frequently noticed feeding function of the mother is neglected. While this point requires further study, it seems possible that there is some block between mother and daughter. That this is not on the ordinary social level is suggested by the ease with which the mother gives permission and goes about her task while the kids play. Rather it seems on a deeper level, possibly connected with physical functioning of some sort. The energetic, masculinelike enthusiasm of story 1 seems to be related to this and may suggest some feminine-role rejection on Betsy's part.

4. Some of the structural aspects of her personality as they appear so far are:

a. Inner control is used but there is possibly some hesitancy that needs to be explored.

b. Conscious control is used actively but not to the point of constriction.

c. Imaginative capacities are excellent.

d. Anxiety level is active but not distorting, seems structured around feminine-role problems and a developing sexual awareness.

e. Emotions are easily handled and used in complex fashion.

Picture 3. [Laughs] They are doing some trading horses—this horse belongs to this white man, and this man is showing a ring to the white man, and the white man wanted the ring and finally they made a trade of the ring for the horse.

1. The organization and logic are excellent. The fairly involved plot suggests a higher IQ estimate, possibly superior to very superior (125–135).

2. This again is like story 1 in its active interactional characteristics. It further stresses the possibility that Betsy is somewhat rejecting the

more traditional feminine-role activities and finding herself more interested in masculine activities.

3. The "trading" plus the active movement of this story seem to imply a strong interest in excelling and excellence generally. This is not a compulsive perfectionism but rather suggests a good strong interest in skills and superior performances. It is to be presumed that Betsy would therefore be approved by schoolteachers and find schoolwork of interest.

4. The "ring" and its attendant trading scene is an original response of good quality.

Picture 4. That's a bed and he's got a nightgown. Instead of going to sleep he's crying—instead of making a prayer he's crying (?) 'cause he is punished by his mother. Really pictures of somebody?

1. This picture is emotionally significant to Betsy in some way. She approaches it very obliquely, as she has not other pictures; and she attempts to test its personal relevance (are these really pictures of somebody?). A further attribute quite uncharacteristic of Betsy is her selecting first the bed. Certainly a more characteristic approach for her would have been to say something like, "This boy is crying by his bed," or some other formulation that went more directly to the heart of the plot.

2. In addition to being a disturbing picture for her, it also arouses the first basically negative ideas (picture 1 she likes too much to call negative). The boy is crying and was punished. It is possible that she finds herself unable to cope with the notion of a lone person or that the suggestion of passive and negative tone here is frightening to her. If this is the case, one would see some anxiety behind her forceful, active behavior and suspect some depressive moods that appear to relate to the withdrawal of personal contact. She has difficulty being succorant and receiving.

3. It should be noticed that her intellectual organization holds up fairly well. She presents quite complex ideas (instead of) and still gives us a plot.

Picture 5. This fence goes to this corner and then comes through here again. Dead cows' bones here, fire here, and somebody sitting here (ditch) looks like a German.

1. This story, while it has some very constructive elements, is not basically a coherent plot. Rather it is an identification of specific aspects of the picture. It may be that this forlorn stimulus, with no people in it, is something with which she cannot cope. Perhaps she

has not yet worked out the inner maturity to permit her to be without people. This would, of course, suggest that her marked emphasis upon energetic interaction is, as partially implied in story 4, still in the exploratory phases and that this experimentation with people is incomplete.

2. Her poor organization here suggests, as in 4, that she can be upset emotionally and that some reactive swings occur. A part of this is probably the mood swings suggested by 4. Considering that her assertive attitudes appear to be in part defensive, it may be that mild temper periods constitute another form of emotional unsteadiness for her.

3. The "fire" in this story has already been commented upon on page 68; the details will not be repeated here. The importance lies in observing that even though at times her outer control is not consistent her imagination and inner vitality persist. The reference to the "German" is, in a sense, a forced effort to bring the much-needed people into view. It is an original observation but not one of good quality.

Picture 6. A blind man sitting down here, thinking away about when his death will come in the future.

1. The story suggests that Betsy can from time to time accept calm and ease. More generally, of course, she rushes in with enthusiasm and vigor. We have seen the high emphasis upon inner feeling categories in earlier stories. This story, while of a slightly more negative quality, reflects the same strong introversive tendency seen in other stories and presents a further elaboration of her quite complex inner control.

2. The specific content here of the man thinking of the future is most likely a fairly direct reflection of her own feelings. Her active social experimentation is also a worry about the future, an effort to define the outer world so she can live in it comfortably.

Picture 7. This fellow is coming back from the store—Frank—and these folks are going to the store—his wife, Annie, Mrs. Joe Pirio, and me.

1. The organization of this story is only fair. She adequately describes the major stimuli, though she does not really complete a story. She does, however, put the persons in motion and, if one is willing to accept "going to the store," she does give fairly good plot development.

2. It is also of special note that she does sense and respond to the

"busy" aspects of this card. Her response to it may be profitably compared with that of Charlie Charging Bull. He emphasizes the details: the line is incomplete, this is broke, the wheels don't start. For Charlie, these details are the unusual, idiosyncratic responses. For Betsy, the emphasis upon people in action is the unusual part. She may not be entirely at ease with people, she may not be quite sure how it comes out, but she has cast her lot with personal interaction. She specifically mentions five people in the story, and by name. One of them is herself—a further direct connection of her involvement with people.

3. We may also suggest that Betsy will work well with the school. Here she portrays her ability to deal readily with adults.

Picture 8. This woman is telling this girl to go to the store and get two loaves of bread and two bottles of jam.

1. Here she does escape into details, albeit details with a rather pleasing future. She reacts to the two stimuli adequately and sees an appropriate interaction between them. She does not, however, indicate any outcome. As with the previous pictures, this failure to complete an action suggests some feeling of unresolved affect. In this case, it would appear to be affect related to the mother. What this is is not clear from the picture, though there has been some suggestion in picture 2. Again, here, she overlooks the direct maternal connection. No affect expressed, no direct interaction of two persons. Instead, she picks unusual details. They are, however, not stimulus-determined details, as with Charlie, but concept-determined ones. She expresses no affect toward them and, in fact, treats the whole picture rather casually.

2. From these observations, it may be suggested that:

a. There is some hesitancy experienced in connection with the mother.

b. This appears to reflect itself in some aversion to the feminine household role.

c. Her somewhat masculine orientation seen in other cards appears to be substantiated here.

3. It is of further interest that in this picture she deliberately separates the figures. The girl is to go away to the store. In no other story does she base her plot on a separation of characters. There may be agreement, or as in 7, people may be going places, but she does not separate two central figures. This would seem further evidence of the maternal problem. Yet it should not be overlooked that there

is no aggression or hostility here—and in a girl who is easily able to express such ideas if she wishes. In addition, the chore she is sent to perform is not an unpleasant one: to secure bread and jam. It would appear that while there is some affect-resistance between mother and daughter, the daughter still sees her positively. She resists household tasks, but feels a little ashamed of herself for doing so. If one were to hazard a guess as to the nature of the hesitancy, comparatively mild as it is, one would have to look into the issue of the mother's sexuality. The rejection of the biological relationship (see also 2) in calling her "woman" and in not permitting interaction, yet the choice of a highly nurturant evasion, suggests an over-all sound relationship but some underlying problems having to do with the mother's own problems. This may be exaggerated by Betsy, considering her present active but restraining interest in males.

Picture 9. This man is teaching these boys how to practice their dances, and he's showing them how to motion their hands the way he does.

1. Good easy story, especially when seen in comparison with 8. She leaves the boys and man together, though she separates the mother and daughter. She would appear to be more at ease with the (pleasing and strong?) father.

2. She is slightly depreciating of the boys here, in not giving them a more active part as she did in 1. This would suggest the easy positive relationship to the father and an unsettled and cautious interest in the boys.

Picture 10. This boy's name is Haskiba and he's just thinking of a way of getting married. This woman is making some of that dried yucca fruit Annie showed you, and these men are saying how many times after they used to make it that way.

A family picture seen as a marriage and food drama! She takes the isolated boy and explains his separation not as rejection by the group but as voluntary opportunity to think about an interpersonal relation. She puts the woman to work and provides her with an approving audience of males. Good feeling for people, easy concepts of interpersonal relations, sexuality being seriously debated in her own mind. It should also be noted that she moves directly to the boy in this picture and deals with the more apparent group second.

Picture 11. This boy is standing on a hill and looking the place over and it's a beautiful place, and he's singing. He's thinking he's going to ask his mother to move their camp over here.

Here is Betsy's real easy affect in operation. A girl of vigor and sensuality, with appreciation of aesthetics and the relation of man to it.

Picture 12. Here's a snake and somebody lying there—looks like this boy went astray and he just went asleep. And these bats came around and they're going after his ears.

1. Betsy is not particularly distressed by this scene. She admits that snakes exist and that bats are flying about and are "going after his ears." She does leave the boy lost and vulnerable—an indication of some general anxiety.

2. Her anxiety, however, is not pervasive or of neurotic quality. Here her response might be compared to Charlie's, in which the fear, attack, and guilt possibilities of this picture are accentuated.

TAT Analysis Summary

Mental approach

Level. Superior to very superior intelligence (125–130 IQ).

Efficiency. In general, should be excellent. Has the energy and the directness of approach necessary for adequate functioning. At times, however, if she should become unsure of herself, it seems probable that her efficiency would be reduced because of her tendency to lose her organizing capacities. This, however, is of minor importance and her attack upon problems should be forceful, direct, and generally successful. There is a suggestion that the directness of this approach is modified by some slight anxiety and a tendency to overact.

Organization. Her organization capacities are good and she is able to utilize them in both routine and creative areas. These capacities, however, are subject to the influence of emotional factors and are occasionally disrupted.

Creativity

Very creative. Produces creative ideas readily and with ease. Imaginative capacities are good and used frequently as an attack upon emotional problems.

Behavioral approach

General. Active, vigorous girl who approaches the outer world in a direct and slightly demanding fashion. Her approach to daily events suggests a certain superficial confidence in the outer world, both in her ability to handle it and in its eventually giving in to her. This is the picture of a somewhat "spoiled" child who, basically somewhat afraid of real contact with the outer world, denies this fact by affirming complete confidence in it. She has a rather playful contact with reality which suggests that the first impression she makes upon people is uniformly good and which also betrays her real doubt as to the stability of her grasp upon it.

Peer relations. Her peer relationships should be excellent and she should be a constructive member of any group. She is somewhat more masculine than feminine in her interests and orientation toward peers. She seems to try to avoid the usual feminine household tasks and prefers more masculine diversions and duties. She does not seem to be avoiding girls but would seem more readily identified with boys.

Adults. Her relationship to adults is also excellent. She is able to recognize this potential control and authority but is not unduly impressed by it. This suggests good confident relations with parents and ability to work well with adults in general.

School. Schoolwork should be very good in all areas. Intellectually she is a superior student and her drives toward action and superiority should serve her well in classwork. Relationships with teacher and students should be satisfactory and co-operative.

Specific problems. There are suggestions that Betsy may have tendencies toward:

1. Overactive aggression, especially when she does not have her own way and when her superiority is questioned (temper), and/or,

2. Periods of depression or moodiness for essentially the same reasons. It may be that the periods of moodiness are closely related to her intimate ties with other people and that, while being refused her own way would give rise to (1), any removal of affection (real or imagined) would give rise to (2).

Family dynamics

Relation to parents. In general her feelings for her mother are good and she has adequately handled any external control which her mother may enforce. The mother seems, however, to be rather permissive and not to have unduly dominated her daughter.

This girl seems to have rejected somewhat the usual household feminine role (if this is as one would expect in the Navaho tribe) and, while she feels slightly guilty about it, may refuse or at least protest against household duties. Her more masculine interests and energy pattern tend to confirm this possibility.

She is not quite at ease with her mother for another reason which will have more far-reaching influence upon her development than her feminine-role rejection. This is the problem of her sexual adjustment, which is discussed more fully later. Since there seems little hostility to her mother, the author would suggest that this girl's orientation in the feminine sexual role has been communicated fairly directly to her by her mother, whose own sexual adjustment is suspect (some rejection).

We have no data on other family members except the statement that the relation to the father seems sound and, considering the masculine trends, may imply closer feeling for him than the mother.

Family atmosphere. Family atmosphere generally good and, with the exception of the sexual area, conducive to adequate maturity of the children within it. No specific hostilities or undue domination of one member by another.

If it is important in the Navaho tribe (and this family), there should be trouble getting Betsy to accept household feminine tasks.

Inner adjustment

Basic emotional attitude. Basic emotional attitude is slightly aggressive.

Impulse life. Has good acceptance of inner life. She seems quite vital and intense and, with the exception of feminine-sexual area, is on her way to a very sound mature adjustment. Her inner life is quite fluid and active and is used fairly well in solving emotional problems.

There is, however, a suggestion that this acceptance is not as complete as her general adjustment would imply. Somehow she does not get quite enough support from her inner life to enable her to handle her problems. While her general solutions are forceful and direct, she is aware of her more tender side. She would like to relax and for once be compliant and succorant but is unable to do so.

System of control. Inner control is used well, though it is not completely effective. Conscious control is needed to handle some of these unsolved problems, though this is by no means constriction. Outer control is not adequately established as yet and this imbalance of control gives rise to the occasional temper and moody periods already mentioned.

Anxiety. There is some general anxiety and insecurity upon which the somewhat overreactive activity and vigor is based but these are by no means pervasive and do not particularly handicap her adjustment. (See also "Sexual adjustment.")

Adjustment mechanisms. Above-normal conscious control, over-reactive vigor and activity, slight rejection of feminine role.

Emotional reactivity. Betsy is especially aware of other people and generally dependent upon them for stimulation and support. She must have them in her environment in order to feel safe. She is actively concerned with problems of her relations to them and has not reached any adequate solution. She is genuinely driven toward contact with them, but is not completely able to accept them emotionally.

Maturity. In Betsy's case it is hard to say what this concept implies. In many ways, and to all overt appearances, this girl has reached adequate maturity for her age and developmental level. She is, however, in a fairly active and flexible period and has not yet reached a mature handling of her impulse life. She shows signs of concern over typical adolescent and immediately preadolescent problems and worry about the future and her relation to it.

Emotional reactivity

Drive toward outer world. Drive toward outer world is strong, though she is somewhat unable to accept all stimuli. Occasionally she retreats from outer world contact. She always puts her best foot forward but is actually a little wary of the world.

Emotional ties to people. Generally spontaneous and vital though some restraint in sexual area. She has not yet reached sufficient maturity to be completely free in her dealings with reality.

Sexual adjustment

There is some specific sexual anxiety and consequent rejection of the usual feminine role. She is very sex conscious yet is confused over the significance of her sexual life. This is not, however, neurotically rigid and the prognosis is not markedly hampered by this.

She has difficulty accepting herself as feminine, though she is aware of herself as a love object.

Summary

This is the record of a girl whose general adjustment both to self and to her environment is good. She is a rather pampered child who approaches the outer world with vigor, strength, and confidence. Her adjustment, however, is somewhat uncertain and her appearance of excellent social adjustment is based more on her above-normal conscious control than on an adequate balance of inner and outer control. She is a somewhat masculine girl whose rejection of some of the feminine role leads her to boys' interests and tasks. Raised in a very genial family, her general outlook on life and her techniques for adaptation are constructive and suggest an excellent prognosis. There is, however, evidence of specific sexual anxiety which arises largely from her mother's own uncertainty in this area. The father is an adequate Navaho man and presents no specific problem to his daughter. The family seems to have had considerable contact with whites and not to have rejected this contact in any way.

Betsy is a girl of very facile impulse life who has developed her fantasy to a usable degree but seldom escapes her problems through it. Her first approach to new situations is vigorous and direct, though not without some anxiety. She may retire once she has tackled a problem and finds it too difficult, but her first reaction is somewhat of a challenge rather than either complete acceptance or rejection.

Rorschach Analysis *

Mental approach

This girl's intellectual capacities are superior, as shown by good form quality, originality, variety of content, and good organization. Her intellectual efficiency, however, is below her potentialities. It is effected by the emotional conflict which seems to occupy her mind and leads her to overplay her imagination and take refuge in tiny details instead of making more meaningful whole concepts.

Imagination

She has remarkable imaginative capacities and perceives twelve original concepts in thirty-one responses. She uses both imagination and creative powers to aid her in solving the emotional conflict with which she seems to be struggling.

Behavioral approach

Her basic emotional attitude includes aggression, impulsiveness, and passion. There is a need and appreciation for warm affectionate feelings. It appears that suddenly for some reason her ready and passionate responsiveness has become questionable to her, and much of her

* This Rorschach record was administered by Dr. Dorothea Leighton. It was scored and interpreted by Dr. Alice Joseph. The summary is reproduced here with their permission.

energy is called upon to solve this problem, which affects her with the force of a fresh trauma. She gives no evidence of anxiety, but she appears to be definitely aware of the conflict within her.

Control

Her control, which is exceedingly complex and intricate for a girl of her age, functions in the following way: there is a first immediate violent reaction, desire and fear, that cannot be mastered by outer control. So inner control, calling up her imaginative abilities, comes into play. She uses inner control effectively and to an unusually high degree for her age, but there are certain very disturbing emotions which do not yield to this treatment. So she tries to inhibit them. The disturbance is superimposed on an originally natural and spontaneous acceptance of the outer world which, apart from this one side, appears to her very friendly and serene. It is this fact that suggests mainly the existence of a fresh trauma. From the content of the answers which use inhibitive determinants and inner control, it is probable that the drives she cannot accept are of a sexual nature. Her conscious control is good, neither too much nor too little, and is refined by a rather strong tendency toward introspection.

Inner adjustment

The present conflict has no neurotic quality and does not affect deeply her basic personality structure. It is probably temporary, and to some extent connected with her physiological and inner maturation. Her imaginative and creative capacities seem sufficient to achieve a solution. She is an introvert, and her tendencies are also introversial.

Maturity

Her maturity is rather more than would be expected for her years, but still not anything excessive or such as would indicate overadjustment.

Summary

Betsy is a very intelligent, spirited girl, evidently just blossoming into adolescence and not yet master of the new impulses this has given her. In her contacts with people she will probably appear still rather egocentric, with vivid alternate moods of enthusiasm, aggression, opposition, and withdrawal into herself. There may also be a slight display of self-consciousness.

Life History *

This child attained an IQ of 126 on the Arthur and 111 on the Goodenough.

She is the oldest of seven children, one of whom died at about one year. She is a lively girl, almost always on the go, talking a good deal when with her family, laughing and joking. Her job at home was taking care of her family's sheep and those of her aunt. In this work she usually had the company of an eighteen-year-old girl cousin, but the report was that Betsy did most of the herding. She was a little moody at times, and had spells of not wanting to do anything she was told. One of these moods hit her when asked to do the Battery.† She was pouty and did a poor job. Later she repented and asked to be allowed to repeat it. The moodiness was not apparent when she was seen at her aunt's sheep camp, where she was a pet and the youngest girl, instead of the oldest one and expected to share the family responsibility. It was not evident at school either, though there she seemed definitely quieter than she did at home.

Betsy appears to get along well with her peers. She is too lively not to have fusses with them at times, but these are not serious and do not last long. Her next younger sister complains that Betsy does not do her share of the housework at home, but also says that at school she likes to work with Betsy "because she works fast," and likes to go for walks with her and their friend "because Betsy sure makes us laugh." There was a good deal of family rivalry between Betsy's siblings and their cousins, and Betsy took her full share of this. She often stood up against her cousins for the benefit of her brothers and sisters. She seems fond of her siblings, and if she has a pet it is the youngest girl. Her nearest sister is her principal companion at school with the addition of a relative whom they both find very congenial.

Adults who know Betsy speak freely in her praise. She is respectful and responsive and does what they tell her, but adds something of herself in the doing. Her mother related with satisfaction that, when asked if she were going to a prospective Squaw Dance, Betsy replied she did not know if she was or not. She always left it up to her parents and did whatever they said. She is not as passive as this might imply, but certainly is in general quite easy to handle.

---

* This life history summary was prepared by Dr. Dorothea Leighton and is reproduced here with her permission.

† A special group of tests of emotional response and moral ideology.

She goes to a boarding school run by some Protestant missionaries. They report that she and her sister are quite outstanding in the school as well behaved, hard working, generally nice children. Both are said to do good work. Betsy is thought to be more timid than her sister. Both are thought to be good influences on the other children.

The family consists of the mother and father, three boys and three girls, with Betsy the oldest child. The seventh child, who died, came next to last in the family. The family seems extremely happy and devoted. The parents are very congenial and affectionate, and are greatly interested in each child. The children fall naturally into two groups, the three oldest and the three youngest. As long as they were home, the three oldest carried most of the work responsibility for the children, but in their absence the youngest girl who was only five was a remarkably good little mother to her two young brothers. The parents delighted in signs of intelligence or wit in their flock, and told stories about them on every occasion. They were also proud of their various manual or domestic abilities, and mentioned them frequently. Their decision as to which child was smartest varied from time to time. At first they settled on the oldest boy, but when they came home after dark one night and found that the five-year-old girl had managed to light the gasoline lantern without ever having been taught they wondered if perhaps she was not even smarter than her brother. They all have very individual personalities, and taken as a group they are certainly an unusually attractive bunch of little Navahos.

The father is a quiet, pleasant man with a twinkle in his eye who has made his living as a silversmith for the past few years. He has worked at it for traders and also independently. His wife learned with him, and they enjoy working together very much. He also depends to some extent on the crops he can raise, and on the flock of sheep they have lately started to build up. Both husband and wife try to pay their debts and to live as much as possible on a cash basis, which is very unusual among this group. They have been able to accumulate rather more than an average amount of manufactured goods, but most of their wealth is invisible, and consists of small bills at the various traders, instead of the large, never-paid accounts of most of their friends and relatives.

The father takes great interest in the children. He is said to spend some time each morning instructing them in the way they should behave. He represents somewhat the old Navaho way of doing things, but is broad-minded, intelligent, and liberal toward innovations. He thinks most highly of his oldest son, the third child, and probably finds more companionship in him than in the girls, but he is proud of them all.

He seems to be quite unusually devoted to his wife, and much more expressive of his affection than most Navahos. This is in his family tradition to some extent. A local trader says that this man's father was the only Navaho he ever saw hold his wife's hand in public. In any case, there seems to be the same sort of mutual regard and trust between them that is held up to whites as a marriage ideal. His wife depends on him for advice and counsel in matters with the family and with other Navahos, and he leans on her where it comes to relations with white people.

Betsy's mother is an attractive woman of perhaps thirty. She comes from another area of Navahos, but has a few relatives here. She went to the same mission school as Betsy for eight or nine years. She has apparently made a satisfactory integration between mission and Navaho ways, and has used what she learned at school to the advantage of her family both economically and in raising their general standard of comfort. There is a hint that on first leaving school she was very strongly in favor of white ways, and then had a reaction against them, but at present a compromise that seems to work very well has been reached. She is lively, talkative, and fun-loving, but takes her responsibilities toward her family quite seriously. She works very hard and expects her daughters to do likewise, though the writer does not think she exerts more pressure on them than most Navaho mothers, if as much. She does not know much about Navaho arts and crafts except the silverwork that she learned with her husband. She neither weaves nor grinds. She is more charitable than many educated Navahos towards the uneducated ones, and is in considerable demand to interpret for them and to write their letters.

She knows very little about Navaho religion, and is not much affected either by what the missionaries taught her about Christianity. Of the Navaho religion she retains some of the fears and a small amount of respect for the efficacy of native medicines and ceremonials. On the mission side, she has had all the children baptized, but did not hesitate to change the name of one of them after this when she took the notion. She does not expect her schoolchildren to take missionary efforts too seriously, but was careful to keep them from telling the teachers that she was on her way to a native dance once when she visited them.

She is proud of her children and competitive for them. The writer does not think she has definite aims in view for them, but wants them to do well. At times she plays and jokes with them as if she were their own age, but she is very definitely their boss and they look to her for direction and advice. There seem to be less inhibitions in the interpersonal relations of this whole family than in most Indian families the writer has known.

She is proud of her husband, also, and she often tells how smart he is to be able to learn not only to speak English but also to read and write it without ever going to school. She admires him for his wisdom and for his lack of jealousy and seems to feel herself very fortunate to have married him. She said that each time she had a baby she would decide that getting married was a terrible thing, and wonder why she had ever done it, but at all other times she seemed content with her lot. After the birth of the seventh child in twelve years, she began to have a lot of trouble with hemorrhaging and pain each month, so she went to the hospital at the mission and had her uterus removed. She was very weak for a long time, and greatly impressed, as was her husband, with the need for taking care of herself. She is rather relieved to be done with having children. She astonished the female population of the area by living through the operation, and seems to have been really rather surprised herself.

Since Betsy was the first child, the parents experimented somewhat with her, but this the rest of the children escaped. For one thing, she was the only one of the family to escape the cradle board. She was also the only one to have her birth hair cut off when it grew long enough to do so. Her great-uncle told her parents she looked awful that way and as if nobody loved her, so they did not do it to the rest of the children. She was nursed and ceased mostly of her own accord when she began to walk around and eat other food, at a little more than a year. She talked fairly soon after starting to walk, learned the process easily, and has always talked well and rather freely. Toilet training was not very definite, but was accomplished without particular difficulty. It has been said that Betsy was very spoiled at one time, but she does not appear so now, and certainly takes her responsibilities without fussing. She first went to a public school for about six months, but then got sick and never went back. She went to the mission school three years ago, and apparently enjoys it very much. The second year she took her sister, and this year her brother went with them. This is something of a drain on the family cash, but parents and children alike are eager for the education and apparently have their hearts set on getting it at the same place as did the mother.

All three children gained a good deal of weight and rounded out considerably at school. At home they are so active there would be difficulty in having them eat enough to get fat. Except for some undernutrition Betsy seemed in good physical condition. Her only sicknesses have been some stomach pains when she was three years old for which she had a medicine man, jaundice when she was in the public school, and mumps two years ago.

Her attitude on religion was tapped when it was jokingly asked if the cycle of four ceremonials, of which only two had been performed, was to be completed. Her mother joined the joke and said maybe, but Betsy expressed very sharp displeasure at the idea. It is interesting that her first drawing was one of the church at her school, which she painted blue.

Summary

This is the oldest daughter and first child of a very affectionate couple who seem to have made a good compromise between Navaho and white ways of living. She is bright and lively, more so at home than at school, where she is rather timid. She is the family sheepherder in the summertime, and apparently prefers this job to domestic duties. The first three children have followed their mother's educational footsteps, and the rest look forward to doing so some day. The father is uneducated, but it has not stood in his way and he has made up for it to some extent by learning English in his jobs. At present he earns most of the family cash as a silversmith, in which work his wife delights to help him. Betsy apparently resents a little her position as oldest and the responsibilities it entails; at least she seems happier at school and in her aunt's family than in her own, though she is devoted to her own.

Part 3

THE PICTURES

CHAPTER 12

The stimulus properties
of the pictures

An important part of the process of interpretation resides in the understanding of the stimuli that the pictures present to the subject. In earlier chapters a number of general variables descriptive of the stimulus value of the pictures were presented. These were given largely to suggest the range of variation in the pictures and as leads to differential reactions of subjects. The interpretation of the individual record normally proceeds picture by picture through the set administered. For this reason, the interpreter finds himself in need of specific picture-by-picture knowledge in addition to knowledge of general factors in terms of which all pictures may be described.

An analysis of each picture is presented in this chapter. There are six categories of analysis:

I. **Murray's Description** as a reminder to the reader of the card.

II. **Manifest Stimulus Demand** of the card. The manifest aspects of the card usually observed by subjects and utilized in their stories will be described. As will be recalled from the earlier discussion of the concept of stimulus demand, there appear to be certain aspects of the card which may be taken as "given" and variations from which may be thought to be either "avoidance" by the subject or "misinterpretations" and "distortions." However, the level at which the "given" is understood to be presented and the manner in which it is described can bear significant relationships to the interpretations made by the subject. The object on the floor in 3BM is described by Murray as a "revolver." Similarly, the figure is described as a "boy." If now we presume that any other reference to these objects constitutes a perceptual misrecognition, we are assuming that to most normal subjects the reality of these objects is unquestioned. This then encourages us to see perceptual distortion in the subject who calls this a woman and says that she has mislaid her keys. Yet in large numbers of normal subjects just such "reinterpretations" occur.

In Rosenzweig and Fleming's study,[117] for example, in fifty men and fifty women from ages twenty to forty (occupation and social class not stated), it is noted that among male subjects 50 per cent claimed the figure to be female and 44 per cent, male. Further, only 20 per cent also attributed youth to the figure which the original description implies is a "boy." Similarly, only 28 per cent of these subjects identified the floor object as a gun or other weapon. In contrast, there is seldom any doubt but what the figure in card 1 is a "boy." Here Rosenzweig and Fleming's subjects agree with us. All of their male subjects so identified him, both with respect to sex and age. This would lead us to suggest that the "boy" of card 1 is indeed "given" and that deviations in subject response (i.e., girl, woman, old man, etc.) are to be seen in the possible light of misconceptions. However, in 3BM, the "given" is clearly not a "boy" in the same sense. It is rather a "huddled figure" of either sex and indefinite age. The present writer would be in accord with Rosenzweig and Fleming's [117] subjects in seeing the figure either as male or female, though he would be inclined to have expected a slightly greater preponderance of "male" than "female" interpretations.

The point is that considerable caution should be used in deciding what is "given" and hence what may be thought to be a distortion with special interpretive significance. In subsequent discussions of specific cards, the attempt will be made to describe the manifest stimulus demand of each card in this light. It should be recognized that the definition of reality is a touchy matter and, generally speaking, an issue to be determined by consensus of those persons presenting no symptoms suggestive of reality disorientation. Our concern, of course, is to so define the manifest stimulus as to enable us to develop a definition of distortions but not to prematurely define as distorted the ordinary "range of possible interpretations" to be expected in a person of adequate reality contact. This is not to say that some of the possible interpretations of objects within the usual range do not lend themselves to personality interpretations. In fact, it would be our position that most of them do. However, there is quite some difference in seeing these as misperceptions and hence suggestive of personality distortion, or as "normal variations" and hence reflective of personality needs still well within the normal range.

Within the category of manifest stimulus demand, three subcategories will be used:

a. Adequate Stimulus Notation refers to those major segments of the stimulus which reflect an adequate accounting of the card. By adequate accounting is meant the most generally noted details and those out of which the usual subject builds his story. Thus, in number 1, the boy and the violin should be noted, and a statement of a relationship between the two included. Absence of direct or indirect reference to any one of these may be thought to reflect some blocking out of stimulus areas worth special interpretive attention. Similarly, in card 3BM, a "huddled figure" of either sex and indefinite age—most frequently young, if age is noted—should be observed.

b. Other Details Often Noted refers to frequently observed details, other than those referred to in (*a*), that are not basic to the plot but which may be reasonably expected in some normal subjects. Thus, in number 1, a parental figure is frequently introduced. In 3BM, the object on the floor is often seen as a gun or other weapon.

c. Seldom Noted Details refers to the fact that some subjects observe details seldom seen by other subjects. These are generally suggestive of special preoccupation or special detail compulsions. The furrows and small outbuildings in number 2 or the specks of light in the dark background of number 14 are examples of this.

III. Form Demand. Cards differ in the form pattern which they present to the subject and hence possibly reflect different degrees of task difficulty.

IV. Latent Stimulus Demand. Each stimulus probably presents, in addition to form and manifest content stimuli, a particular emotional issue.

V. Frequent Plots. This refers to the usual ways in which subjects integrate the preceding features and the particular stories which they tell.

VI. Significant Variations. The writer has gained the impression that some variations of response bear more close observation than others.

CARD 1

I. Murray's Description. A young boy is contemplating a violin which rests on a table in front of him.

II. Manifest Stimulus Demand.

a. An adequate accounting of this picture would appear to be one in which reference is made to the boy, the violin, and some statement of a relationship between them.

b. The only other detail frequently noted in this picture is some reference to an introduced figure of a parent or, somewhat less frequently, to another adult such as a music teacher or relative other than parent. There is some slight tendency for this figure to be introduced more frequently by males than by females.

c. Seldom noted details: object under violin noted as sheet of music, table, or cloth.

III. Form Demand. The form of this picture is a simple one involving only the major stimulus elements under II-*a*.

IV. Latent Stimulus Demand. This picture appears to be one dealing with the general issue of impulse versus control, or the question of the relationship of personal demands to those of outside cultural agents.

V. Frequent Plots. The two basic plots to this picture are:

a. The boy is obliged to practice by parent, he rebels and prefers to play or do some other self-directed activity. In middle-class subjects, the boy usually at least temporarily accepts this pressure.

b. The boy is self-directed and ambitious and is now either dreaming of becoming or will become an outstanding violinist.

VI. Significant Variations. In a sense, any deviation from the foregoing may be thought of as a significant variation. The violin may be seen as broken, the boy sleeping, the object under the violin seen as a book, or the violin seen as a train. These, however, are all what we might call rare details, at a level of frequency· less than noted under II-*c*, Seldom Noted Details. In general, unless such rare details occur with some frequency in normal subjects, they will not be mentioned. Similarly, no particular psychodynamic implications of a particular variation will be indicated but rather attention will be called to variations that will bear special analysis in the normal ways. In this picture, then, in addition to the basic characteristics of the plot and the character, special attention should be paid to:

a. Any introduced figure, most frequently expecting this to be a parent, and to the attributes of such a figure and its relationship to the boy. Of special interest here will be a possible introduction of peer figures (with respect to play) especially in plot 1, and other impersonal figures who, especially in plot 2, may serve as audience or critics.

b. The way in which the issue of impulse and control is handled, noting particularly the ending of the story.

c. There is some temptation to assume that the violin and/or its strings may have special sexual significance. If the subject pays particular attention to them, this hypothesis could be entertained, recalling our previous cautions as to interpretation.

CARD 2

I. **Murray's Description.** Country scene: in the foreground is a young woman with book in her hand; in the background a man is working in the fields and an older woman is looking on.

II. Manifest Stimulus Demand.

a. An adequate account of this card would include: some reference to a number of persons, some reference to the country or farm aspects, and some accounting for a relationship between the figures. It should not be overlooked that references such as "family working on a farm" or even the cryptic "family harvest" quite adequately account for the basic stimulus. More frequently, however, the individual figures are identified separately. They are quite generally seen as presented in Murray's description.

b. Other details often noted are the details of farm (rocks, buildings, production) and of the three figures (girl has books, woman is leaning against tree, and man is working).

c. Seldom noted details include the possible pregnancy of the older woman and, in decreasing order of frequency, the horse, the outbuildings in the background, the furrows, the details of dress of the women, and the musculature of the man. A "lake" and the second man and horse, which may be seen in the far background, are probably in the category of rare details. A rare detail of some interest is the posing of the young woman at the left as though standing in front of a large picture or mural (the rest of the card being the mural she is viewing).

III. Form Demand. The form demand of this card is somewhat greater than 1, calling for the subject to integrate three major form elements, the people, and to take into account some aspect of the background scene. In the subject prone to compulsive observation of stimuli, this card is a particularly good one in that it provides such a wealth of detail for observation.

IV. Latent Stimulus Demand. This picture's basic emotional stimulus is in two areas:

a. The stimulus of interpersonal relations proper and the challenge of a number of people together. It is basically the only card in the series that directly presents the subject with a group scene. Its particular stimulus, of course, deals with the relationship of younger to older and of male to female. To this extent, it is useful for eliciting feelings toward interpersonal interaction, toward parent-child relations, and toward heterosexual relations.

b. The contrast between the new and the old, as represented by the story of the girl going off for education as opposed to the farm folks. In this respect it is a useful picture in activating attitudes toward personal mobility and ambition and the extent to which the individual sees the traditional as valuable or as inhibiting.

V. Frequent Plots. The two most frequent plots to this picture deal with the issues presented in the discussion of latent stimulus demand. First, there is the plot of the young girl leaving the farm, possibly for further education relevant to returning to the farm, or for opportunities which the present home scene cannot provide. Second, there is the story portraying a focus upon the family *status quo,* i.e., the story of the family members hard at work gaining a living from the soil (somewhat more frequently seen as unproductive than productive).

VI. Significant Variations. Special points of importance here deal with:

a. The extent to which stimulus details are utilized.

b. The figure who is chosen as the hero-figure.

c. The extent to which splits occur among the three figures presented. For example, the story may be split so as to unite the two women (man is hired hand) or to unite the two younger persons (husband and wife with mother-in-law). Similarly, predominance may be given to any one of the three figures as the dominant force with the other figures subordinate. In any of these possible formulations, the attributes of each person and the nature of the interaction between figures is worth special note.

CARD 3GF

I. Murray's Description. A young woman is standing with downcast head, her face covered with her right hand. Her left is stretched forward against a wooden door.

II. Manifest Stimulus Demand.

a. The basic requirements of this card are only the woman and some explanation of the unusual position and generally negatively perceived situation.

b. The door is sometimes noted but is not necessary to an adequate plot.

III. Form Demand. The single figure is the only basic form.

IV. Latent Stimulus Demand. The emotional demand of this picture is that of its negative dramatic quality. In a sense, the stimulus is the question: why would a person be depressed or in pain and what will she do about it? In responding to this stimulus the familiarity of the subject with negative emotions, his basic optimism or pessimism, and the passive or assertive nature of his defenses are often revealed.

V. Frequent Plots. The woman is generally seen at some point in an unhappy chain of events. She is often crying or in pain. Ideas of guilt and despair and possible suicide are often found.

VI. Significant Variations. In a sense, any happy and constructive story is a misperception of this negative picture, unless the subject can logically account for the downcast head and the position of the woman. Points of special interest here will be the outcome in terms of whether or not the woman overcomes her difficulty, the use of any introduced figures and the role they play in either having created the trouble or in getting her out of it, and the previous event to which the difficulty is attributed.

CARD 3BM

I. Murray's Description. On the floor against a couch is the huddled form of a boy with his head bowed on his right arm. Beside him on the floor is a revolver.

II. Manifest Stimulus Demand.

a. The huddled form of a person, generally seen as young, of either sex. The figure is in a situation of a negative character calling for some explanation.

b. Other details consist of the object on the floor, most generally seen as a gun or other weapon. It is entirely possible, however, to see this as another object (a bunch of keys, for example) without distortion. The "couch" itself is often mentioned though seldom plays a central part in the story.

III. Form Demand. The figure and the "gun" are the only two forms of importance. It would appear that roughly one-fourth to one-third of subjects concern themselves in some way with the object on the floor, whether seeing it as a gun, other object, or merely indicating awareness of it without identifying it.

IV. Latent Stimulus Demand. The picture presents a lone figure in what is generally a negative circumstance. Unless the story is unusually logically constructed, it would be expected to be negative in quality. It is, like 3GF, a stimulus saying to the subject: what could make a person sad and what could he be expected to do about it? As such, it arouses associations of loss, guilt, attack, and aggression. It is important that this is a lone figure and hence attitudes toward the isolated self tend to be aroused.

V. Frequent Plots. The stories usually deal with a person who has been attacked or who is himself guilty over his own precious misdemeanor.

VI. Significant Variations. The "gun" is perhaps the most important single point for special attention. There is some tendency to think that it can readily lend itself to symbolic statements of sexual concern. This might be the case where it is treated either with special concern or intentionally ignored in a story that could readily have utilized it. In either case, any suggestions derived along these lines should be carefully checked with other data.

CARD 4

I. Murray's Description. A woman is clutching the shoulders of a man whose face and body are averted as if he were trying to pull away from her.

II. Manifest Stimulus Demand.

a. An adequate accounting will include reference to the man, the woman, and some explanation of the position of these figures.

b. The other details include the second "woman" in the background, seen often as a real person, an artist's model, or a poster or picture of a woman.

III. Form Demand. This card has no particular form aspects of importance, other than the two primary large details (the man and the first woman) and the small detail (the second woman) in the background.

IV. Latent Stimulus Demand. Attitudes toward heterosexual relationships are of course the central issue of importance in this card.

The contrast possible between the first and second woman permits also the dealing with the direct'issue of sexuality and "good and bad" women.

V. Frequent Plots. The plot's central issue is generally some explanation of the reason for the woman's appearing to restrain the man and of the direction of action of the man. In middle-class groups at least, the woman is most generally seen as the moral being who is offering moral advice to the more impulsive and irrational man. In about half of the instances the picture in the background is brought into the explanation.

VI. Significant Variations. The treatment of the balance of influence between the man and woman is of special interest here, as is the extent to which the second woman is used as a sexually threatening object or explained in a less conflictful way. Special attention should be paid to the way in which the drama is resolved and whether the outward directed goals of the man are attained or abandoned.

CARD 5

I. Murray's Description. A middle-aged woman is standing on the threshold of a half-opened door looking into a room.

II. Manifest Stimulus Demand.

a. An adequate accounting will refer to the woman and some explanation of why she is entering the room.

b. Other details often noted are the objects in the room. Not infrequently figures are introduced, normally seen as in the room portrayed.

III. Form Demand. The form of this picture lends itself to special preoccupation with minor details. Generally, however, the task is simple, set by the two large details of the woman and the room.

IV. Latent Stimulus Demand. This is a picture especially likely to portray attitudes toward the maternal figure, especially when seen as prohibitive and supervisory. In adolescents, particularly, the apprehension of adult control of sexual exploration is often brought out.

V. Frequent Plots. The woman is usually seen as having surprised someone in the room or as having heard something which she comes to investigate.

VI. Significant Variations. A special point of interest here lies in the problem or persons in the room. It not infrequently occurs that some voyeuristic tendencies are displayed through the woman not announcing herself. Similarly, apprehension over possible maternal punishment results in denial of all affect and emphasis merely upon inspection of the contents of the room. It is possible for the scene behind the room to be brought into the story. Variation along this latter line often parallels more elaborate stories with plot lines that have more reference to the scenes prior to the one presented.

CARD 6BM

I. Murray's Description. A short elderly woman stands with her back turned to a tall young man. The latter is looking downward with a perplexed expression.

II. Manifest Stimulus Demand.

a. An adequate accounting calls for reference to the woman, the man, and some explanation of the relationship between the two.

b. Other details often noted: the hat and the window are very seldom mentioned and are in no way a necessary part of the basic stimulus.

III. Form Demand. Only two large details are involved, the woman and the man.

IV. Latent Stimulus Demand. This card deals most generally with the attitudes of the subject toward maternal figures and particularly toward separation or discord in that relationship. It may also very profitably be structured, especially for working adults, in terms of the reaction to the possible authority of the mother as reflecting the stable and traditional. Thus the breaking of the relationship reflects ability to activate new ideas and projects. Similarly, a good portrayal of the subject's degree of independence is given.

V. Frequent Plots. The most frequent plots to the picture present the man as the son who is either leaving or presenting sad news to the woman seen as a mother.

VI. Significant Variations. The extent to which the man is an independent agent is the most important point to observe here. This is, of course, best seen in the content of the problem presented and in the outcome. Secondarily, the reaction of the mother to the son's problem will bear scrutiny and often reflects the subject's image of maternal control. It is also of interest to note whether or not the subject accepts the general mother-son version of this or whether he refuses to discuss this relation directly and hence gives other interpretations—woman and a salesman, man is friend bringing news of her son or husband.

CARD 6GF

I. Murray's Description. A young woman sitting on the edge of a sofa looks back over her shoulder at an older man with a pipe in his mouth who seems to be addressing her.

II. Manifest Stimulus Demand.

a. An adequate accounting will refer only to the woman, the man, and some explanation of the relationship between them.

b. Other details often noted: the sofa and the pipe.

III. Form Demand. The two large details, the woman and the man.

IV. Latent Stimulus Demand. This is a picture of sexual advance of the older man. It is useful in portraying attitudes toward heterosexuality, especially in its temporary aspects.

V. Frequent Plots. In middle-class subjects this is usually a sophisticated heterosexual scene in which the man is proposing some sort of activity. In women, particularly, there is considerable variation in the reaction of the woman and in the activity proposed by the man.

VI. Significant Variations. The manner in which the subject responds generally reflects his confidence in unstructured interpersonal situations. Easy and friendly relations are more generally found in upper middle-class groups than in lower middle-class groups, reflecting a greater ease and experience in temporary, unexpected personal contacts. The person who mistrusts interpersonal relations, especially in their sexual implications, tends to propose some difficulty or disruption in the relationship. A surprised or startled reaction in lower middle-class women is often elicited.

CARD 7BM

I. Murray's Description. A gray-haired man is looking at a younger man who is sullenly staring into space.

II. Manifest Stimulus Demand. An adequate accounting requires only the two men, the one on the right normally seen as the older, and a statement of some relationship between them.

III. Form Demand. There are only two large details, the two men, that require attention.

IV. Latent Stimulus Demand. This is a card dealing with hierarchal personal relations, normally taking the form of younger and less experienced versus older and more experienced. It is particularly stimulating of attitudes toward authority, toward the influences of external demands (in the person of the older man), and to a somewhat lesser degree attitudes of personal activity or passivity (especially as seen in the person of the younger). More specifically in younger subjects, the older man becomes a parental figure and images of the father are stimulated. In older subjects, the older man may carry the implication of a more impersonal authority and hence attitudes toward rules and policies, especially in a work setting, are stimulated.

V. Frequent Plots. The plots to the story follow closely the latent stimulus, taking the form most frequently of a father-son or of a professional relationship. In any formula, the older is most frequently advising the younger. Especially in middle-class working males, the father-son theme is sometimes replaced by a boss-employee one.

VI. Significant Variations. Points of special interest here deal with the extent to which extreme reactions of crime or discord are given versus the more usual plots. The nature of the relationship stated between the men—how close in goals, how authority-oriented—should be particularly noted. The outcome becomes most important in terms of whether the young man follows the advice mechanically, integrates it into his own plans, or rejects it with hostility.

CARD 7GF

I. Murray's Description. An older woman is sitting on a sofa close beside a girl, speaking or reading to her. The girl, who holds a doll in her lap, is looking away.

II. Manifest Stimulus Demand.

a. The two central figures are all that are required for an adequate story, plus an explanation of their activity.

b. Other details frequently noted are first the doll in the girl's hands and, less frequently, the book from which the woman may be reading.

III. Form Demand. The form demand here is simple, consisting of the two large details of the figures plus the small details of the doll and book.

IV. Latent Stimulus Demand. This picture is, of course, primarily a mother-child stimulus, giving attitudes toward maternal relations and toward the presumed characteristics of older women. In middle-aged subjects, it is also frequently perceived as primarily a "child" story and feelings toward young children are revealed. The fact that the girl is "looking away" is seen by some as evidence of the child's rejection of the mother.

V. Frequent Plots. Predominantly seen as mother and child, the plots attribute most frequently some sort of "mother" relation: teaching, advisory, consoling. Secondarily, reading for pleasure or entertainment is sometimes seen.

VI. Significant Variations. The question of the form blocks that are related to each other is of special interest here. That is, is the content primarily descriptive of the mother-to-child form areas or, for example, of the child-to-doll area, or the mother-to-doll area? This often gives important clues to covert maternal relations.

CARD 8BM

I. Murray's Description. An adolescent boy looks straight out of the picture. The barrel of a rifle is visible at one side, and in the background is the dim scene of a surgical operation, like a reverie-image.

II. Manifest Stimulus Demand.

a. An adequate accounting must deal with the foreground boy, the reverie-image in the background, and some explanation of the reason why these are in seemingly different planes yet together.

b. The other details frequently noted are the rifle and some details of the surgical scene, the doctor or patient, and, less frequently, the "knife" in the hand of the "doctor."

III. Form Demand. The form problem set here is of considerable importance in that it presents two blocks of form (the boy and the background scene) which, while both "real" enough, do not appear to be occurring in the same reality plane. This is further complicated by the rifle which, while equally real, is not placed so as to fit logically into the other form blocks. Similarly, the rarely noted window or bookcase in the upper right is present but not consistent with the placement of the other forms. The task, of course, is to construct an explanation appropriately relating these seemingly unrelated forms.

IV. Latent Stimulus Demand. This picture is a stimulus test of the subject's reality orientation as well as of his ambition and future planning skills. Secondarily, it permits hostile and attacking fantasies to emerge.

V. Frequent Plots. The surgical plot is the more frequent, in which the boy is seen as dreaming or imagining the background scene. Most frequently, this relates to his ambition or future career plans. Frequently, the scene is reversed and the boy becomes the image in the mind of a doctor—usually as thinking of his son who also will become a physician. Occurring in roughly one-fourth of the instances, the rifle is related to the boy and then the surgical scene is caused by the boy's shooting someone.

VI. Significant Variations. The major interest beyond the usual content concerns is the way in which the main form elements are related. Of special interest will be the possible response to the knife or other specific anatomical details of the operating scene, suggestive of aggressive tendencies or of castration fears.

CARD 8GF

I. Murray's Description. A young woman sits with her chin in her hand looking off into space.

II. Manifest Stimulus Demand. An adequate account requires reference to the woman and to her "dreamy" pose.

III. Form Demand. The woman is the only detail of general importance.

IV. Latent Stimulus Demand. This lone figure is usually taken as a stimulus to self-oriented fantasy of the minor future planning sort. It stimulates a positive daydream, in middle-class women often taking the form of marriage and family, of ambition of a short-range domestic variety.

V. Frequent Plots. The plots follow closely the latent stimulus, being usually a story of a woman daydreaming of some pleasant domestic or closely related event.

VI. Significant Variations. This is a rather highly stereotyped picture, the only variation being the infrequent possibility of plots other than those suggested.

CARD 9BM

I. Murray's Description. Four men in overalls are lying in the grass taking it easy.

II. Manifest Stimulus Demand.

a. An adequate accounting requires some attention to the reason for the lying-down positions and for the group of men.

b. Other details frequently noted are the specification of the number of men and their identification as laborers, tramps, soldiers.

c. Less frequently, one or more of the men may be seen as Negro and the man in the left front as "younger." Similarly, details of clothing or body parts may be noted.

III. Form Demand. This card presents many possibilities of form notation (the clothing, positions, body parts) but the more usual and only necessary forms are the four men.

IV. Latent Stimulus Demand. The basic stimulus here is probably that conveyed by the relaxed positions and relates to issues of ease, not-work, and lack of responsibility, and the relationship of passive enjoyment to superego. Secondarily, the close physical proximity of the bodies readily stimulates apprehension over body contact and sometimes male homosexual concerns. Closely related to this is the possibility of interpreting the scene in terms of peers, "buddies," and male companions which may reflect the male subject's ease with his own sexuality.

V. Frequent Plots. The dominant plot here appears to be that of men of some inferior class position who are relaxing and resting. In middle-class subjects, work is a normal accompaniment, either before this scene or after it.

VI. Significant Variations. Singling out of individuals is of special interest and most frequently occurs with respect to the "younger" person or with one of the others seen as Negro. It is also possible to utilize the "Negro" perception as relating to latent homosexual aggression fantasies.

CARD 9GF

I. Murray's Description. A young woman with a magazine and a purse in her hand looks from behind a tree at another young woman in a party dress running along a beach.

II. Manifest Stimulus Demand.

a. An adequate accounting will include the two women plus an explanation of the "hiding" of the one and the running of the other.

b. Other details frequently noted include reference to the beach and water, to the long dress of the one woman, to the tree.

III. Form Demand. This picture also lends itself to some detail observation, but the basic form demands include only the two figures.

IV. Latent Stimulus Demand. This stimulus in most groups is seen as a conflict of either a sibling nature or of two women over a man. It is basically a picture reflecting female peer relations.

V. Frequent Plots. Most frequently, the plots to this picture are of two women in conflict, frequently over a man, and somewhat less frequently a story in which the background woman has done something wrong. Co-operation as a basic plot occurs in about one story out of ten.

VI. Significant Variations. The point of central interest here is probably the interpersonal relations between the two women.

CARD 10

I. Murray's Description. A young woman's head against a man's shoulder.

II. Manifest Stimulus Demand.

a. An adequate accounting will refer to two figures in some kind of close physical position. In general, the figure on the left is seen as male and that on the right as female. However, both figures are sufficiently vague as to sustain alternative interpretations. Rosenzweig and Fleming [117] report that 100 adult subjects see the left figure as male in 100 per cent of the instances. The right figure is seen as female in 98 per cent of the men and 96 per cent of the women. The writer's own experience would be more in accord with Eron [112] whose subjects generally so identify these figures in slightly over 40 per cent of the instances. This does not include a related interpretation of mother and son in 12 per cent of his nonhospitalized cases. Thus it appears that this is not unequivocally a stimulus of older male and female, but rather a stimulus of closeness and sensuality, and that with some ease the subject may interpret either figure as male or female. This does not deny, however, the more probable interpretation of older male on left and female on right.

III. Form Demand. Two central, large details only, the two figures.

IV. Latent Stimulus Demand. This is a picture of close physical contact and deals with two primary issues. First, how does the subject handle close physical contact and sensuality? Second, how does he react to love-objects, especially toward possible separation? When so phrased, it also is reflective either of the subject's view of his spouse or of the intimate emotional (though not generally sexual) relation between his parents.

V. Frequent Plots. There are three basic plots here, all involving the two figures in close embrace. Following Eron, they may perhaps be called contentment or nurturance of partner, departure of one partner, or reunion. They occur in about this same order of frequency.

VI. Significant Variations. The identification of the figures is probably the central point of variation here. Despite the author's observations on the relative ease of seeing these figures as of either sex, he would scrutinize carefully those interpretations which do not follow the more usual identification of the left figure as male and the right as female. It should not be overlooked that in middle-class American society this is the strongly "preferred" interpretation, rather than merely the interpretation that follows logically from the physical stimulus. The subject's ease with the close physical contact may be specially scrutinized.

CARD 11

I. Murray's Description. A road skirting a deep chasm between high cliffs. On the road in the distance are obscure figures. Protruding from the rock on one side is the long head and neck of a dragon.

II. Manifest Stimulus Demand.

a. Here Murray's description is probably also the best description of the manifest stimulus. It should be noted, however, that the obscure figures are not necessarily human and are frequently perceived as bugs, a pack horse, etc. The "dragon" also may be seen as other animals and either as coming out or entering the cavern on the rock. Some explanation in the story would also be expected to account for the elemental or "prehistoric" quality of the scene.

b. Other details frequently noted include some details of the rock and chasm and less frequently the smaller "fleeing" figure in front of the form block on the bridge.

III. Form Demand. This picture is more complex in form than many of the earlier listed ones, both in providing more form areas and in the general vagueness and poorly defined identity. Formwise, this is a difficult picture and strains the subject's imagination more. It is thus a good picture for testing the subject's range of imagination and his ability to deal with irregular and poorly identified stimuli.

IV. Latent Stimulus Demand. This is a stimulus of the unknown and the uncontrolled. It reflects the subject's fear of attack (the "man" attacked by the "dragon") and his ability to deal with lack of social restraint. More generally, it may be described as an "elemental" picture in that the scene is raw and unsocialized and the plots told to it need not deal with properly controlled social events. In subjects fearful of such uncontrolled emotions, either strong aggression or succorance demands are readily expressed. In such cases, the subject's response to the "dragon" is of special interest. It may be used to reflect assertive feelings—being seen as coming out of the cliff and attacking people below. It may also be used to reflect succorance demands—being seen as a protecting animal or as going into the cliff in search of a refuge.

V. Frequent Plots. Stories of aggression and/or escape seem the most frequent to this picture, with the "dragon" seen as coming out of the cliff in possible attack upon the obscure figures near the bridge.

VI. Significant Variations. Stories in which the subject portrays difficulty in controlling the animals (dragon, bug) or those in which the hero is pursued by the animals often reflect an inability to control instinctual or sexual drives.

CARD 12M

I. Murray's Description. A young man is lying on a couch with his eyes closed. Leaning over him is the gaunt form of an elderly man, his hand stretched out above the face of the reclining figure.

II. Manifest Stimulus Demand. An adequate accounting will include the two figures plus their unusual position.

III. Form Demand. The two figures are the only basic forms, though the outstretched hand may be treated as a separate detail.

IV. Latent Stimulus Demand. The relation of the potentially passive and dependent to some superior uncontrollable force is the basic emotional stimulus here. It will reflect the subject's passivity, his attitude toward a controlling force (including in some subjects the attitude toward a therapist), and potentially, in some subjects, homosexual concerns.

V. Frequent Plots. Plots of hypnotism, illness of the young man, or some religious rite are frequent here. In these the older man will be the hypnotist or the minister or doctor.

VI. Significant Variations. The boy's reaction to the potentially passive dependent status is of particular interest, including the extent to which the boy has willingly submitted or been forced.

CARD 12F

I. Murray's Description. The portrait of a young woman. A weird old woman with a shawl over her head is grimacing in the background.

II. Manifest Stimulus Demand.

a. An adequate accounting will include only the two figures plus some explanation of their being together in this position.

b. Generally, the interpretation of subject is about as Murray gives it. However, recently we have seen in female subjects over seventy interpretations in which the "weird old woman" becomes a gently smiling and helpful person. Close examination of the face of the older figure suggests that "weird" and "grimacing" are not necessary connotations.

III. Form Demand. The two figures are the only major details, though the facial feature of the older woman can be differentially perceived.

IV. Latent Stimulus Demand. In subjects in the middle-age range, this appears to be a stimulus relating older to younger. Thus, for the mature woman, threats of old age appear prominent. In the younger adult, apprehension over control by an older woman appears more prominent. A basic stimulus selected by many subjects, especially women, is one which portrays the old woman as some symbolic representation of a part of the younger: her evil self, her self when aged, etc.

V. Frequent Plots. Most generally, the younger woman bears a family relationship to the older woman who is influencing or advising in some way. In about one-third of the stories, the older woman is seen as adversely influencing. In about one-third of the stories, a second plot will appear in which the older woman is a symbolic representation of the younger woman.

VI. Significant Variations. Of importance here is the issue of whether the subject sees the two figures in the same reality plane (mother-daughter) or whether one is a symbolic representation (my bad self, me when old, etc.). In addition, if treated in this latter fashion, the particular ideas toward the good and evil or other parts of the self should be specially viewed. In the light of the possibility of some, especially older, subjects seeing the background woman as kindly, responses to her should probably be watched more carefully and attention paid to the extent to which projection rather than reality observation is involved in attributing adverse influences.

CARD 12BG

I. Murray's Description. A rowboat is drawn up on the bank of a woodland stream. There are no human figures in the picture.

II. Manifest Stimulus Demand. An adequate accounting of this picture would include some reference to the boat, the woodland scene, and probably an explanation of the boat being unattended. The assumption of the need for some explanation of the "no people" is based upon the general feeling that the majority of subjects will feel compelled to offer such explanation. This is again, as in 1 and 10, and perhaps 12F, a case where the real stimulation of the card must be described in terms of the usual complex social assumptions made about the situation reflected in the card, and where merely describing the actual physical objects present is clearly an oversimplification.

III. Form Demand. This picture presents many possibilities of detail observation, details of the trees, flowers, stream, faces in the ambiguous tree forms, etc. Only a response to the readily identifiable boat and the woodland nature of the scene is generally to be expected, however.

IV. Latent Stimulus Demand. Here, the stimulus appears to be of two qualities, one represented by the absence of people and the other by pastoral, quiet, idyllic nature. These point to special sources of interpretation. The first is to see whether the subject prefers to introduce people or merely to accept the scene as presented. Many subjects, of course, are quite enchanted by not being required to deal with people here and accept the nature aspects willingly. Others will introduce people. The second is the question of the extent to which the subject can handle the possible sensitivity and relaxation of this scene. Some insight into the ability to handle positive, comforting emotions may be gained here.

V. Frequent Plots. Sheer fun and adventure stories appear frequently here. These usually include some people who have left their boat for reasons dealing with the particular adventure in progress. It should be recalled, however, that, while less frequent, the bright and cheery aspects of this picture are not so apparent that quite sinister stories cannot readily be presented. In the light of the more generally perceived positive aspects of the stimulus, however, the author, in the case of the sinister stories, would look for inabilities to accept positive emotions, sensuality, and possibly the feeling that without the social control provided by the presence of people the subject may fear his instinctual life will get out of hand.

VI. Significant Variations. These have been really indicated. They are the presence or absence of people and the treatment of the possible sensuous and relaxed elements.

CARD 13MF

I. Murray's Description. A young man is standing with downcast head buried in his arm. Behind him is the figure of a woman lying in bed.

II. Manifest Stimulus Demand.

a. An adequate accounting will include the man with downcast head, the woman, and some explanation for their being together in this fashion.

b. Other details frequently noted include references to books, the bed, and the nudity of the woman.

III. Form Demand. The two major details are the two persons.

IV. Latent Stimulus Demand. This is a stimulus of sexuality and, in the light of the usual responses of middle-class subjects, for them it might even be called a stimulus of illicit sex or of sex accompanied by guilt or other negative reactions. Generally, it suggests subject's attitude toward sex partner and particularly toward the reactions prior or subsequent to intercourse. Relations between sexual and aggressive feelings are often portrayed.

V. Frequent Plots. The plot of illicit sex followed by guilt is possibly the first plot in frequency in middle-class adult subjects. Somewhat less frequently appears the plot in which the woman is ill or dead and the man (often a husband) is expressing remorse or grief.

VI. Significant Variations. The variations of the two persons to either the plot of illicit sex or (not unrelated) death or aggression are of special interest. One may particularly observe: how well does the subject construct a plot to this "shocking" picture; is his form level disturbed by its content?

CARD 13B

I. Murray's Description. A little boy is sitting on the doorstep of a log cabin.

II. Manifest Stimulus Demand.

a. An adequate accounting would include the boy and, normally, some explanation for his seeming aloneness.

b. Other details frequently noted are the details of the cabin, especially whether or not containing people and, less frequently, attention to the possibility that the boy is holding something in his hands.

III. Form Demand. The smallness of the boy in comparison with the cabin, plus the general absence of other people, may generally lend a quality of smallness and aloneness to the boy. In any event, the boy and his relationship to some wider concept are the major stimulus demands here.

IV. Latent Stimulus Demand. The potentially underprivileged and/or deserted boy suggests an underlying stimulus of loneliness and insignificance that encourages the respondent to explain his feelings toward such states and toward their causes. The latter are normally seen in terms of either the environment of lack or of parental absence or neglect.

V. Frequent Plots. This is frequently a deserted or at least left-behind boy of a less-privileged family. He is generally waiting for the return of his parents. Occasionally it is seen as a stimulus to the need for escape from unpleasant surroundings and dreams of ambition are attributed to the boy.

VI. Significant Variations. The relation of the boy to the absence of parents, if so interpreted, is of special interest, as is the explanation of the relation of the boy to his present environment.

CARD 13G

I. Murray's Description. A little girl is climbing a winding flight of stairs.

II. Manifest Stimulus Demand. An adequate accounting includes the girl and the flight of stairs plus an explanation of her reason for being where she is.

III. Form Demand. It seems possible that the general massive grayness of the background and the stairs place this picture in much the same category as 13B, a stimulus of the lone small person in an environment that is overwhelming. Here, however, the background lends itself more to impersonal than to personal interpretations.

IV. Latent Stimulus Demand. The small person struggling against some impersonal but overwhelming environment. This picture also lends itself to projection of symptoms associated with defenses against the feeling of being overwhelmed by one's own anxieties.

V. Frequent Plots. The plots to the picture usually take the form of a girl climbing the stairs exploring, by choice or necessity, some unknown situation.

VI. Significant Variations. Of special interest here is the situation that will confront the girl as she proceeds as well as the presence of obsessive preoccupation reflective of inability to handle the gray impersonality of this picture.

CARD 14

I. Murray's Description. The silhouette of a man (or woman) against a bright window. The rest of the picture is totally black.

II. Manifest Stimulus Demand. An adequate accounting will include the single figure and some reference to his activity or, usually, his thoughts at the time. While Murray proposes that the figure may also be a woman, this seems much less a reasonable interpretation than for 3BM, for example.

III. Form Demand. The figure-ground characteristics of this card tend to support the interpretation of a person standing in the room, with his back to the subject and facing the outside light. However, in a small percentage of the cases (8 per cent in Eron's hospitalized group), the figure is seen as climbing into the room from outside. Small objects can also be seen in the "totally black" background though these occur generally only in disturbed or anxious subjects. Some, who do not report a suggestive white speck, do still wonder what might be lurking in the dark.

IV. Latent Stimulus Demand. This is most frequently a stimulus to self-ambition fantasy and daydreaming. It is thus reflective of the degree of ambition and organization of the subject's future planning. This includes, of course, the interpretation in which ambition is rejected and the subject returns to some routine activity identified not with the outside (or the future) but with the room behind him.

In many ways it would be more appropriate merely to identify this stimulus as one encouraging the verbalization of self-fantasy and to observe that in many middle-class groups this is closely related to fantasies of ambition, often work-oriented. In other persons, and in some of the middle-class persons, fantasies of suicide or other depressive fantasies appear.

V. Frequent Plots. Predominantly the figure standing at the window, most frequently at night or very early morning, thinking of the outside world, particularly as it relates to his future plans.

VI. Significant Variations. Plots other than the more frequent one just suggested are of special interest, particularly since the range of plots appears quite limited here. Of special interest are the responses in which objects are seen in the dark.

CARD 15

I. Murray's Description. A gaunt man with clenched hands is standing among gravestones.

II. Manifest Stimulus Demand.

a. An adequate accounting will include the old man plus some explanation for his being among gravestones.

b. Other details frequently noted include the clenched hands sometimes seen as holding something, or as being restrained as by handcuffs or rope.

III. Form Demand. The man and the basic scene are the only two major form elements. Due possibly to the general stern and darkened aspects of the scene, there are a number of small details that lend themselves to a variety of special interpretations. Thus the gravestones may be seen as chairs in an auditorium, the clenched hands as holding a lamp, a prayer book, etc. These border on perceptual distortions, as does seeing the man as a woman.

IV. Latent Stimulus Demand. This is normally a sad picture lending itself especially to thoughts of sadness, death, and hostility. The slightly ghoulish aspects of the card tend to stimulate ideas of sadness. It is provocative of death and aggression fantasies. It does permit, also, the focussing upon the man as a sympathetic figure in which case sadness at the loss of a loved figure may become the main stimulus.

V. Frequent Plots. The most frequent plots are those of sadness at loss of a loved one, or the interpretation of the scene as religious. Less frequent are plots of fear, loneliness, or of an unreal or symbolic nature.

VI. Significant Variations. It is of special interest to see whom the subject proposes as dead or ill and the extent to which guilt feelings are aroused. Considering the potential for unreal, symbolic, and wanton aggression here, special attention should be given to such plots.

CARD 16

I. Murray's Description. Blank card.

II. Manifest Stimulus Demand.

III. Form Demand. This is a white card without further form of any kind. It is possible, of course, for the subject to accept the stimulation of the white and to associate to it his responses. Echo responses of this sort—white for my purity, blankness for my mind, white rabbit, or white snow—may perhaps be accepted as self-conscious evasions and generally considered rejects.

IV. Latent Stimulus Demand. One suspects that the basic stimulus of this card may best be described only in terms of the individual's frame of mind at the time of presentation. It would appear to reflect the anxieties or problems that have been gradually accumulating over the previous stories. The card is thus less useful when given at the beginning of a series.

V. Frequent Plots. Accordingly, the plots vary widely, the largest single category of response possibly being autobiographical, though here too, of course, specific plots vary.

VI. Significant Variations. It is of special interest here to note the way in which the subject constructs his story. Does he begin at once telling a story and permit the examiner to himself imagine the "stimulus" through the implications of the plot? Does he first describe a stimulus and then tell a story about it? Is he willing to accept his own fantasy readily or does he qualify and/or avoid it with reference to the card, with echo associations of whiteness, etc.?

The extent of hostility to the examiner or possibly, if in therapy, to the therapist may also be reflected in this card.

CARD 17BM

I. Murray's Description. A naked man is clinging to a rope. He is in the act of climbing up or down.

II. Manifest Stimulus Demand.

a. An adequate accounting includes the man and the rope plus an explanation of the setting. This normally implies a reference to whether the man is going up or down the rope.

b. Other details frequently noted include specific reference to the muscles or the nudity. Not infrequently, the background gray will be referred to in identifying the scene.

III. Form Demand. The impression of movement is strong here and, while in essence the only major form consists of the man, the rope, and the background, it would seem that attention to the movement is an essential part of the stimulus.

IV. Latent Stimulus Demand. This is an extremely useful picture because it reflects the subject's concept of the relation of the individual to his environment and images of his prowess or vulnerability to environmental forces. Narcissistic, exhibitionistic, and competitive ideas are readily aroused here as are notions of fear and escape.

V. Frequent Plots. The man may be seen as an athlete showing his prowess or as an escaped prisoner. Normally, the figure is the hero in the general sense and the sympathy of the storyteller is with him. That is, the escaped prisoner is normally escaping from evil forces. Most frequently, he will be seen as going up the rope. (Eron [*] reports

---

[*] Eron, Leonard D. Frequencies of themes and identifications in the stories of schizophrenic patients and non-hospitalized college students. *J. consult. Psychol.*, 1948, *12*, 387–395.

46.7 per cent of his hospitalized and 40 per cent of his nonhospitalized populations see him that way.)

VI. Significant Variations. It is useful to note the nature of the environment in which the figure is found as well as whether or not other figures are introduced to assist, hamper, or observe him. The subject's desire for recognition and display or his fears of vulnerability should be noted. Attention may be paid to the possible descriptions of nudity or physical build.

CARD 17GF

I. Murray's Description. A bridge over water. A female figure leans over the railing. In the background are tall buildings and small figures of men.

II. Manifest Stimulus Demand.

a. An adequate accounting includes the woman and some explanation of the drama of the scene. This may include specific references to other details.

b. Other details frequently noted include the bridge, the water below, the small figures of men.

III. Form Demand. The picture includes a wide variety of forms but the woman and the general "strangeness" of the scene are the basic stimuli. The other form details refer to the variations and details of the plot.

IV. Latent Stimulus Demand. The depressive, irregular, or dramatic aspects would appear to be the major emotional stimulus. The specific plots are individual efforts to explain these qualities. Along these lines, depression, suicide, female homosexuality, and criminality are all possible associated ideas.

V. Frequent Plots. Plots of suicide or female unhappiness are frequently developed. If related to small male figures, she may become the girl friend or lookout for a gang. In this case, attitudes toward a possibly departing or deviant love-object are often reflected.

VI. Significant Variations. It is of special interest to see whether the plot revolves entirely around the woman or whether she is seen as related to the other small figures. In the former case, the self-oriented feelings, usually negative, dominate the plot. In the latter, the idea of self as related to others forms a stronger part of the subject's ideas.

CARD 18BM

I. Murray's Description. A man is clutched from behind by three hands. The figures of his antagonists are invisible.

II. Manifest Stimulus Demand.

a. An adequate accounting here would clearly parallel Murray's description—including reference to the men, the hands, and the unusualness of the scene (invisible antagonists).

b. Other details frequently noted include the facial features (anxious, tense) and the clothing (disheveled).

III. Form Demand. The man and the three hands are, of course, the major form stimuli. The unusual placement of the hands is also specifically stimulating of explanation.

IV. Latent Stimulus Demand. This is a stimulus of the fearful person attacked by unknown forces. As such, it reflects the extent of the subject's feeling of control or hopeless susceptibility to the aggression of others. Fears of mysterious sources of influences, sometimes within the individual himself, are aroused. Fears of drug or alcohol addiction also appear.

V. Frequent Plots. The man is most generally seen as fearful, or anxious, and being attacked or restrained. He himself is also frequently seen as drunk and as disheveled.

VI. Significant Variations. A point of special interest is whether the basic "mysterious force" is within the person or whether it is "behind" him. Similarly, the extent to which the plot is disrupted by an inability to satisfactorily explain the three hands in the picture is of special note.

CARD 18GF

I. Murray's Description. A woman has her hands squeezed around the throat of another woman whom she appears to be pushing across the banister of a stairway.

II. Manifest Stimulus Demand. An adequate accounting will refer to the two figures and some explanation of the position of the two. It should be pointed out that, in the light of the high frequency of "helpful" or "positive" stories to this picture, it might be well to relate its description in more neutral terms. In particular, the words "squeezed" and "pushing" seem overstated. This does not mean that a large, normal population cannot "misperceive" a stimulus. It is apparent that they can. If we assume this to be essentially an aggressive picture, then the normal subjects would appear to prefer to ignore it. This relates more to their preferences and stereotypes (as in 10) than to any perceptual distortion *per se*.

It is also not clear that the second figure is "another woman." The figure is seen as male about as frequently as it is seen as female and somewhat less frequently seen as a child (male or female) or as a "young" man or woman.

III. Form Demand. The two figures and their unusual position.

IV. Latent Stimulus Demand. This would appear to be an aggressive stimulus, much as Murray initially described. It remains true, however, that approximately half of normal adult subjects see this as a helpful, supportive picture. (In Rosenzweig and Fleming,[*] 46 per cent give plots of this sort.) However, the fact that notions of injury, anxiety, cruelty, or distress are reported may suggest that even this group at some level recognizes the aggressive scene for what it is and attempts to avoid it by turning it into its opposite. This would, in essence, appear to be more relevant to the character of the group of subjects than to any need to redesignate the picture.

It might therefore still be appropriate to propose this as a stimulus of aggression and to concern ourselves with the ways in which subjects attempt to deny and cover up this recognition. In this light the figure on the left becomes particularly important.

V. Frequent Plots. As suggested, help and consolation constitute the single largest category of plot. This is followed by direct plots of cruelty and aggression.

VI. Significant Variations. The success and ease with which subjects provide a "nonaggressive" plot is of special interest. Similarly, the relation of the figure on the left to the plot requires special attention.

CARD 19

I. Murray's Description. A weird picture of cloud formations overhanging a snow-covered cabin in the country.

II. Manifest Stimulus Demand.

a. An adequate account would include the snow-covered cabin, sometimes differently interpreted, and the outside elements, sometimes seen as bad weather, sometimes as abstract forces.

b. Other details frequently noted include the detail of the "windows," the outside forces, and the black figure directly behind the cabin.

III. Form Demand. In addition to the two major form elements to which we just referred, this picture presents a wealth of analogous

---

* Rosenzweig, Saul, and Fleming, Edith. Apperceptive norms for the Thematic Apperception Test. II. An empirical investigation. *J. Pers.*, 1949, *17*, 483–503.

details which permit a wide range of interpretation. The subject's ability to make a coherent story out of this ambiguity is one of the most useful aspects of this picture.

IV. Latent Stimulus Demand. The basic stimulus of this picture may profitably be seen as "newness and unusualness." As such, it provides useful clues to the subject's ability to cope with the new and unusual and with his differential reactions to structure (in earlier cards) versus lack of structure (in this card).

The basic stimulus may also be conceptualized in terms of the potentially isolated individual (the cabin) in the presence of impersonal forces of potential evil (the outside snow or other threatening elements). The ability to tell a coherent story here usually reflects some security feelings, some independent thinking, and a good reality grasp. Stereotypic thinkers or persons without firm security feelings often reject this card, either totally or as "bad art" or merely as "weird."

V. Frequent Plots. The usual plot refers to some unit (cabin, boat, shack) as subjected to outside, potentially bad forces (rain, storm, snow, evil, evil figures, spooks). The plots then may emphasize either the safe warmth within the house or the possible harm to be done by the outside forces.

VI. Significant Variations. Of particular interest here is the ability to tell a coherent story. Also of importance is the extent to which comfortable coping with outside forces is presented versus fearful anticipation of evil. Part of this will consist of the descriptions given of the outside (especially whether personal or impersonal) and of the inside (whether desolate or warm and protected). A number of special interpretations may occur here: the "windows" as eyes, the black figure as a witch. These usually reflect special preoccupations related to guilt.

CARD 20

I. Murray's Description. The dimly illuminated figure of a man (or woman) in the dead of night leaning against a lamppost.

II. Manifest Stimulus Demand. An adequate accounting will include the figure (not necessarily the larger part) and some reference to the setting. The details in the setting and the dim light are frequently included. The figure is more generally male.

III. Form Demand. This is a single form picture, though it may be noted that the relation of the single person to the distant lights may contribute to a stimulus of "aloneness."

IV. Latent Stimulus Demand. This picture is a stimulus of indecision, indefiniteness, loneliness. Into this feeling the subject may insert direct loneliness, aggression, or other personal feeling.

V. Frequent Plots. The subject is generally alone and waiting for some specific person (often a date or spouse). Uncertainty or loneliness are a large part of this plot.

Secondarily, a plot reflective possibly of the dark aspect is one of crime or potential aggression, in which the figure is waiting for a gang or is a holdup man waiting for a victim.

VI. Significant Variations. The relation of the figure to the environment is an item of special interest here. Where does he place himself with respect to the potential loneliness aspect of the stimulus?

Some notes on administration

The procedure indicated by Murray was discussed in Chapter 3. This procedure is an entirely sound one which is preferred by many workers in this field. It seems to the writer especially appropriate when exploration of the test itself and the sources and ramifications of the subject's fantasy is a special interest of the investigation. For ordinary purposes of clinical study and when knowledge of special groups of subjects is the central focus, the author would recommend a somewhat modified procedure. This is the procedure suggested in Chapter 3. Its special features are as follows:

1. A set of twelve to fifteen pictures is an adequate sample of the fantasy for ordinary purposes. This set should be selected along the lines suggested.

2. The set may be administered in one session, normally lasting from forty-five minutes to 1½ hours.

3. The same set of pictures should be used for all subjects within a given research population. As much as possible other related investigations should also utilize the same set, with special additions as may be suggested by the particular focus of the problem.

Technique of Administration

The standard procedure of administration, and the one for which the set was centrally designed, is the individual interview format. In this the examiner presents the instructions and the pictures and the subjects respond verbally. The examiner then records in written form the responses. The data to be recorded consist of all remarks made by the subject from the presentation of the first picture to the completion of his story to the last picture in the series. This implies that any remarks of the subject which he himself indicates are not part of his responses are nonetheless to be recorded. This includes side remarks and criticism of the testing situation, the examiner, the previous pictures.

The instructions to be followed are those provided by Murray. The basic format is as follows:

This is a test of imagination, one form of intelligence. I am going to show you some pictures, one at a time; and your task will be to make up as dramatic a story as you can for each. Tell what has led up to the event shown in the picture, describe what is happening at the moment, what the characters are feeling and thinking; and then give the outcome. Speak your thoughts as they come to your mind. Do you understand?

The author proposes one specific and one general modification of these instructions. First, eliminate the reference to "one form of intelligence." This is a minor modification and no harm is done by including it. However, to the extent that it encourages the subject to think of the creation of stories as a sort of test, closely related to the intelligence test with which he may be familiar, it is probably inadvisable. Second, these instructions can be modified in any way that is basically an elaboration upon them. The objective is not to repeat identically these words for all subjects, but to be sure that all subjects understand the task that is set for them. Thus, if it is necessary to repeat them two or three times for a subject, do so. If the subject appears not to comprehend the notion of "telling a story," this could be equated in as many ways as seem necessary to get over this idea. References to scripts, scenarios, fairy tales, stories your mother told you, plots of books, etc., are entirely legitimate. The points to be conveyed to the subject are:

1. He is to tell a story. This is a sequence of events with some development of time in it. It includes a beginning, a middle, and an end. The middle refers to a description of what is present in the picture as he sees it. The beginning refers to some notion of how this came about, how things got to be this way. The end refers to some explanation of what might happen in the future, how it will all come out.

2. In so doing, he is to use his imagination. This means that he is to give whatever seems to him a good explanation of the picture. In so doing, he may be told that people think up all sorts of different things to the picture and that it is his own ideas that the examiner is interested in.

3. He is to describe the situation as he sees it and he is to propose feelings, actions, ideas, characterizations.

It is generally well for the examiner to repeat the instructions after the first and second stories have been given if the subject does not complete his stories with the usual outcome. If such reminders do not produce traditional endings, the author would not insist, but rather would assume that the failure to give endings is a datum to be used in interpretation and not a failure of the subject to understand the instructions.

It is strongly recommended that stories be recorded by picture number rather than merely by sequence. This is a precaution against losing track of the actual picture to which the story was told. While in most normal subjects the picture can be identified from the story alone, in some cases this is not true. It is also strongly advised that each record be identified with the name or code number, age, sex of the subject, plus any other identification information pertinent to the purpose for which the record was taken. Similarly, each record should be marked with the date of administration and with the name of the test administrator. This is a reminder that such records may be used in later months for research purposes and that the memory of the examiner should not always be relied upon to provide these cues.

After the last story has been given, the subject should be asked to select the two cards which he likes best. To assist in this process all the pictures may be spread out in front of him and the subject allowed to rearrange them or pick them up if he chooses. After he has selected two, he should be asked to give his reasons for his selection. As an aid in the process he may be reminded of the story he told to them and asked if he wishes to change or add to his story in any way. Following this, the process should be repeated with respect to his two least-liked cards. If the subject claims that he likes them all equally, or dislikes them all equally, he should still be encouraged to select these four pictures. It is sometimes helpful here to rephrase the best- and least-liked issues, suggesting that you want him to select the two where he liked best the stories he told perhaps or where he liked them least. If the subject asks, "What do you mean, did I like the people, or the art work?" the author would be inclined to avoid a choice, asking the subject to pick them on any basis he wishes. Subjects seldom have difficulty doing this, though their logic for their choices may vary.

The Role of the Examiner

The role of the examiner is essentially one of encouraging the subject to respond freely without at the same time indicating directions and choices in the subject's manner of response. There appears to be considerable possibility that a specially played role on the part of the examiner—intentional assertiveness, negative criticism of performance, and the like—can influence the resulting productions.* It seems probable, also, that less intentional role-playing on the part of the examiner may also influence the production, though it is by no means clear in what ways. In this situation, it seems most appropriate for the examiner to maintain the "encouragingly neutral" role which is traditional in such situations. Beyond the establishment of initial rapport and the presentation of the instructions and the pictures, the author suggests that the examiner should:

1. Refrain from indicating the content of the subject's response at any point. Thus, when the subject asks what something might be, the examiner's response should convey the notion that the picture area in question can be whatever the subject wishes. This should be presented, however, not as a challenge but as a freedom of choice should the subject so desire.

2. Refrain from interfering with the flow of the subject's thought by the insertion of issues determined by the examiner. Thus, it is proposed that all inquiries be left until the end of the entire series of cards. At that time inquiry is justified on at least two grounds. First, if the subject has presented some remark which the examiner is inclined to see as a basic perceptual distortion or a logical inconsistency of a major sort, the subject should be asked to tell again what he said at that point. Here the interest is one primarily of clarification. The examiner did not quite understand and wishes to be enlightened. Second, if the examiner has some special interest stemming from his on-the-spot analysis of responses, he could inquire further about certain of the subject's responses which appear to relate to this notion. Thus, if specific parental hostility is suggested as a problem, the examiner may want to discuss again his responses to card 6BM or 7BM. This will be especially true, of course, in the discussion following the sub-

* For a particularly useful discussion of these various possibilities, the reader is referred to Chapters 3, 4, and 5 of Seymour Sarason, *The Clinical Interaction* (New York: Harper and Brothers, 1954).

ject's choices of best- and least-liked cards. Here the author would feel free
to encourage the subject to elaborate his original story, criticize it if he
wishes, change it if he wishes. It should be recalled, however, that any
changes or elaborations the subject makes at this stage are not to be seen
as editorial changes justifying alteration of the original responses but as
addenda that may throw light upon the original response as given.

Special Features of Recording the Stories

In recording all that transpires between the initial presentation of picture
1 and the end of the last story, some problems of what to include arise.
Generally, as suggested in the foregoing, all verbal remarks of the subject are
to be recorded. In addition, it may be well to remark briefly on such points
as reaction time, notations of pauses, and extraverbal happenings.

It has not been the present writer's habit to record reaction times. However, many examiners find this useful. If this is done, some systematic way
of stabilizing the time intervals should be developed. It is often best not
to introduce a stop watch into the situation. The examiner can "calibrate"
himself to count seconds and to note the number of seconds elapsed between
card presentation and beginning of story. These may not be exact according to the clock, but they enable comparisons to be made between records
and within records. The primary importance of such notations is the cues
they may give to stories or pictures which have special meaning for the
subject. Such cues would come from a comparison of specific individual
reaction times with the average reaction time for that subject. The average will itself vary from subject to subject, of course, but the author would
suspect that the intra-individual variations would be of most use. In this
connection both unusually short and unusually long reaction times should be
examined.

Notations of pauses are useful in indicating the breaks and hesitations
in the record. For these notations it is felt that recording the time in seconds is being overly specific. Rather, a simple notation of (short pause) or
(long pause) seems sufficient. The writer has made a habit of indicating
short and long pauses by dashes, varying the length of the line somewhat to
indicate the length of hesitation and as a means of indicating records given
in a halting manner where each few words are interspersed by a short pause.

The recording of the behavior of the subject other than his verbalizations
is largely a matter of personal preference. The author is inclined to feel
that such notations are less apt to lead to valid inferences than are the data
of the stories proper, including, of course, pauses, delayed reaction times,
and other formal aspects. If the examiner wishes to record these, however,
they can be noted in the body of the story, with parentheses or other indications that they are not a direct verbalization of the subject. Any remarks
or questions by the examiner should be similarly noted.

Short Cuts to Securing Stories

As has been mentioned, the basic form of recording for which the TAT
was designed is the personal interview, with the subject speaking and the

examiner recording in longhand his responses. There are a number of occasions upon which modifications of this procedure are desired. Some modifications in procedure seem justified.

The first of these may be the need to simplify the task of the examiner. This can be done by shortening the normal longhand procedure or by use of electric recording equipment. There is no objection to either of these procedures provided careful attention is paid to the basic interaction of subject and examiner. The examiner can use shorthand or speed writing, if it really aids him. However, if there is any possibility that this will interfere with the rapport with the subject, effort should be made to re-establish rapport. For example, sometimes children are inclined to want to know just what the examiner is writing down. To this end, they may want to see what he has written or ask for it to be read to them. Being able to reproduce what the subject has just said is of importance in this circumstance. If the examiner prefers to use shorthand, it is often well to explain to the subject that you are doing so if he appears to express any interest in what you are writing down. Some subjects, frequently the smarter children, will test you out by asking for it to be read back. Usually doing so will satisfy them that you are indeed getting just what they said and are not making other remarks about them.

The second way to simplify the examiner's task is to record the responses electrically. In this circumstance, two possibilities exist. Either the recording must be so good and so well concealed that the subject never knows it is being done, or the same precautions must be taken as when using shorthand. Generally the latter is the more practical procedure. In this case, the subject should see the equipment, be allowed to play with the microphone, etc. Frequently, giving the subject the microphone to adjust to his own liking allays his apprehension. It often is helpful in getting a good recording to adjust the microphone distance to an adequate recording distance, of course.

If either the electric recording or shorthand method is used, the examiner should not forget that the simplication of the recording situation may result in increased complications later on. One normally works from a typed record. Getting the shorthand or the electric recording into a typed script should not be forgotten as an important part of the process. If one is adequately supplied with secretarial help, this is perhaps not a problem. If one is not, then recall the time and effort required to get the recording into typed form. For research purposes an electric recording has great advantages. It does require, however, some advance planning with respect to typists.

The second general circumstance for which adaptations of the basic procedure may be required is when tests are desired on a large group of subjects within a fairly limited space of time. This brings to the fore questions of group administration and subject-written records.

Group administration seems entirely feasible if certain precautions are taken. Satisfactory tests have been given either with slides projected on a screen or with a number of subjects using one copy of a picture.

In any format in which a number of subjects take the test in a group, attention should be paid to the number of subjects in the group. In viewing a movie, one of the attributes of the audience in these circumstances would appear to be the degree of anonymity given by the darkness and the large number of people present. The result of this appears to be the opportunity which it gives the person to diminish his own projection, to rely upon the film to exercise the imaginative elements. In this circumstance, individuality is dispersed. In the TAT testing circumstance, we want the individuality to be increased and brought to the fore. This would suggest that group administration yields most profitable data when the size of the group is such that attention may still be focussed upon the individual in that group.

In a group numbering not more than fifteen, this would appear to be still the case. One is able in this circumstance to encompass other individuals and still maintain one's own feeling of separateness. In groups much larger than this, the individual partakes of the qualities of the group and individuality is possibly not emphasized. Therefore it is advisable to administer the slides to forty-five persons, for example, in three or four sessions of ten to fifteen persons each. This is, of course, not as simple as using the entire forty-five in one session, but the yield of individualized stories is worth the extra time. It is still, of course, considerably quicker than forty-five individual administrations. The same applies to administrations in which a number of subjects look at one card. This means that a group of fifteen would be broken down in three or four subgroups. In this case, the examiner should leave the card face up on the table and allow each person to look at it as much as he chooses. This card is then picked up and the next one substituted after the subjects are finished.

In either of these formats, setting a time limit seems feasible. The author would suggest a five-minute time limit per picture, in which the subjects are advised of the passage of the four-minute period and told that they will have one minute more. Of these two general formats, the writer prefers a group of ten or fifteen seeing one projected slide in a room where the light is adequate for writing yet dim enough for good projection of the slide.

In either of these formats, special attention should be given to the forms upon which the subjects write their responses and to the instructions. First, the instructions should be given orally by the examiner. The usual precautions should be taken about repeating them if all persons do not seem to get them. In general, it is often well to repeat them twice anyway, in somewhat altered form. At the same time, the subjects should be provided with a booklet. The first sheet of this booklet should contain the written instructions which the examiner will give orally. The subject is then able to read them at the same time as they are spoken. The remaining sheets of the booklet should contain one full 8½ by 11 sheet for each of the stories to be written. Each sheet should be numbered, preferably at the top, with the number of the picture, and accompanied by a short sentence saying something like, "Now write your story to the first picture here." The subsequent sheets could bear similar notations. The last sheet may be divided into two halves. The top half would be marked with a notation requesting a selection (by number) of the two best-liked pictures and a request for the subject to write his reasons for these selections. The bottom half may be similarly marked with a request for the two least-liked pictures.

A further modification is to provide the subject with a special booklet in which both the pictures and a space for writing the story are provided. In this booklet, it is often useful to reproduce the picture on the left-hand side of a double page. The right-hand side is then a blank page headed by a notation such as, "Write your story to this picture here." Depending somewhat upon the research focus of a study in which such a booklet is used, there should be some introductory pages to such a booklet asking for personal data relevant to the problem at hand. In such a format, profitable use has been made of a personal history and short autobiographical form, a sentence completion test, and a request for the subject to "Draw a Person."

Data from these modifications of the basic testing procedure appear to be quite useful. While it is apparent that such modifications work best with subjects of average and above intelligence who are of high school or advanced educational experience, they have considerable use in groups. One loses, of course, the advantage of some of the hesitations, pauses, rejected stories, alternative stories, etc.; nonetheless the resulting stories appear to be adequately imaginative, individually varied, and interpretively meaningful.